ArtScroll® Series

Rabbi Nosson Scherman / Rabbi Meir Zlotowitz

General Editors

Food *for*

Published by

ArtScroll
Mesorah Publications, ltd

Yom Tov

Teaching

Hadracha

Warmth

Thought

Stories that tantalize
your spiritual taste buds

Rabbi Yitzchok Hisiger

FIRST EDITION
First Impression … March 2017
Second Impression … November 2019

Published and Distributed by
MESORAH PUBLICATIONS, LTD.
4401 Second Avenue / Brooklyn, N.Y 11232

Distributed in Europe by
LEHMANNS
Unit E, Viking Business Park
Rolling Mill Road
Jarow, Tyne & Wear, NE32 3DP
England

Distributed in Australia and New Zealand
by **GOLDS WORLDS OF JUDAICA**
3-13 William Street
Balaclava, Melbourne 3183
Victoria, Australia

Distributed in Israel by
SIFRIATI / A. GITLER — BOOKS
POB 2351
Bnei Brak 51122

Distributed in South Africa by
KOLLEL BOOKSHOP
Northfield Centre, 17 Northfield Avenue
Glenhazel 2192, Johannesburg, South Africa

ARTSCROLL® SERIES
FOOD FOR THOUGHT
© Copyright 2017, by MESORAH PUBLICATIONS, Ltd.
4401 Second Avenue / Brooklyn, N.Y. 11232 / (718) 921-9000 / www.artscroll.com

ISBN 10: 1-4226-1874-9 / ISBN 13: 978-1-4226-1874-5

Typography by CompuScribe at ArtScroll Studios, Ltd.
Printed in the United States of America
Bound by Sefercraft, Quality Bookbinders, Ltd., Brooklyn N.Y. 11232

Table of Contents

Preface   7
Acknowledgements   9

A Taste of Torah   13
A Taste of Diligence   35
A Taste of Purity   53
A Taste of Insight   67
A Taste of Neshamah   81
A Taste of Compassion   95
A Taste of Warmth   107
A Taste of Tefillah   119
A Taste of Integrity   133
A Taste of The Omnipresent   143
A Taste of Faith   163
A Taste of Clarity   185
A Taste of Leadership   199
A Taste of Hadrachah   219
A Taste of Fortitude   233
A Taste of Ethics   243
A Taste of Sensitivity   253
A Taste of Humility   277
A Taste of Chinuch   287
A Taste of Teaching   309
Nuggets of Wisdom   321
A Taste of Shabbos   333
A Taste of Yom Tov   347
Glossary   375

Preface

Why write stories?

Why write a book?

Rav Shalom Schwadron, the famed *maggid* of Yerushalayim, had been a mashgiach in a yeshivah in Yerushalayim when he suddenly decided to become a *maggid*.

What caused this abrupt change of plans?

In 1915, Sarah Schenirer and her family fled war-torn Poland and found refuge in Vienna. On Shabbos Chanukah, she attended a local shul, a branch of Vienna's Schiffshul located in the Stumpergasse, where the words of the rav, Rabbi Dr. Moshe Flesch, were penetrating and compelling. He referenced the heroine of the Chanukah story, Yehudis, who was willing to sacrifice her own life for the future of Klal Yisrael.

"Mi laShem eilai! [Whoever is for Hashem, join me!]" the rav cried out, echoing the words of Moshe Rabbeinu (Shemos 32:26) and the Chashmonaim of old. "Who will come forth and bring the bnos Yisrael back to their Father in Heaven?" In those days, young girls did not receive a formal Jewish education, and they were being lost to Klal Yisrael as they were swept up by foreign ideologies.

Sarah Schenirer heard and was mesmerized. She took it upon herself to try and change the tragic state of affairs.

The Bais Yaakov movement was born.

The rest, as they say, is history.

Years later, when telling this story, Rav Schwadron would weave a fanciful portrayal of the palaces in Gan Eden belonging to Rabbi Flesch. "When Rabbi Flesch, in wonder, asked the *malachim* in what *zechus* he merited this reward," related Rav Schwadron, "he was told that each of his palaces represents one girl who stayed *frum,* and this was due to his influence on one person, Sarah Schenirer."

Rav Shalom would then relate that after contemplating all this, he said to himself, *If one derashah can leave such an impression, imagine how much nachas ruach I can give the Ribono Shel Olam with many derashos!* At that moment, he decided to quit his job and become a *maggid.*

The power of a story is inestimable.

Each story and each anecdote has the power to influence, motivate, inspire, and rejuvenate.

May the stories in this volume provide food for thought, ultimately leading to positive changes in our lives and the lives of those around us.

Acknowledgments

Rav Yechiel Yaakov Weinberg, author of *Seridei Eish*, once described a meeting of academics that took place in Berlin, the purpose of which was to establish the definition of a Jew.

One person opined that being Jewish is a matter of religion. Others disagreed, stating that even an apostate is considered Jewish. Some asserted that being born to a Jewish mother defines one as Jewish. Others argued that this was not true, because many Jews are descendants of converts.

"A Jew is an individual who follows the commandments of the Torah," said one person.

"That's patently false," claimed another, "for Chazal tell us that a Yisrael who has sinned is still a Yisrael" (*Sanhedrin* 44a).

"If one is born in the Holy Land," averred another, "that makes him a Jew."

The others refuted that claim, pointing to the majority of Jews throughout the ages who were born in the Diaspora.

As this matter was being discussed, a simple Jew entered the room and offered his own solution to the conundrum. "Why all the debating? *Ah Yid iz ah Yid!* A Jew is a Jew!"

Rav Weinberg commented that the last opinion was most correct. A Jew is a Jew. His essence cannot be defined by normal adjectives and descriptions.

We say in Mussaf (on Yamim Tovim and Shabbos Rosh Chodesh),

"*V'romamtanu mi'kol haleshonos* — And You have exalted us above all tongues." One interpretation of this is that Hashem has raised us to a level that is beyond the portrayal of any language, for we are a special breed with special characteristics and potential.

This book is a tribute to Klal Yisrael. Each story and anecdote reflects the beauty of our nation, and why we are all so fortunate to count ourselves as members of this elite group, the *am hanivchar*, the chosen nation.

My gratitude to the Ribono Shel Olam knows no bounds. He has showered me with so much kindness, none of which I deserve. I pray that I become worthy of His munificence.

Heartfelt thanks to **Rabbi and Mrs. Pinchos and Chani Lipschutz** for granting me the unique opportunity to be part of the team at *Yated Ne'eman*. I am fortunate to work for a publication whose singular goal is bringing about the greatest *k'vod Shamayim* possible. Some of the stories in this book appeared, in one form or another, in the *Yated*, and I thank Rabbi Lipschutz for his continuous guidance, compassion, and leadership.

I express my *hakaras hatov* to my dear parents, **Rabbi and Mrs. Yisroel and Reyna Hisiger**, for everything they have given me so selflessly and generously, and for constantly encouraging me to reach for the stars. I am grateful to them, as well, for serving as my on-call editors and proofreaders, and for reviewing this entire manuscript.

My devoted in-laws, **Rabbi and Mrs. Dov and Bashy Morgenstern**, are paragons of humility and *chesed*, who have raised a wonderful family based on the purest ideals of Torah. Their unremitting benevolence, and the warmth and hospitality that pervade their home, reflect their special nature. I thank them for being there for all of us.

I thank my siblings and their children, and my wife's siblings, for their constant support and encouragement.

Special kudos to my brother, **Rav Hershel Hisiger**, who first suggested publishing these stories as a book, and from whose wellsprings of knowledge and keen insight I have benefited considerably.

This book is dedicated in memory of my grandparents, **Reb Tzvi Yehuda (Harry) and Shifra (Sophie) Hisiger** *z"l*, and **Reb Zev (Willie) and Basha (Bessie) Feller** *z"l*, whose fortitude, character, and strength continue to inspire.

My wife's grandparents, **Rabbi and Mrs. Yacov Lipschutz** and **Rabbi and Mrs. Gershon Morgenstern**, have adopted me as one of their own, and the feelings are mutual.

My uncles and aunts are staunch devotees of mine and always have kind words and insightful comments, treating me with benevolence and graciousness.

I am thankful to those who were kind enough to share the stories contained in this book. I have tried my best to give proper attribution to each person. If I have erred, I beg their forgiveness and ask that they contact me. Likewise, I thank the many people who are kind enough to take the time to read my writings each week and comment on them.

I thank the entire staff at the *Yated* — the writers, the editors, the office staff, the graphic artists, and everyone else involved in its production — for their friendship, professionalism, and creativity, and for being such a pleasure to work with.

I am most appreciative to **Rabbi Yechiel Spero** for his friendship, and in particular for matching me up with an exemplary editor, **Mrs. Tova Salb**, whose professionalism and expertise have found expression in every page of this book.

It is a great honor in the world of Torah literacy to join the **ArtScroll** family, led by **Rabbi Meir Zlotowitz** and **Rabbi Nosson Scherman**. They are both legends in their field, whose pioneering courage, wisdom, and creativity spawned an unprecedented revolution in Torah literature. The assistance and counsel of ArtScroll's **Rabbi Avrohom Biderman** in the preparation of this book was invaluable.

The entire ArtScroll team has done another terrific job from start to finish. Thank you, **Mrs. Mindy Stern,** for your insightful editing and comments. Thank you, **Mrs. Faygie Weinbaum**, for your meticulous proofreading. Thank you, **Mrs. Toby Goldzweig,** for entering the editorial corrections, and thank you, **Mrs. Chana Sternglantz,** for doing a fantastic job in paginating the book. Thank you, **Reb Eli Kroen,** for producing a magnificent cover.

Many people have helped me, influenced me, and impacted me over the years. They are too numerous to mention, but I am truly indebted to them all and cherish our relationships.

Finally, I thank my wife, **Itta Brocha**, who has created a nurturing environment for our children, **Shifra**, **Leizer**, **Zevi**, and **Tzvi Yehudah**. *"Sheli v'shelachem shelah hu* — What is mine and what is yours is all from her" (*Kesubos* 63a).

May the Ribono Shel Olam bless us with berachah, hatzlachah, good health, and much nachas for years to come.

Yitzchok Hisiger

A Taste of Torah

Dead for the Day

"*When a man dies in a tent*" (Bamidbar 19:14). *Based on these words, the Gemara tells us that the Torah only establishes a permanent foothold within someone who "kills" himself for it (Berachos 63b). According to one explanation, this means that only the Torah of someone who lives in this world like a guest in a "tent," in total cognizance of its ephemeral nature, will endure forever.*

Through his actions, Rav Efraim Zalman Margulies suggested another interpretation.

Although Rav Efraim Zalman was a very wealthy businessman, he had a fixed rule that until 1 p.m., he could not be disturbed for any business matter, no matter how much money he stood to earn. He told his wife that until 1 o'clock, she was to consider him as "dead."

Once, a merchant came to his house and told his wife that he needed to speak to Rav Efraim Zalman for just five minutes, regarding a deal through which her husband could earn 10,000 rubles, a veritable fortune. The rebbetzin told the man that she had promised her husband not to disturb him under any circumstances until 1 in the afternoon, and she could make no exceptions. The incredulous merchant tried to convince the rebbetzin to call Rav Efraim Zalman, but she would not budge.

When she later told Rav Efraim Zalman about the visitor, he expressed great joy that he had demonstrated to Hashem that five minutes of Torah were worth more to him than 10,000 rubles.

Heilige Shas Yidden

R eb Yankel, a resident of the town of Volozhin, spent a signifi-cant amount of time involved in Torah study. He was an un-pretentious man who dressed simply and lived an austere life, but word among the townsfolk was that Reb Yankel had completed *Talmud Bavli* several times, thanks to his diligence and perseverance.

In fact, the great Rav Chaim of Volozhin would rise when he saw Reb Yankel; the Torah giant clearly felt that this man's achievement warranted such an open display of honor.

This confused the *yungerleit* of the Volozhiner Yeshivah, who were *talmidei chachamim,* well versed in all facets of Torah. Why, they wondered, would their great rebbi stand up for a simple Yid like Reb Yankel? True, he had learned the entire *Talmud Bavli* several times, but did he understand the Gemara he had studied? Did he comprehend *pshat* in all the arcane and intricate *sugyos*? He had done nothing more than read the words of the Tannaim and Amo-raim. Why the great demonstration of honor?

Hearing their objections, Rav Chaim sat down with his *talmidim* and proceeded to teach them a lesson. "As you know, there are two types of *Shasin* that are commonly sold," Rav Chaim began. "There's the Amsterdam *Shas*, which boasts a beautiful print, with easy-to-read letters. It is mistake-free and contains critical correc-tions to errors found in prior editions. It is a pleasure to learn from but is a bit pricey.

"Then there is the Zoltzbach *Shas*, which is not nearly as nice. In fact, it contains mistakes and inaccuracies. It does not have the im-provements and advancements of the Amsterdam *Shas*."

Rav Chaim now explained what he was driving at.

"Would you ever suggest that the Zoltzbach *Shas* possesses less *kedushah* than the Amsterdam *Shas*?" asked Rav Chaim rhetorical-ly. "Of course not. A *Shas* is a *Shas*. It has the full *kedushah* of a *Shas*, whether it is the Amsterdam version or the Zoltzbach version."

Rav Chaim's message was clear. Reb Yankel may have been a Zoltzbach Shas. His grasp of some of the sugyos haShas may have been minimal, and he may not have been fluent in all the masechtos he had completed. He may have forgotten many of the blatt he had learned.

But he was a Shas Yid nonetheless.

Whether one is an Amsterdam Shas or a Zoltzbach Shas, the holiness is there.

Pleading With the Partners

*T*he presence of the talmid chacham in the back row of the Mirrer Minyan in Boro Park, Brooklyn, day in and day out, was as certain as the sun rising each day in the east. Day after day, the wizened iluy sat, surrounded by dozens of tomes, his head buried deep in the sefer in front of him. He was in a spiritual paradise, spending his days the only way he could imagine.

It was no wonder that Rav Aharon Kreiser was recognized as a gaon. Decades of Torah learning had produced one of the great Torah personalities to grace the American Torah world.

Each day, as sure as one could find Rav Kreiser seated at his table in the Mirrer Minyan on 16th Avenue, as soon as it was lunchtime, one would observe a simple but devout Yid entering a local store to pick up two sandwiches and beverages. The Yid would then head to the Mirrer Minyan, where he would take a seat next to Rav Kreiser and place one sandwich and drink in front of the Rav, while saving the other sandwich and drink for himself. This Yid provided the physical sustenance, so Rav Kreiser could continue to imbibe the spiritual nutrition of which his neshamah could never get enough.

One day, when this Yid came with the lunches and drinks to the Mirrer Minyan, he noticed something strange. The building, for some inexplicable reason, was locked. This had never happened before. He looked right, he looked left, and then he stared above. Nothing. No sign. No clue. Why was the *beis midrash* closed? Something did not make sense.

Spotting some milk crates nearby, the Yid grabbed a few and began stacking them next to the building. Once they were at an adequate height, he climbed atop the crates and craned his neck, so that he could peer through one of the windows into the *beis midrash*.

Then he saw the most perplexing sight. The *aron kodesh* was wide open, and there, right in front of the Sifrei Torah, standing with his arms outstretched, was a man. Pressing his face a bit closer against the window, the Yid saw that the man standing there was none other than Rav Kreiser.

As he tried to keep his balance on the precariously piled milk crates, the man suddenly heard Rav Kreiser's voice. *What*, he wondered, *could Rav Kreiser be saying?* He placed his ear against the windowpane, trying to make out what his friend and daily lunch partner was uttering. And then he heard it.

"*Bava Kamma*, how could you?" cried Rav Kreiser. "How can you let Rav Nachum be ill? *Kesubos*, how is it possible? How can the *tzaddik* Rav Nachum be so sick?"

The Yid realized that Rav Kreiser was referring to the rosh yeshivah of Yeshivas Mir Yerushalayim, Rav Nachum Partzovitz, who was in poor health.

"*Kiddushin*, what's going to be?" continued Rav Kreiser. "How can you abandon Rav Nachum?"

"*Bava Basra*, you can't let go of Rav Nachum."

And so continued Rav Kreiser, crying, pleading, and beseeching.

> *In light of Rav Nachum's great hasmadah and yegiah, Rav Kreiser viewed the masechtos as partners with the unforgettable Mirrer rosh yeshivah. Hence his plea on behalf of the great gaon.*

Like Bread

Reb Shalom Ziskind was about 20 years old and learning at Beth Medrash Govoha in Lakewood, New Jersey, when he received a call from Rav Avraham Abba Freedman, who was sending a student from Detroit, Michigan to New York. The boy wanted to switch out of public school and into yeshivah for 12th grade. Rav Freedman, a *chinuch* leader in Detroit, asked Reb Shalom to bring the boy to the Skulener Rebbe, Rav Eliezer Zusia Portugal, for a *berachah* and some words of *chizuk*.

Reb Shalom went to the Rebbe's *tisch*, where he met the 17-year-old boy, who was among 50 or 60 men — mostly Chassidim — standing around the Rebbe and drinking in his words. It took some time until Reb Shalom was able to bring the boy over to the Rebbe. Then he whispered in the Rebbe's ear that the boy was studying in a public school in Detroit and was thinking of transferring to a yeshivah.

All of a sudden, the Rebbe's face lit up. He stopped everything, took the boy's hand in his own, and asked him, "Do you understand Yiddish?"

"Yes," he replied.

The Rebbe then told him, "I want you to know two things: First of all, Torah is like bread. Until you taste it, you can't know what it is like. You must go to yeshivah to taste it. And second, the future of Klal Yisrael depends on boys like you."

This boy was on cloud nine for the rest of the night. He decided to go to Yeshiva Torah Vodaath, and from there he went to Lakewood. He eventually became a rebbi in Los Angeles, where he influenced hundreds of *talmidim* over many years.

It is true: The future of Klal Yisrael depends on boys like him.

The Wife's Reward

*R*av Shlomo Brevda, a close talmid of Rav Aharon Kotler and a talmid muvhak of Rav Yechezkel Levenstein, is known for publishing the works of the Vilna Gaon as well as many other sefarim. He is also remembered as a beloved maggid who traveled worldwide for 60 years, delivering the mussar lessons of his great rebbeim.

Rav Brevda related an important lesson he learned from Rav Aharon Kotler, rosh yeshivah of Beth Medrash Govoha. As much as we admire men who study Torah, said Rav Aharon, we should admire their spouses even more, for they do not feel the husbands' pleasure in Torah study and the ecstasy of breaking through to an exciting *chiddush*. Yet they work at home, day and night, keeping the home clean and caring for their children. In the next world, however, they will receive more reward than their husbands.

Rav Brevda said that he heard this from Rav Aharon over 60 years earlier, when he explained that sometimes, inevitably, men waste time in the middle of learning, so they can never be sure that they have fulfilled their purpose in this world. Yet, women have no direct enjoyment from their husbands' learning and still they never cease their housework, so they deserve even more reward.

When a young man asked Rav Aharon, "Are you saying that my wife will get more out of my own Torah learning than I will?" he answered emphatically in the affirmative.

"Believe what I say!" Rav Aharon continued. "Women sacrifice more than men, especially in our generation, and are assured that they will be rewarded in full."

Application Exception

Each year, by a certain date, the list of *talmidim* who would be joining Yeshivas Ponovezh in Bnei Brak was finalized. Once that time arrived, the Ponovezher Rav, Rav Yosef Shlomo Kahaneman, was adamant about not accepting additional *talmidim*, and he firmly upheld this rule.

One time, right after the deadline, an exceptionally wealthy individual approached the rav and asked him to accept his grandson into Ponovezh. The rav refused, explaining that the list had been completed, and once the date of registration had passed, no exceptions could be made.

The *gvir* was disappointed. "If this is true," he remarked, "then I have no gripes. However, if I hear that the rav has made an exception for someone else, I will demand an explanation."

Immediately following this exchange, the rav exited the yeshivah building together with Rav Dovid Povarsky, rosh yeshivah of the yeshivah. On the steps to the entrance of the yeshivah, they encountered Rav Chaim Kanievsky, who was a relatively young *talmid chacham* at the time. Rav Chaim had come to ask the rav to accept a certain *bachur*, a relative of his, into the yeshivah. Upon hearing the request, the rav agreed to take the *bachur* into the yeshivah, no questions asked.

Once Rav Chaim had gone on his way, a startled Rav Povarsky turned to the rav. His question didn't need to be articulated: How could the rav, moments before, have turned down the wealthy gentleman, refusing to accept his grandson, and then immediately accepted Rav Chaim's relative?

The query didn't faze the rav.

"*Rav Chaim iz der Torah alein,*" the rav answered simply. "Rav Chaim is the Torah itself. *Eim ken men nit upzogen* — Him, I cannot refuse."

> The Ponovezher Rav already recognized the greatness of the humble gadol in Bnei Brak, Rav Chaim Kanievsky, when he was still young.
>
> And there was no saying no to the Torah alein, the Torah itself.

Avoiding Bitul Torah

R av Chaim Kanievsky was presented with the following query: A person wishes to buy an apartment and has two options. He can purchase an apartment on the highest floor of a building and thus be able to fulfill the *mitzvah min haTorah* of *maakeh*, constructing a fence around a porch or roof area of a certain height (*Devarim* 22:8). However, because the apartment is higher than 20 *amos*, he will have to light his Chanukah menorah by his doorway and there will be diminished *pirsumei nisa* (publicizing of the miracle). Alternatively, he can buy a first- or second-floor apartment that is within 20 *amos* of the ground, and while he won't have the opportunity to fulfill the mitzvah of *maakeh*, he will be able to light his menorah at his front doorway or at a window, causing increased *pirsumei nisa*. Which is preferable?

Rav Chaim's response was succinct: "*L'matah, mi'shum bitul Torah.*" The person should purchase an apartment on a lower floor, said Rav Chaim, in order to minimize *bitul Torah*. That is, by not having to ascend and descend various flights of stairs when entering and exiting, the person will not be wasting time that could be used for *limud haTorah*.

Saved for Torah

*R*av Yitzchok Karpf was raised on the Lower East Side of Manhattan of the 1920's and 30's, by parents who desired a Torah education for their children, a rarity at the time. He later became a son-in-law of the famed Torah pioneer, Rav Shraga Feivel Mendlowitz, and enjoyed a career as a star rebbi and maggid shiur at Yeshiva Torah Vodaath and later Mesivta Beth Shraga, influencing generations of talmidim.

Rav Yitzchok's son, Yisrael Meir, was born with Down syndrome. Yisrael Meir, who was unable to attend a mainstream yeshivah, did not learn how to read Hebrew in school. However, Rav Karpf wanted him to know how to daven, so he asked a kindergarten rebbi from Torah Vodaath to teach his son how to read *lashon hakodesh*. When the rebbi succeeded in this task, Rav Karpf felt very grateful to him.

At the time, this rebbi's teaching salary was not sufficient for his growing family, and he was considering the field of watchmaking. Rav Karpf got wind of this and approached the menahel of Torah Vodaath, Rav Nesanel Quinn.

"We have such a big yeshivah," said Rav Karpf. "Surely you can find an additional position for this talented rebbi." Rav Quinn agreed and appointed the rebbi as a dorm mashgiach. Along with the menial aspects of his new position, the rebbi was "thrown a bone" and honored with an occasional *vaad* for the older *bachurim* of the yeshivah; these *vaadim* were, by all accounts, an astounding success.

With time, it emerged that this kindergarten rebbi was no simple educator; he was something extraordinary. And thanks to Rav Karpf's persistence, an outstanding talent had been uncovered.

> *The former kindergarten rebbi's name is Rav Moshe Wolfson, who eventually became the mashgiach of Yeshiva Torah Vodaath and rav of Beis Medrash Emunas Yisrael in Boro Park, where he continues to inspire hundreds.*
>
> *All thanks to Rav Karpf's gratitude for his help and appreciation for his talents.*

"Do You Know It Is Zees?"

*S*ometimes, in our busy and hectic lives, we become consumed *with what we must do, and with telling our children what they must do, and we forget or neglect to tell our children just how wonderful Torah learning and Torah living are. Yet Rav Nosson Tzvi Finkel, rosh yeshivah of Yeshivas Mir Yerushalayim, demonstrated — through his deeds and his words — the beauty of a Torah life and the wonderful blessings Hashem grants us. Rav Nosson Tzvi reminded us all to appreciate the things we do, viewing them not as compulsory, but as the greatest way of life one can imagine.*

Rav Nosson Tzvi was frequently visited by 13-year-old boys seeking the *berachah* of the rosh yeshivah upon their bar mitzvahs. In addition to wishing them mazel tov, Rav Nosson Tzvi would *bentch* each boy that he grow up to become a *talmid chacham* and a *yerei Shamayim.*

But Rav Nosson Tzvi wasn't finished. He had a message that emanated from his heart, which was saturated with *ahavas haTorah*. He would take the boy's hand and softly and gently ask the *bachur*, "Do you know that the Torah is *zees* [sweet]?"

The Greatness of the Maharil Diskin

*R*av Yehoshua Leib Diskin, known as the Maharil Diskin, was a gaon and tzaddik. Rav Yosef Dov Soloveitchik, who was known as the Beis HaLevi, succeeded the Maharil Diskin as rav of Brisk when the Maharil moved to Eretz Yisrael. Whenever the Beis HaLevi would write a letter to the Maharil, his hand would shake from fear and awe. According to the Beis HaLevi's grandson, Rav Yitzchak Zev Soloveitchik, this happened a number of times. And Rav Baruch Ber Leibowitz, later rosh yeshivah of Kamenitz, related that Rav Chaim Soloveitchik (the Beis HaLevi's son and Rav Yitzchak Zev's father) said that he was prepared to walk even 30 miles to hear the chiddushei Torah of the Maharil Diskin.

The Maharil Diskin's hands used to tremble all day — but not on Shabbos. When those who were close to him first noticed this, they surmised that he had a certain fear that was calmed on Shabbos. They later found out that he was constantly writing out the *Sheim Hashem* with his fingers, to fulfill the *pasuk* that states, "*Shivisi Hashem le'negdi samid* — I have set Hashem before me always" (*Tehillim* 16:8). On Shabbos, however, he did not want to write even in such a way that leaves no imprint.

Once, in the middle of the day on Yom Kippur, the Maharil Diskin suddenly felt his strength leave him and he became so weak that he fainted. A tumult ensued and his *talmidim* called for a doctor. They tried to revive him, but the Maharil Diskin remained unconscious. Among those present was Rav Moshe Eliezer Dan

Ralbag, the Maharil Diskin's cousin and prized *talmid*. He leaned over his unconscious rebbi and asked him a deep question based on a Gemara in *Perek Merubah* in *Maseches Bava Kamma*. To everyone's surprise, the Maharil Diskin suddenly awoke and exclaimed, "*Dos iz ah kasha!* [That's a real good question!] *Dos iz ah kasha!*"

It was Torah that was able to revive him.

One Daf

The Maharil Diskin used to deliver an in-depth *shiur* on Gemara, Rashi, and Tosafos for two hours each day to an elite group of *talmidim*. During the winter of 5638 (1878), when he first arrived in Eretz Yisrael, he completed only the first *daf* of *Maseches Bava Basra* on the *sugya* of *hezek re'iah*. For 40 days, he taught his *talmidim* that one page of Gemara, without repeating himself or revising what he said even once. They delved deep into the *sugya*, covering its entire length and breadth.

When the 40 days were up and each distinguished *talmid* understood the material according to his ability, Rav Yehoshua Leib perceived that they felt that they had finally merited to understand a *daf* of Gemara and were pleased that they no longer needed to study that *daf*.

But Rav Yehoshua Leib had a vital lesson to impart to them.

"If you imagine that you are now in full comprehension of this *daf*," he told them, "you are mistaken. At this stage, we are likened to the little *cheder* boys who have finished learning *aleph-beis* and are sure that they now know all there is to learn. Our comprehension of this *daf* is a drop in the ocean compared to the depth of the Tannaim and Amoraim. However, it is impossible to tarry longer over one page, for then we would never get to learn the whole Torah."

Reflecting on Rav Yehoshua Leib's remark, Rav Yaakov Oren-stein said, "You can be sure that the slightest trace of pride or

self-satisfaction that may have crept into the hearts of the talmi-
dim was instantly erased."

❖ ❖ ❖

The Chazon Ish also had what to say about this vignette, but
he focused on a different aspect: the fact that the Maharil was
able to spend so much time on one page of Gemara. The Chazon
Ish said that this is the sign of a true talmid chacham: "A true
talmid chacham can learn one page of Gemara for 40 days, and
40 pages of Gemara in one day."

One must be able to study a given topic for days on end,
plumbing its depths and uncovering every nuance of that par-
ticular subject, while also being able to study a larger number of
pages of Gemara in rapid succession in order to learn as much
of the Torah as possible.

Food for Tosafos

A group of *bachurim* entered the office of the Kamenitzer rosh yeshivah, Rav Baruch Ber Leibowitz, to describe their physical deprivation. They complained about their inability to comprehend the *sugya* while suffering from hunger. On his lofty level, however, Rav Baruch Ber found it difficult to understand how hunger could be an impediment to in-depth learning.

One intuitive *bachur* understood the need to explain it to the rosh yeshivah according to his frame of reference, so he stated, "We are sufficiently nourished for Gemara and Rashi, but for Tosafos, we need additional food!"

This description had its desired effect, and the situation immediately became a matter of urgency. The rosh yeshivah turned to his son-in-law, Rav Reuven Grozovsky, and began to make plans to travel to America to raise funds — for the study of Tosafos.

Taanis Versus Tosafos

Yerushalayim of old was home to a holy Jew named Rav Nachum Shadiker. As part of his lofty *avodas Hashem*, which included lengthy *tefillos* and continuous Torah learning, Rav Nachum undertook many voluntary fasts. These *taaniyos* were often trying and taxing, but Rav Nachum persisted. His connection to the material world was tenuous; he lived in a spiritual realm, where service of Hashem was all that mattered.

On one of these fast days, as evening approached and the sun began to set, Rav Nachum called over one of his sons and asked him to bring a cup of water. After Rav Nachum drank the water, his son remarked that while his father may be feeling weak from the fast, in just a few minutes the sun is going to set, signifying the end of the day. Couldn't he have held out for such a short length of time so that he could complete the fast?

Rav Nachum surprised his son with his response. "No," he said, "I am actually feeling all right; I am physically fine. However, I am currently studying a particular Tosafos, and because of my fast, I was having trouble plumbing its depth and understanding its profundity. I therefore asked you for the cup of water, so that it can refresh me and allow me to analyze the Tosafos with full concentration.

"True, the fast is almost over, but studying the words of Torah is more significant and important than fasting many, many voluntary *taaniyos*."

It Has to Be Alive

Rabbi Shmuel Kaufman, longtime *mechanech* in Detroit, learned in Telshe Yeshivah in Cleveland when he was young. One morning, right after breakfast, he was walking to the dormitory and was greeted unexpectedly at the entrance by the rosh yeshivah, Rav Eliyahu Meir (Elya Meir) Bloch. At the time, Rav Elya Meir, who had lost his family in the Holocaust, had not yet remarried and was living in the dormitory with the *bachurim*.

"Shmuel," he said, "come to my room. Let's talk in learning."

Although surprised by the invitation, Shmuel was not nervous, as he had just said a *chaburah* the day before, and so he had *chiddushim* to tell his rosh yeshivah. The session went well, as he repeated most of his discourse of the previous day.

The next morning, once again, he walked to the dormitory after breakfast and again Rav Elya Meir was waiting for him at the door with a friendly greeting. "Shmuel, come to my room and let's speak in learning."

This time, Shmuel wasn't as confident as the day before. He had to rack his brain to remember the remnants of the *chaburah* that he had not yet told the rosh yeshivah. Nevertheless, he made a fine presentation, not letting on that he was somewhat rattled.

The next day after breakfast, he told his friend, "Let's go around to the back entrance of the dorm. I don't want to run into the rosh yeshivah again. I used up my entire *chaburah*."

They walked around to the back entrance, but sure enough, standing right there was Rav Elya Meir, waiting for his *talmid*. Now Shmuel knew that he was in trouble. He had nothing left to say on the Gemara. What in the world did the rosh yeshivah want from him?

"*Nu*, Shmuel," said Rav Elya Meir, "say a *shtickel Torah*."

Shmuel was at a loss for words. "What does the rosh yeshivah want from me?" he finally asked. "The first day I said part of my *chaburah*, and yesterday I used it all up. I've got nothing left to say."

Rav Elya Meir said to him with a smile, "I just wanted to convey to you that you must always have something to say on the Gemara — not only when you prepare a *chaburah*, but on a daily basis. How can a day of learning pass without gaining some new insight into the Gemara: a *kasha*, a *terutz*, or a *sevarah*?

"We call it *Toras chaim*. It has to be alive. Everyone must find something new that excites him and causes him to think and probe. Otherwise, *heist dos nit gelerent* — it is not called learning."

— *heard from Rabbi Yitzchok Tzvi Schwarz*

Tanu Rabbanan

Rav Nachum Partzovitz, rosh yeshivah of Yeshivas Mir Yerushalayim, was once walking up and down the aisles of the yeshivah's *beis midrash.* Two *bachurim*, who hadn't been fully engaged in their learning, noticed the rosh yeshivah drawing near. Somewhat embarrassed by their lack of intensity, they turned to their Gemaras, feigned a look of *hasmadah,* and began to chant loudly, "*Tanu Rabbanan* — Our Sages taught," using words commonly found in the Gemara.

During that *z'man*, the yeshivah was learning *Maseches Nedarim.* The rosh yeshivah stopped by their seats and said simply, "*Sheker saneisi va'asa'eivah* — I have hated falsehood and abhorred it," quoting a *pasuk* in *Tehillim* (119:163). Rav Nachum then continued: "In all of *Maseches Nedarim*, the words '*Tanu Rabbanan*' do not appear."

> In that brief moment, the bachurim were taught an unforgettable lesson in honesty, while also witnessing the astounding Torah greatness of the rosh yeshivah.
>
> Rav Yitzchak Oheiv Tzion shared this story with Rav Chaim Kanievsky, who confirmed that the words "Tanu Rabbanan" do not appear in Maseches Nedarim at the beginning of a phrase, though he pointed out that the words do appear within a longer phrase: "Man tana leha de'tanu Rabbanan…— Who is the Tanna who related this Baraisa…" (Nedarim 27a).

My Brothers' Simchah

Rav Naftali of Ropshitz once observed a simple Jew dancing on Simchas Torah with gusto. The man went around and around, singing and dancing with a genuine *simchah*, a huge smile spread across his face as he held onto the Sefer Torah with great passion.

The Ropshitzer was a bit surprised. This man was unlearned and knew little in the way of Torah. What was he so exuberant about? How was he capable of mustering such elation on Simchas Torah?

Intrigued, the Ropshitzer approached the man and shared his puzzlement. The man flashed the Rebbe another big smile and explained.

"True," he said, "I am not learned and I don't know much Torah, but my brothers, my fellow Yidden, are celebrating the completion of the entire Torah and I am rejoicing in my brothers' *simchah*! I am exhilarated with their accomplishment. How can I not dance?"

"Is This the Ketzos?"

Tzvi, a diligent yeshivah *bachur* from Lakewood, spent his mesivta and *beis midrash* years *shteiging* at a respected American yeshivah. Soon after, he went on to learn in a prominent Yerushalayim yeshivah, where he hoped to continue his *aliyah ba-Torah*. Tzvi had recently authored a *sefer*, an impressive treatment of many of the complex *chakiros*, questions, and postulations found in the *Ketzos HaChoshen*, the *Nesivos HaMishpat*, and other *sefarim*, along with contemporary *sevaros* and explanations.

While working on his *sefer*, Tzvi had benefited from the works of Rav Yechiel Michel Ber Dzimitrovsky. Rav Dzimitrovsky had published, with beautiful elucidation and footnotes, the now standard and widely used editions of *Ketzos HaChoshen* and *Avnei Miluim* (the *sefarim* of Rav Aryeh Leib HaKohen Heller, who was known as the Ketzos, after his most famous *sefer*, the *Ketzos HaChoshen*) and the *Nesivos HaMishpat*, which was written by Rav Yaakov Lorberbaum, a contemporary of the Ketzos. Tzvi wanted to meet Rav Dzimitrovsky and thank him for all he had done for him and for Klal Yisrael.

Tzvi found Rav Dzimitrovsky's address and headed to his home. As he approached, he realized that his lack of fluency in the Hebrew language would present a problem when he arrived. How would he convey that he was seeking the author of the well-known commentary on the works of the Ketzos?

When he arrived at the address he had been given, he knocked hesitatingly. Answering the door was a young girl, who looked at the yeshivah *bachur* with questioning eyes. Tzvi looked back, opened his mouth to speak, but found himself at a loss. Stammering, he finally blurted out, "*Zeh Ketzos?* [Is this the Ketzos?]"

The girl smiled. "*Kein* [Yes]," she responded, demonstrating that her father's efforts for *harbatzas haTorah* had so permeated his own home that it was the very essence and identity of his family.

> The meeting between the young, budding talmid chacham and the accomplished marbitz Torah was a productive one. That first encounter flourished into a wonderful kesher between the two.
>
> Yes, Tzvi had found the right address, the address of "the Ketzos."

A Prior Commitment

*T*here was a Gerrer Chassid, a world-class genius and masmid, who was also an exceedingly humble man and a hidden tzaddik. In his later years, he suffered from Alzheimer's. The condition had a devastating impact on him and he spent most of his days confused and disoriented, at the mercy of foreign caretakers. He was incapable of even opening a sefer. His family monitored his condition and supported him around the clock, but it was a source of overwhelming sorrow to them to see their brilliant father in this state, to have to answer his confused questions, and to realize that he could not recognize even his closest family members.

During the winter of 2015, his grandson got married, and the father of the *chassan* discovered, to his surprise, that there is a wonder drug that could bring about an amazing turnaround for a few hours; after taking it, the patient returns to himself to some extent, albeit for only a short amount of time. The drug's side effects are too damaging for it to be taken regularly, but it can be taken once every few months. The family planned to give the pill to their father on the day of the wedding, so he could partake in the *simchah* and speak to the guests. What could bring the family more joy than that?

Several hours before the wedding, the father was given the pill, and he became more lucid than he had been in months. "Abba," his son said, "I am marrying off my son. We are taking you to the wedding." The elderly man, suddenly remembering his son and grandson, trembled with excitement and was happy to embrace them, but he announced that he did not intend to go to the wedding.

"Why?" cried the disappointed family members. They presumed that his faculties were still impaired.

"I have missed many hours of learning," the man replied.

He proceeded to sit and learn for 15 hours, taking notes in his notebook in his compact handwriting.

Only one of his sons was capable of deciphering his father's handwriting, and he went to the house to determine whether the notes were sensible or if his father's mind was impaired as before. Perusing the notes, the son was astonished: His father had written many pages of notes on *Maseches Bava Basra* and a few on *Maseches Pesachim*. The notes on the previous pages in the book, which had been written several years earlier, were also mostly on *Maseches Bava Basra*, with a few pages on *Maseches Pesachim*!

Teaching the Beauty of Torah

*A*ccolades of greatness are often used loosely, but in the case of Rav Efraim Zuravin, they are quite apt. The fact that his name is not familiar to many is part of his genuine gadlus, which came along with great anivus.

I didn't know Rav Efraim personally, but I have memories of Rav Efraim from the period when he was the rosh kollel of Rav Shlomo Lesin's kollel in Lakewood, which was located just a few blocks from my home. Once in a while, I would stop in at the kollel to surreptitiously catch a glimpse of him learning. I had been told about his greatness by talmidim of his and felt that I had to seek him out. I thought that, to some extent, I knew a secret that much of the world — beyond his circle of talmidim and admirers — did not.

When Efraim was 11, his family moved from Baltimore to Lakewood. He would go to Beth Medrash Govoha on Shabbos afternoon to watch Rav Aharon Kotler deliver his *shiur*, even though he didn't understand a word. When Shabbos was over, he would walk over to the wall of the *beis midrash* where the *mareh mekomos* for Rav Aharon's *shiur* had been posted, and he would take down the paper and place it in his drawer. *One day*, he thought to himself, *I, too, will be able to understand these things.*

Rav Efraim kept those papers for the rest of this life. They were among his most prized possessions.

Years later, when Rav Aharon's son, Rav Shneur, was looking for someone to write his father's *chiddushim* and prepare them for publication, he found no one more capable than that very individual, who, as a boy, had collected those small papers. Rav Efraim was a 32-year-old *yungerman* when he was selected for this task. He is credited with transmitting the *shiurim* of Rav Aharon Kotler to the greater Torah world and future generations of *talmidei chachamim*.

A *maggid shiur* at his yeshivah once asked Rav Efraim why he delivered such dazzling, difficult *shiurim*, which, in the *maggid shiur's* opinion, were beyond the grasp of some of the *bachurim*.

Rav Efraim responded, "I want to show them the beauty of Torah in all of its depth. I want the *shiur* to be the catalyst for them to love and appreciate the beauty of Torah."

Rav Efraim's shiur wasn't a vehicle through which to demonstrate his brilliance or creativity. His goal was what should be the goal of every maggid shiur and marbitz Torah: to get his listeners to appreciate the beauty and majesty of Torah. And while not every bachur had the ability to comprehend every detail of Rav Efraim's shiurim, there was no question that each one emerged with an appreciation of the magnificence, depth, and splendor of Torah.

"We" Should Read It

In Czarist Russia, the minister of education had decreed that the yeshivos must add various secular subjects to their curriculum. "I am just trying to make you more effective as rabbis and teachers," explained the minister.

An emergency meeting of rabbanim was held to discuss how to respond.

One of the rabbanim suggested that a delegation meet with the minister and read and translate to him the *tefillah* of "*Ahavah Rabbah.*" In this daily *tefillah*, which is recited right before *Krias Shema* of Shacharis, we express the love that HaKadosh Baruch Hu has for His nation and how He lovingly gave us the Torah. We beseech Him, in the *zechus* of our forefathers, to allow us to study and understand these life-giving words.

"If we could get him to understand how dear each word of Torah is to us," argued the petitioner, "perhaps he would understand why we consider this decree so terrible."

Rav Yitzchak Blazer, a great *mussar* personality, known in the Jewish world as Rav Itzele Peterburger, arose and declared, "I believe that if we would read and translate the *tefillah* of *Ahavah Rabbah* to ourselves, the decree would be rescinded."

If only we could all appreciate the preciousness of each word of Torah…

A Taste of Diligence

Two Much

As a *bachur*, Rav Yitzchok Karpf was greatly influenced by his encounters with Rav Elchanan Wasserman, during Rav Elchanan's visit to the United States to raise funds for his yeshivah in Baranovich. Every afternoon, Torah Vodaath would send a different *bachur* to assist him.

One afternoon, it was the turn of Yitzchok's *chavrusa*. Since he had a strong desire to form a bond with this *gadol*, Yitzchok decided to go along. When they arrived at the house where Rav Elchanan was staying, the two boys knocked on the door. Rav Elchanan himself opened the door, and upon seeing two *bachurim*, exclaimed, "*Tzvei? Ich hub nit der pleitzes far der bitul Torah fuhn tzvei!* [Two? I can't accept responsibility for the *bitul Torah* of two *bachurim*!]"

Young Yitzchok Karpf learned an enduring lesson about the severity of *bitul Torah*.

Lernen

He did not realize it at the moment, but it was to be the last time that Rav Chaim Dov Keller, today rosh yeshivah of the Telshe Yeshivah in Chicago, would be seeing his beloved rebbi, Rav Elya Meir Bloch, rosh yeshivah of Telshe Yeshivah in Cleveland.

Many years later, the scene remained vivid in Rav Keller's mind and he shared the following memories in The Jewish Observer:

When Rav Keller entered the rosh yeshivah's room in the hospital with some others, Rav Elya Meir was not there. Only after a while did the rosh yeshivah enter, dragging his slippered feet and leaning heavily on his stepson, Reb Mordechai Glicksman. Perspiration beaded his forehead and he had considerable trouble breathing. Rav Keller winced at the sight.

Rav Elya Meir, who had always greeted all *b'seiver panim yafos* and with genuine warmth, could not gather the strength to say, "*Shalom aleichem.*" Not even a nod. He merely acknowledged his visitors' presence with his eyes. With great difficulty, he was helped to an armchair and sat there breathing heavily.

After a few moments, he said three words: "*Ah shvere mishpat* [A hard, painful judgment]." This was the only time Rav Keller ever heard the rosh yeshivah utter a complaint about something personal.

Finally, the rosh yeshivah caught his breath, managed a weak smile, extended his frail hand, and said, "*Shalom aleichem.*"

Then he explained: "It's a hard judgment. But it's not the pain. From the time that I was young, I've never known what it means to sit idle. I would be learning myself or with others, or writing or speaking or reading, or even fixing something around the house. But to just lie in bed and do nothing is a terrible punishment."

Thus did Rav Elya Meir see himself just before he passed away. And thus do his thousands of talmidim and admirers remember him. Rav Elya Meir could never sit idle. There was too much to be done.

The rosh yeshivah was an ish ha'eshkolos, a possessor of a host of talents: He was a rosh yeshivah and rebbi, whose shiurim were masterpieces of profundity. He had gifts of oratory and writing. His energy was boundless. His interest in his family,

his talmidim, his yeshivah, the city of Cleveland, and Klal Yisrael was remarkable.

With all his pressures and commitments, which took so much of his time and energy, he maintained strict *sedarim* for his own learning, which could not be violated except for emergencies.

Aside from that, like other great men in Telshe, he had made a *kabbalah* to learn one hour a day in which he was not to be interrupted at all — even for an emergency— at times expending extraordinary effort to keep this *kabbalah.*

Soon after his last major operation, Rav Keller stayed with the rosh yeshivah overnight. The rosh yeshivah was critically ill, with tubes attached to various parts of his body. He could not move and he could hardly talk. After a while, he said one word: "*Lernen* — Learning."

Rav Keller took a *Chumash* and learned with him the *parashas hashavua* with Rashi. From time to time, the rosh yeshivah's eyes would turn to the clock on the wall. When a half-hour had gone by, he said: "*Genug,* enough." Extremely fatigued, he closed his eyes. Some time later, he looked at the clock and again said, "*Lernen.*" Rav Keller learned aloud for another half-hour. When the time was up, the rosh yeshivah said, "*Genug,*" with a smile of satisfaction. He had finished his hour of learning.

Rav Chaim Mordechai (Mottel) Katz and Rav Mordechai Gifter, the other roshei yeshivah of Telshe Yeshivah, once visited Rav Elya Meir in the hospital. He said to them, "*Mi'yom amdi al daati,* from the time that I arrived at my full senses, I never missed my *kabbalah* to learn at least an hour a day, with one exception: when I was wheeled into the operating room before dawn and did not regain consciousness until after the stars came out. But now I feel that stopping to learn may be a case of *pikuach nefesh,* since I am so weak that the learning may endanger my life. However, I will not permit myself to forgo learning unless you *pasken* that I should."

Their *psak* was, of course, that he should not learn.

> *Rav Elya Meir possessed outstanding ahavas haTorah and an inner calm, which came from unbelievable self-discipline and seder — an all-pervasive order — that allowed him to accomplish so much in his 60 years.*

And at the center of all of this was Torah, for Torah was the essence of his life.

Life-Giving

"**G**edolah Torah she'hi nosenes chaim la'oseha va'olam hazeh u'va'Olam Haba — Great is Torah for it confers life upon its practitioners, both in this world and in the World to Come" (*Pirkei Avos* 6:7).

Rav Yosef Shalom Elyashiv was a living embodiment of this. Torah gave him life. To him, life was Torah and Torah was life.

Rav Leibel Lisker, a nephew of Rebbetzin Shaina Elyashiv, was in Eretz Yisrael and went to see Rav Elyashiv. He did not arrive during the time set aside for *kabbalas kahal*, when Rav Elyashiv met with the public, but since he was related, he was given special treatment and was usually able to enter the Elyashiv home whenever he came.

This time, however, Rebbetzin Elyashiv informed him that while he was welcome to enter, Rav Elyashiv was not home. When Rav Lisker explained that he had an important *shailah*, the rebbetzin graciously told him, "The rav is learning at the Ohel Sarah *beis midrash*, where he locks the door so that he is not disturbed. However, I'll tell you what I do when I need him, as I have a pre-arranged system with him. Go to a particular window of the *beis midrash* and knock three times. When you do, he will open the door. Tell him that I advised you to do this and you will then be able to present your *shailah*."

Rav Lisker proceeded to Ohel Sarah and was about to knock on the window when he heard two people inside the *beis midrash* engaged in a heated exchange of Torah. Not wanting to disturb Rav Elyashiv and his *chavrusa*, Rav Lisker waited. After about 10 minutes, though, Rav Lisker decided to utilize the "secret," and he knocked on the window three times. Soon enough, Rav Elyashiv opened the door and welcomed in Rav Lisker.

Upon entering the *beis midrash*, Rav Lisker looked around, but he saw no one except for Rav Elyashiv. What had happened to his *chavrusa*? He looked again just to be sure, but there was no one there.

His suspicion was confirmed after he witnessed this a number of times: Rav Elyashiv was his very own *chavrusa*. He was able to learn by himself in the manner that one learns with a *chavrusa*. With his unusual *kisharon* and *hasmadah*, he was capable of using the give-and-take style of a regular *chavrusashaft*. This was the result of — as well as the means of attaining more of — the clarity that he possessed in Torah.

Rav Elyashiv himself said, "I never in my life learned with a *chavrusa*." But he explained that this is a challenging way to learn and he did not recommend it to others, because it is difficult for most people to gain clarity without the nature of *chavrusa* learning.

A person was once observing Rav Elyashiv studying a *shtickel Torah* in the *sefer Tzafnas Pane'ach* from the Rogatchover Gaon. The *sefer* is a particularly complicated one, yet Rav Elyashiv was reading through it with surprising speed. The observer couldn't contain himself and asked Rav Elyashiv, "How is the rav able to do that? How can you learn through such a complex *sefer* so quickly?"

Rav Elyashiv's response was simple: *"Durch lernen, lernen, lernen* — Through learning, learning, learning."

Rav Elyashiv once made an observation regarding the *lechem ha-panim* that, in actuality, reflected his own devotion to unremitting *limud haTorah*.

The halachah is that the *lechem hapanim* must remain on the *Shulchan* in the *Beis HaMikdash* "*tamid* — always" (*Shemos* 25:30). What does *tamid* mean? The Mishnah in *Maseches Menachos* (99b) records a *machlokes* between the *Chachamim* and Rabbi Yose. The *Chachamim* state that as one set of Kohanim pulled the previous week's breads from the *Shulchan*, other Kohanim immediately placed the new breads on the table, with each handbreadth of the old loaf being replaced by a handbreadth of a new one. In this way, the *lechem hapanim* was on the *Shulchan* continuously.

Rabbi Yose disagrees. As the Gemara explains, he maintains that even if the Kohanim were to completely remove the old bread from the *Shulchan* before the other Kohanim placed the new bread on the table, it would be considered *tamid*. Thus, according to Rabbi Yose, as long as the breads were on the *Shulchan* at some point every day and night, this sufficed for the requirement of *tamid*.

Rabbi Ami deduces from Rabbi Yose's words that even if a person learns a *perek* of Torah in the morning and a *perek* of Torah at night, he fulfills the requirement of: *"Lo yamush Sefer haTorah hazeh mi'picha ve'hagisa bo yomam va'lailah* — This Book of the Torah shall not depart from your mouth; rather you should contemplate it day and night" (*Yehoshua* 1:8). Just as one may fulfill the mitzvah of *tamid* by ensuring that no full day or night passes without the presence of *lechem hapanim* on the *Shulchan*, so may one fulfill the command of *"ve'hagisa bo yomam va'lailah"* by ensuring that no full day or night passes without Torah study.

Rav Elyashiv remarked that we can similarly apply Rabbi Ami's observation to the opinion of the *Chachamim*. Thus, according to the *Chachamim* who require the *lechem hapanim* to be on the *Shulchan* at every moment, one's *limud haTorah* must also be constant and undisturbed to fulfill the requirement of *tamid*.

How apt a thought for one whose life was one long period of tamid, of ceaseless Torah learning, truly fulfilling "ve'hagisa bo yomam va'lailah" in every sense.

Five Minutes

A serious *bachur* learning at Yeshivas Mir Yerushalayim had a very close friend who was getting married in the United States in the middle of the *zman*. The *bachur* would not have left yeshivah in the middle of the *zman* to fly in for the wedding, but due to unforeseen circumstances, many of the *chassan's* friends, and even some of his family, would not be able to be at his wedding. In this unusual situation, the *chassan's* close friend in Eretz Yisrael felt that his presence at the wedding would make a huge difference to the *chassan*. No doubt, he would be fulfilling the Torah dictum of gladdening the heart of a groom.

Still, unwilling to make the decision on his own, the *bachur* presented his dilemma to Rav Yosef Shalom Elyashiv: Should he or should he not leave yeshivah for a short period in the middle of the *zman* to attend the *chasunah*?

Rav Elyashiv listened to the entire question, taking in all the particulars of the situation. Before he gave the *bachur* specific direction and guidance, he sighed and said, almost to himself, "If people would understand the value of even five minutes of *limud haTorah*, such questions wouldn't even come up." He then proceeded to give the *bachur* personal guidance for his particular situation.

To Rav Elyashiv, five minutes was an eternity; five minutes of limud haTorah was unequaled.

With this in mind, one can comprehend the very real mesirus nefesh that Rav Elyashiv demonstrated in setting aside time each day to meet with and advise people from all over the world.

In *Parashas Yisro* (*Shemos* 19:14), we are told how Moshe Rabbeinu descended from Har Sinai and approached Klal Yisrael to instruct them to sanctify themselves and wash their clothing before receiving the Torah. Rashi explains that the intent of the *pasuk* is to highlight the fact that Moshe, as the *manhig* of Klal Yisrael, ignored his personal affairs and needs and went directly from the mountain to the people.

What exactly were Moshe Rabbeinu's personal "affairs"? The Rambam (*Hilchos Melachim* 12:4) tells us that the *chachamim* and *nevi'im* pine for the *yemos haMashiach*, not so that Klal Yisrael can rule over the world, but so that they can fully devote themselves to Torah. The "affairs" of the *chachmei Yisrael* are Torah, so what exactly were the affairs of Moshe Rabbeinu that he abandoned in order to proceed directly to Klal Yisrael?

Rav Elyashiv, in explaining this Rashi, said that of course Moshe Rabbeinu, the *avi hanevi'im*, was the greatest *masmid* in the world, dedicating his every available moment to the study of the holy Torah. And that is precisely what the *pasuk* is informing us. Moshe Rabbeinu's "personal affairs" constituted his Torah learning. The greatness of Moshe, explained Rav Elyashiv, was that as he descended from Har Sinai, his desire was to engage in Torah study, yet he put aside his own affairs — his precious *limud haTorah* — in order to address the needs of his people, the nation of Klal Yisrael.

> *Rav Elyashiv could have been describing his own sacrifices for Klal Yisrael.*
>
> *Rav Elyashiv gave away his most precious commodity — his time — for his fellow Yidden. For him, time wasn't money. Time was limud haTorah. Time was irreplaceable in his eyes, as he showed again and again.*
>
> *Yet, he sacrificed that which was most precious to him to be mechazeik Yidden, to dispense advice, and to articulate clear psak halachah when asked.*

Rav Altusky's Goral HaGra

*R*av Chaim Dov Altusky was a shining example of a Jew who is totally dedicated to Torah, with every fiber of his being. His *Chiddushei Basra* series, based on the shiurim he delivered to thou-

sands of talmidim for over 50 years, is studied in batei midrash all over the world. From 1965 to 1997, he completed the 60 sefarim of the series, at an average of one sefer every six months.

Along with his father-in-law, Rav Chaim Pinchas Scheinberg, Rav Chaim Dov founded and nurtured Yeshivas Torah Ore in New York and later in Yerushalayim.

Rav Altusky basically lived in Yeshivas Torah Ore. He learned the whole day in the *beis midrash* with *tefillin* on his arm and head, toiling in Torah with all his strength. He ate his meals in the *beis midrash* or in a small room at the back, and returned home each night at the exact same time. He was like a machine that never tired out.

Rav Altusky carefully weighed and measured every second. When Rav Shmuel Hominer, a great *talmid chacham* and prolific author of *Eved HaMelech* fame, passed away, Rav Altusky considered going to the *levayah,* as the two had had a personal connection. But Rav Altusky, who so valued his time, was unsure if this was the right way to spend his time.

In order to decide, Rav Altusky made a *Goral HaGra*, a complex formula learned from the Vilna Gaon, which is used to determine a course of action. It involves turning the pages of a *Tanach* in a specific order and then reading a certain *pasuk.* Rav Altusky did the *goral* and came up with the *pasuk:* "And Shmuel said to Shaul, 'Tell the attendant to go on ahead of us,' so he passed ahead. 'You stand here now and I will let you hear the word of G-d'" (*I Shmuel* 9:27). From this, Rav Altusky deduced that while others should attend the *levayah,* he should stay behind and learn "the word of Hashem."

People generally use the Goral HaGra when faced with life and death decisions, such as whether to do surgery or whether to go on an important journey. For Rav Altusky, learning or not learning for a few hours was no less crucial a question.

The Elter Zeide's Example

*R*av Shmuel Aharon Yudelevitch, author of Me'il Shmuel, was a son of Rav Shabsai Yudelevitch and a grandson of Rav Yitzchak Yaakov Yudelevitch. Growing up in the world of the old yishuv of Yerushalayim, he inherited a spiritual legacy of Torah greatness. He married into a family of Torah royalty, as well; his wife, Resha, was a daughter of Rav Aryeh Levin, known as the tzaddik of Yerushalayim, who was menahel of Yeshivas Eitz Chaim. Rav Shmuel Aharon was a Torah giant whose righteousness and fear of G-d matched his achievements in the study of Torah.

Even as a youngster, Rav Shmuel Aharon was recognized for his special nature. Some of his peers once chided him for not joining them in their games, instead spending his time learning Torah.

"Don't shut yourself off from us like that," they complained.

"Please, leave me alone," he answered. "You are permitted to play, while I am permitted to study."

Some of the children didn't take too kindly to this response. "Who exactly do you think you are? Do you think you're the *tzaddik* of this generation or something?"

"No," young Shmuel Aharon answered in all seriousness. "But I am a great-grandson of Rav Leibchik Ponovezher, who is blind."

Shmuel Aharon was referring to his illustrious great-grandfather, Rav Yehuda Leib Hellman, known as Rav Leibchik Ponovezher, who, despite his blindness, studied Torah with astounding dedication, completing *Talmud Bavli* numerous times and authoring a *sefer* on the mitzvos of the Torah.

"When I visit my great-grandfather," Shmuel Aharon told his friends, "and I observe the way he learns Torah completely from memory, it creates an obligation. All the Torah that my *elter zeide* ever learned is stored in his mind, and now he is still able to learn Torah. I feel duty-bound to fill my mind with Torah and live up to his example.

"So as I said, you can play, but I must learn, because I have a blind great-grandfather and you do not!"

"All I Want Is a Gemara"

*R*av Aharon Paperman, an American-born talmid of the Telshe Yeshivah in Lithuania, served as a chaplain for the American Army during World War II. After the war, he went to the DP (displaced persons) camps to assess the condition of the survivors and to try to address their concerns. During that period, he visited the DP camp in Bari, Italy, along with a high-ranking United States Army officer.

While there, he met Reb Yaakov Hirsch, one of many human skeletons, wearing a prison uniform that hung loosely on his emaciated figure. Rav Paperman approached Reb Yaakov Hirsch and asked, "Reb Yid, what can I get for you? *Vuss darfts du?* What do you need? Perhaps you want a sweater to protect you from the cold, a pair of shoes, or maybe something to eat."

"No," replied the man. "I don't need any of these things."

Rav Paperman persisted. "Can I get you something? Anything?"

Looking at him, the Yid said, "When Hitler took me to Auschwitz five and a half years ago, I was in middle of learning *Maseches Bava Kamma*. Since then, I have not seen a Gemara. What I really need is a Gemara *Bava Kamma*!"

Rav Paperman was stunned by the purity of this Jew. He had just been through the seven levels of Gehinnom, but the only thing he wanted was to once again embrace a Gemara *Bava Kamma* and learn from its life-giving words; the ultimate elixir for him was learning Hashem's Torah.

Rav Paperman explained to the officer what the man was asking for. The general was so impressed by the request for a book of the Talmud that he told Rav Paperman that he would help him pro–cure one. He said that there was a bombed mansion where the Nazis had dumped Jewish books and artifacts. The army had not yet gone through the contents of that mansion, and he would take Rav Paperman and Reb Yaakov Hirsch there in his jeep, so they could search for the book.

Rav Paperman and Reb Yaakov Hirsch accompanied the officer

to the house. Rav Paperman began searching through the *Sheimos* piles there. When he found a Gemara *Bava Kamma*, Reb Yaakov Hirsch asked if they could open the Gemara and learn for a few minutes right then and there.

The general was very moved and told the survivor, "I salute you for your unwavering faith."

The *simchah* on the man's face energized Rav Paperman as he continued his life-sustaining efforts.

> *Reb Yaakov Hirsch eventually made his way to the United States. He operated a grocery store in Crown Heights, Brooklyn, and always had a Gemara on the counter. Rav Gedaliah Schorr, rosh yeshivah of Yeshiva Torah Vodaath, lived on the next block and would frequent the store and speak with the proprietor in learning.*
>
> *The Admorim of Skulen and Sadigura lived nearby, as well. When one of their families placed an order, Reb Yaakov Hirsch would deliver it himself. When he left the grocery with this order, his wife knew he wouldn't be back for a long time, as he would take advantage of the opportunity to speak in learning with the Rebbe.*
>
> *All he ever wanted was a Gemara.*

Learning With Effort

Rav Yitzchak Scheiner, rosh yeshivah of Yeshivas Kamenitz in Yerushalayim, related the following, which he said his wife, Rebbetzin Esther Leah Scheiner, had witnessed firsthand.

A certain *iluy* visited the city of Kamenitz and asked a powerful question that no one could answer. No one, that is, except the rosh yeshivah, Rav Baruch Ber Leibowitz; Rav Baruch Ber had an answer to the question, and it took him half a minute to come up with it.

But then he immediately recanted and said, "No, I made a mistake. It is not the correct answer. I am wrong."

Rav Baruch Ber closeted himself in a room and spent an hour reviewing the subject. When he finally emerged, he said, "Now I have an answer." He then repeated the same answer that he had shared before, word for word.

Everyone listening was surprised. "Rebbi," they asked him, "you said an hour ago that it was wrong! How can you say the same thing now?"

Rav Baruch Ber responded, "Don't you understand? When I said it before, it was without effort, without working hard to learn the *sugya*. After an hour's effort, even if I am saying the exact same thing, it is correct."

The Grand Bechinah

A *talmid* once remarked to his rosh yeshivah, Rav Mordechai Gifter, that it is no *kuntz* for the rosh yeshivah to remember every Tosafos, since he is an *iluy*.

"You are making a mistake," responded Rav Gifter. "When I learn a Gemara or a Tosafos, I look at it as if it is the last time that I am going to see this Tosafos before the grand *bechinah* in the *Beis Din Shel Maalah.* That is why I remember it.

"If you would learn that way, you could do the same."

Meriting Torah Comprehension

A *talmid of Rav Yehoshua Leib Diskin related that when Rav Yehoshua Leib was rav in Lomza (early in his career), his day of learning and giving shiurim always ended with a nightly study session with an outstanding talmid for a six-hour period. The chavrusa described these sessions:*

"When reaching a difficult point during the regular nightly learning hours, the rav would sink deep in thought, standing motionless for a long time, as he grappled with the questions and answers that seemed to overtake his whole being. After a while, he would awaken from this trance, his eyes bright with revelation, and cite several explanations to this one difficulty.

"There were times when, even after intense concentration, the answers still evaded him. In such an instance, he would ask me to repeat the Gemara aloud, word by word, while he paced the length and breadth of the room, totally absorbed in his efforts to grasp the true *pshat*, until he would begin to cry.

"Turning to the wall, he would cry out in prayer, '*Aneini Hashem aneini* — Answer me, Hashem, answer me (*I Melachim* 18:37). Enlighten my eyes with Your Torah.' He would then put *tzedakah* in a *pushka* for the poor of Eretz Yisrael and humbly pray for Divine assistance in the merit of Rabbi Meir Baal HaNeis.

"Rav Yehoshua Leib's holy countenance would then light up in comprehension of all that had eluded him and, like a triumphant warrior returning from battle, he would return to his seat to continue learning."

Just Learn

Rav Chaim Kreiswirth, rosh yeshivah of Yeshivas Mercaz HaTorah and rav of Antwerp, knew all of *Shas* — *Bavli* and *Yerushalmi* — by heart, verbatim, with Rashi and Tosafos. Throughout his life, he continued reviewing and sharpening his knowledge, always with the same joy and vitality.

He was often seen sitting by himself, his eyes either closed or only half open, reviewing the Gemara by heart. Every now and then, he would put his finger to his lips. At first, it seemed strange, but then people realized what he was doing. Whenever he reached the bottom of a page in his review, though there was no Gemara in front of him, he would moisten his finger from force of habit as if to turn to the next page.

The following is Rav Chaim's advice to growing in Torah learning: "The best thing to do in order to develop application to learning and to succeed in learning — and this is borne out of experience — is simply to learn. Chazal have told us that unlike other pursuits, with Torah, a full vessel can receive more, but an empty one cannot hold anything" [Midrash Lekach Tov: Shemos 28:3].

He also said, "One must learn even when one doesn't have any desire to do so, though I personally was never in a position when I didn't want to learn."

Never a Merchant

When he was first married, Rav Moshe Landynski was supported by his father-in-law, Rav Yisrael Neiman. At one point, Rav Neiman felt that Rav Moshe — who would later become the rosh yeshivah of the Radin Yeshivah — should accept a rabbinical position in a prominent city. Rav Moshe rejected the idea.

When the period during which he promised to support Rav Moshe and his wife had ended, Rav Neiman reasoned, "A person with a mind like Rav Moshe's will be an asset in my tree business. I'll take him on as a partner." This time, Rav Moshe accepted the job.

Part of the job involved going out to the woods and examining the quality of the trees. The first time Rav Moshe went to the forest, he returned with his coat torn to shreds.

"What happened?" his father-in-law asked.

"While I was in the forest," Rav Moshe explained, "I became so involved in my Torah thoughts that I forgot why I had gone there. When darkness fell, I decided to return home, but since I couldn't see, I bumped into many trees and branches on the way. That's how I tore my coat."

Realizing that Rav Moshe wasn't suited for business, Rav Neiman told him, "Return to your learning. You'll never be a merchant."

A merchant? No.

A great talmid chacham and well-known rosh yeshivah? Most definitely.

What's His Name?

At a time when Volozhin Yeshivah was gaining wide acclaim and reports of its distinction reached Rav Moshe Landynski's town of Kinishin, Rav Moshe yearned to study there, but he had three children and hesitated to leave home. He consulted his wife on the matter, explaining the spiritual advantages of studying in Volozhin. Even though she was fully aware of the difficulties of managing her household alone, she wholeheartedly approved of the idea, as did her father, who promised to help her while Rav Moshe was in Volozhin.

Rav Moshe's total immersion in Torah study while he was in Volozhin was unmatched. His son, Rav Mordechai, related that one time, one of his father's *chavrusos* was absent for a *seder*. Fearing that the *chavrusa* wasn't well, Rav Moshe asked a number of *talmidim*, "Where's the black-haired *bachur* who learns with me?"

"What's his name?" they asked.

"I don't know. I never had time to ask him," he replied.

Later, when Rav Moshe was rosh yeshivah in Radin, he was greeted by a man who had studied with him *b'chavrusa* for six years in Volozhin. As they began to review the *sugyos* that they had studied together in Volozhin, the man was taken aback by Rav Moshe's recollection of every Torah thought they had probed years before. One detail, though, eluded Rav Moshe: the man's name. That was because Rav Moshe's mind was always occupied solely with Torah.

Rav Shmuel Dovid Walkin related that yet another time, someone once asked Rav Moshe for information about a certain *bachur* for *shidduch* purposes. Rav Moshe replied that he didn't know the *bachur*.

"But he's your *chavrusa*," the *shadchan* said in surprise.

"Really?" Rav Moshe replied. "Is that his name? We never discuss mundane issues."

What Is a Masmid?

Rav Moshe Landynski served as the rosh yeshivah of Radin Yeshivah when World War I broke out. Rav Yisrael Meir Kagan, the Chofetz Chaim, who was the founder of the yeshivah, was plagued by a dilemma: Should the yeshivah remain in Radin, which meant falling under German rule, or should it flee to Russia, which involved many dangers, especially during wartime?

Ultimately, the Chofetz Chaim and a large group of *talmidim* fled to Russia. Some *talmidim*, though, had to remain behind in Radin, because their citizenship papers made it highly dangerous for them to transfer to Russia. Rav Moshe remained with those students who had stayed behind in Radin, seeing to all their needs.

Since it was wartime and food was hard to come by, Rav Moshe's primary concern was providing his students with sustenance. For this purpose, he secured a vast quantity of onions and opened an onion stall in the market, which he personally managed. With the proceeds from his sales, he supported the yeshivah's students.

Rav Moshe told Rav Simcha Wasserman, "My involvement in the onion market didn't cause me to neglect my Torah study, and I would review my studies as usual, even in the market. A *masmid* isn't only one who studies all day, but one who uses every available moment of his time for Torah study. While weighing onions for customers, I would review nine chapters of Mishnayos by heart."

A Taste of Purity

Ambassadors

W*e strive for purity in our lives: purity of heart, purity of thought, purity of action, purity of motive. We hope to serve Hashem solely for the sake of Heaven, with no other agenda or goal in mind.*

Rav Naftali Amsterdam, one of the leading disciples of Rav Yisrael Salanter, once made a commitment in writing to bring all of world Jewry back to Torah observance.

Someone asked him how he intended to carry out his resolution. Rav Naftali answered, "This resolution means that I will fulfill all of the laws in the *Shulchan Aruch*! By doing so, I will serve as a living *Shulchan Aruch*, a manifestation of what it means to devote one's life to Hashem. Thus, I will inspire people to return to the ways of the Torah."

In the fifth chapter of Hilchos Dei'os, the Rambam lists a number of distinguishing characteristics of a talmid chacham. He describes how a talmid chacham should set himself apart from society in his conduct: in the way he eats and drinks, in the way he dresses, in the way he does business, and so forth. The Rambam then concludes, "A person who does all these things and the like is an example of what the pasuk (Yeshayah 49:3) describes as 'Avdi atah, Yisrael, asher becha espa'ar — You are My servant, Yisrael, in whom I take pride.'"

The Torah enjoins us to emulate the ways of Hashem so that we will be His ambassadors in this world.

The Ketzos in Kletzk

During World War II, Yeshivas Eitz Chaim in Kletzk, like many other yeshivos in Poland, was forced to relocate, settling in Vilna. A group of 39 students of the yeshivah was subsequently sent to a labor camp in Rachota, Siberia. They were placed in the harshest of seven forced labor camps, known as Camp Number One, which was designated for political prisoners, and where they endured unspeakable physical and spiritual torment.

One of the most trying aspects of their labor camp experience was food. The 3,000 inmates received a lunch of meat and potatoes, but it didn't occur to the *bnei Torah* from Kletzk to partake of the nonkosher fare. Under conditions of hunger and deprivation, these brave men skipped their meal, subsisting instead on the daily ration of 400 grams of bread. They gave the nonkosher food to the non-Jews in the camp, who thought that these Jews had lost their minds.

A member of the group, Rav Leib Rotkin, along with some others, was of the opinion that because their lives were in danger, they were permitted to eat the food, yet none of the Kletzker *talmidim* had even the slightest temptation to taste it.

After the war, members of the group were reunited with their rosh yeshivah, Rav Aharon Kotler, at his yeshivah in Lakewood, Beth Medrash Govoha. One time, as his *talmidim* reminisced about their experiences in Siberia, Rav Aharon asserted, "You should have eaten the food. Your lives were in danger, and you were permitted to eat anything at all."

Rav Rotkin responded, "We came to Siberia from the yeshivah in Kletzk, where the very walls were saturated with the words of the *Ketzos HaChoshen* and the *Nesivos HaMishpat*. How could we put *treif* food into our mouths? It was not possible."

"How Much Would I Give!"

Rabbi Yosef Karmel, the national director of the American division of Lev L'Achim, related the following story:

Rabbi Chaim Weintraub was involved with the Mitchazkim program of Lev L'Achim, which reaches out to high school youth, a population once considered unreachable by kiruv experts. Today, there are over 100 Mitchazkim groups throughout Israel, led by Lev L'Achim mentors, who steer the young men onto a course that eventually brings many of them to yeshivos.

When Reb Chaim's son Shloimele turned 3, the family gathered to cut his hair at his *upsherin*. The next morning, Reb Chaim wrapped his son in a *tallis* and took him to a *cheder*, where a rebbi continued the ceremony, showing him the sweetness of Torah. The Weintraubs then dropped little Shloimele off at his *gan* (kindergarten). At lunchtime, Shloimele complained to his *morah* that his head was hurting. She told him to lie down on a cot to rest and called his mother to come and pick him up. By the time Mrs. Weintraub got to the kindergarten, Shloimele's *neshamah* had left his body. A sweet 3-year-old, one day after his *upsherin*, suddenly departed. At the *shivah*, Reb Chaim and his wife were inconsolable. They could barely speak.

And then, a group of Reb Chaim's "street boys" arrived, all wearing yarmulkes out of respect. One of the boys stepped forward to address Reb Chaim and his rebbetzin.

"We have decided," he declared as his friends looked on, "that as a *zechus* for your son, we will all refrain this Shabbos from smoking, from driving, and really from all *chillul Shabbos*."

Reb Chaim smiled and thanked the boys. After the boys left, the family noticed that it was a different Reb Chaim sitting before them. The light had returned to his eyes.

"Did you hear what those boys are doing?" he exclaimed. "It's unbelievable!"

A friend of his had observed the whole scene and was confused.

"I don't get it. Why are you so touched?" he asked. "These boys are totally secular. So they won't smoke or drive for one Shabbos. Who cares? Next Shabbos they will be right back to being *mechallel Shabbos*. What's the point?"

Reb Chaim shook his head slowly and said, "Imagine if a *malach* would arrive right now to inform us that this coming Shabbos we will be able to have our Shloimele back with us — just for Shabbos, one solitary Shabbos. How much would I be willing to pay for that privilege? I'll tell you. I would sell my *dirah* and the clothes off my back. I would take on debts for the rest of my life just to have Shloimele back for one Shabbos.

"The *Aibeshter* is in pain, as only a father can be, for every lost *neshamah*. Imagine the *simchah* He will experience when an entire group of his lost sons comes home for Shabbos! And don't worry. Next Shabbos I will invite them all to my home and they will have to refrain from *chillul Shabbos* again. The next week, I'll think of something else. Soon they won't turn back!

"I will never see my Shloimele in this world again. '*Hashem nassan, va'Hashem lakach, y'hi Sheim Hashem mevorach* — Hashem has given, and Hashem has taken away, blessed be the Name of Hashem' (*Iyov* 1:21). There is nothing I can do.

"But *HaKadosh Baruch Hu* will yet have His *kinderlach* back! And there is something I can do about that."

Selflessness Amid Tragedy

It was on a short Friday, 18 Teves, 5758 (1998), in Kiryas Tosh, located in the suburb of Boisbriand, Quebec, when tragedy struck. Rav Mordechai, the eldest son of Rav Meshulem Feish Lowy, the holy Tosher Rebbe, was *niftar* suddenly from a massive heart attack at the age of 50.

The Rebbe, who was already quite old at the time, was not immediately notified, as he had not yet davened Shacharis. The Rebbe was known for his lengthy *tefillos*, so his son-in-law urged him to daven Shacharis quickly; later, the Rebbe would be an *onein* and unable to daven. The Rebbe sensed that something was wrong and complied. Only after he finished davening was he told the tragic news.

The *levayah* was scheduled for Friday afternoon, close to the *z'man* of Shabbos. Everyone was waiting, yet the Rebbe did not emerge from his private room. What was he doing during this hour, while the *aron* was waiting and the *levayah* was being delayed? What was going on behind the scenes?

Did the Rebbe need the hour to compose himself, to prepare emotionally for the heartrending *levayah*? Was he preparing a *hesped*? Hardly.

During this hour, the Rebbe was on the phone with a man from Montreal who was experiencing severe *shalom bayis* difficulties; he had left his wife and five small children a few weeks earlier and refused to return. This *yungerman* was not a Chassid of Tosh and had no connection to the Rebbe at all. However, a few weeks before, a rav in Montreal had called the Rebbe, begging him to intervene and save the foundering marriage. The Rebbe promised to pay for cleaning help for the family, to ensure that the children got private tutoring, and to do whatever he could to ease the difficult situation in the home. Unfortunately, the husband had made up his mind and refused to return. The Rebbe, to whom *shalom* meant the world, was distressed that no progress was being made. He couldn't bear the thought that this family unit would break down.

Now, as he prepared to bury his beloved son, the Rebbe found his chance. He utilized his private tragedy to help another family achieve *shalom*. He called the *yungerman* and said to him in a tear-choked voice, "I am preparing to go to a *levayah*, so I have only a short amount of time. However, I beg you to make *shalom* with your wife and go home to your family. Please, do this in the *zechus* of the *niftar* who left this world at a young age. This will ensure that his *neshamah* will go straight to Gan Eden."

The *yungerman* was shaken. "Who is the *niftar*?" he asked.

"My eldest son," the Rebbe replied.

"The Rebbe is preparing for the *levayah* of his son and he called me?" the *yungerman* cried, overcome with emotion.

"What better way to bring honor to the *niftar* and perpetuate his legacy than by making *shalom*?" the Rebbe said. "Please, don't refuse me at this crucial time. I can't go to my son's *levayah* unless you promise me that you will return home."

"Rebbe, what can I say? It's so hard."

"I will help you. I'll provide money for household help so that your wife won't be stressed and anxious. I will pay your bills and give you whatever you need."

The *yungerman* was moved to the core. "I promise I will go home," he said. "But Rebbe, it's Erev Shabbos. The Rebbe must go to the *levayah*."

"I am not going until you go home and call me from your house to tell me that you arrived," the Rebbe firmly declared.

And so it was. The *yungerman* did as he was told and called the Rebbe to assure him that he was back home with his wife and children. Only then did the Rebbe join the throngs who were waiting to accompany his son to his final rest.

The family returned from the *levayah* only a few minutes before Shabbos. The Rebbe was calm and serene, strengthening his family members. "*Kinderlach*, you must stop crying now," he said. "It's almost Shabbos. Mordche is in the highest place in Gan Eden."

That Shabbos, the Rebbe davened for the *amud* as usual. The only time he showed emotion was during *Kabbalas Shabbos*, when he said the words, "*L'hagid ki yashar Hashem* — To declare that Hashem is just" (*Tehillim* 92:16), as he accepted the *din* upon himself.

On Motza'ei Shabbos after Havdalah, the Rebbe finally allowed himself to cry.

Holy Socks

Rav Yitzchak Zilberstein was involved in a case of an immigrant from the Soviet Union who knew he was Jewish, but did not know whether he was a Kohen, Levi, or Yisrael. The rabbanim asked lengthy questions, attempting to collect information about the home in which he was raised.

"Do you remember anything that your mother used to do in the house?" they asked him.

The man replied that before each Yom Tov, his mother would purchase new socks for his father. Each time she did this, she would hold a celebration and involve all the children. The immigrant remembered this ceremony well. He described in great detail how his mother would reverently and joyfully present his father with the new socks.

Based on this anecdote, the rabbanim determined that the immigrant was a Kohen. It was obvious that the mother wanted to display her regard for the mitzvah of *Bircas Kohanim*, and to instill that love within her children. Thus, amid much fanfare, she would present her husband with new socks in honor of the Yom Tov, when he would stand without shoes and recite the blessing in shul.

As the grown son recalled, "We children did not know what the ceremony was all about, but it made a strong impression on us."

Holy socks indeed.

Keeping Kosher

*R*abbi Marvin Hier, dean and founder of the Simon Wiesenthal *Center, was, at one time, rav of the city of Vancouver, British Columbia, Canada. Canada, which is now part of the British Commonwealth of Nations, used to be part of the British Empire.*

One time, Queen Elizabeth II of England and her son, Prince Charles, planned an official visit to Canada, and a festive reception was arranged in their honor in Vancouver. Naturally, all the local dignitaries were invited to the event, Rabbi Hier among them. He had no choice but to decline the invitation, though, since a lavish, nonkosher meal was planned for the reception. He sent a polite letter to the planning committee, notifying them that he was unable to attend.

To his surprise, Rabbi Hier soon received a frantic phone call from an official involved in planning the event, who warned him that the queen and the prince would be disappointed if he failed to attend. When Rabbi Hier explained that he was unable to attend because he ate only kosher, the official promised to hire a mashgiach, one whom Rabbi Hier trusted, and he would make sure that the food Rabbi Hier received was fully kosher. Seeing how the organizers had extended themselves for him, Rabbi Hier decided to attend the reception.

When he arrived at the dinner, Rabbi Hier was given a card with his assigned seat number, and he proceeded to his table. At his place was a set of dishes and silverware identical to those of all the other guests, but the mashgiach informed him that the dishes were kosher and had been marked on the bottom. Of course, all the food that would be served to him would be kosher, as well. Rabbi Hier was surprised to discover, though, that the meal consisted of eight courses, each of which would be served at a different table, so that all the guests could get to know one another.

Since he had only a single set of dishes, that meant that Rabbi Hier would have to carry his special kosher dishes with him as he made his way from table to table. And that is what he did: Every time he switched seats, he brought his dishes and cutlery with him.

A different guest, an irreligious Jew, was incensed at the sight. "You have to stop that!" he rebuked Rabbi Hier. "You are humiliating all the Jews here with your behavior!"

But the rabbi was not deterred and insisted on moving his kosher dishes along with him.

Toward the end of the evening, the guests lined up to greet Queen Elizabeth and Prince Charles. When it was Rabbi Hier's turn to shake hands with the prince, the prince leaned toward him and said, "Excuse me, sir."

"Yes, your Royal Highness?" Rabbi Hier asked politely.

"It has been difficult for me to watch you carrying those dishes with you everywhere you go," the prince said. "Why are you doing that?"

"I am an observant Jew," Rabbi Hier explained, "and I eat only kosher food."

This answer piqued the prince's interest. "I didn't know that there is a need for kosher dishes, as well," he remarked. "I thought it was enough for the food itself to be kosher."

The prince listened with great admiration as Rabbi Hier explained the issues involved. Then he shook his hand warmly and brought the rabbi to meet the queen.

Thus began a lengthy conversation on the subject of kosher food. It turned out that the crown prince was very knowledgeable about religion. As the conversation went on, the same irreligious Jew who had reproached the rabbi earlier was unable to bear the sight of a religious rav immersed in conversation with the royal guests.

"Your Royal Highness," he called out, "I am a Jew, as well!"

"Oh?" said Prince Charles innocently. "But I didn't see you carrying your dishes."

Phylacteries in Flight

In July 2014, Rabbi Shay Schachter, then assistant rav of Congregation Knesseth Israel in Far Rockaway, NY, traveled to the Holy Land as an emissary of his shul, to be *menachem avel* the Shaer, Frenkel, and Yifrach families, whose sons, Gilad, Naftali, and Eyal, were kidnapped and murdered by terrorists. Rabbi Schachter was unsure what significance his visit would have or how his expressions of *nechamah* on behalf of hundreds of families would be received, but his fears were allayed before he even stepped off the plane.

In the middle of his flight, the Israeli stewardess asked Rabbi Schachter when he would be returning to the United States. He responded that he would be staying until after Shabbos.

"Just four days? What kind of trip is that?" the stewardess asked innocently.

Rabbi Schachter explained that he was sent by his shul to visit the three families of the boys, to deliver heartfelt letters from their

American brothers and sisters of his shul, and to inform them of the care and concern of their fellow Jews in America.

The stewardess broke down in tears. "This congregation of yours is something unique and something very special," she said, "if this is where their hearts are and this is what is occupying their minds! How incredible!"

The stewardess proceeded to make an announcement to all the passengers. "*Rabbotai*! Come meet a rabbi who was sent by his *kehillah* to perform the great mitzvah of *nichum aveilim* for those whom they feel are their own brothers and sisters. Our plane is safe because we have a *shliach mitzvah* on board with us."

Pandemonium ensued. After Rabbi Schachter was able to finally sit down, a young man seated next to him related that he was 26 years old, from Seattle, Washington, and working in a national zoo. "I am going to Israel for the first time," he told Rabbi Schachter. "I am so inspired by your congregation that I would like to borrow your *tallis* to do a mitzvah that I have not done since my bar mitzvah celebration — in memory of the three boys."

Rabbi Schachter gladly gave the young man his *tallis*, asking him if he knows how to recite the *berachah*.

"Sure, I do," said the confident young man, who promptly took out a small piece of paper from his pocket and recited *Tefillas HaDerech*, the one and only *berachah* he was familiar with.

The young man then asked to borrow Rabbi Schachter's *tefillin*, too. This led to conversations with other passengers, many of whom took photos of this highly unusual scene.

The gentleman wasn't finished. After a few minutes, he turned to Rabbi Schachter and remarked, "Rabbi, I am so inspired, but in my neighborhood, we don't have these boxes. Still, I want to continue doing something special for these three precious souls even after I return home. What would you suggest?"

Without hesitation, a Satmar Chassid sitting in the next row turned to the tattooed and pierced young man and said, "Sweet Jew, if you promise me that you will try and wear these *tefillin* each and every day, I promise to have a pair sent by FedEx to your home in Seattle by the time you get back from Israel."

The two exchanged phone numbers and the deal was done.

Rabbi Schachter's visit to the families was an uplifting expe-rience, but his flight to Eretz Yisrael alone was so out of the or-dinary, and so inspiring, that Rabbi Schachter later commented, "I almost felt like taking the next flight home and calling this trip the greatest success I could have imagined."

The Power of Music

Rav Yerucham Levovitz, mashgiach of the Mirrer Yeshivah in Poland, would deliver a *derashah* to the *talmidim* of the yeshivah at every *Simchas Beis HaSho'eivah* on Succos. On one day of Chol HaMoed Succos in 1936, Rav Yerucham got up to speak as usual, but this time he had a surprise for the *talmidim*. He wanted to teach them a new *niggun*, a very special song.

Rav Yerucham related that the night before, Rav Itzele Peter-burger — who had passed away 20 years earlier — had appeared to him in a dream and taught him a *niggun* to the words of *"Ashrei ish she'lo yishkacheka u'ven adam yisametz bach* — Praiseworthy is the man who does not forget You, the human being who takes strength in You,"* a phrase that we recite in the *berachah* of *Zichronos* in Mussaf on Rosh Hashanah. Rav Yerucham learned the *niggun* well and taught it to his *talmidim*, who sang it with him for hours.

Rav Yerucham exclaimed: "This is a pure *niggun* taken from the *Heichal HaNeginah* in Gan Eden."

Many years later, one of those *talmidim*, Rav Nosson Meir Wacht-fogel, mashgiach of Beth Medrash Govoha in Lakewood, tried teaching the very same song to his *talmidim*, but he encountered great difficulty. For some reason, the *talmidim* could not grasp the *niggun*, and only after a while did they finally catch on.

Some were perplexed by the fact that it had taken them so long to learn the song. Why had it been so difficult?

Rav Nosson commented that the reason they could not grasp the *niggun* was probably that their heads were filled with tunes that were not from pure sources. Therefore, they could not easily learn a pure *niggun* saturated with *yirah* and *bitachon*.

A number of years ago, it was reported that one of the national zoos stopped using the music of German composer and Nazi sympathizer Richard Wagner in its sound system. The zoo attendants noticed that whenever his music was played, the animals became restless and ornery and were harder to manage.

Could it be that the animals understood something about music that we don't?

— heard from Rabbi Yitzchok Tzvi Schwarz

Tying the Laces

Rav Simcha Wasserman once accompanied his father, Rav Elchanan Wasserman, rosh yeshivah in Baranovich, to Warsaw for a convention of *gedolim*. Rav Elchanan's wife had recently bought him new shoes, doing so in a crafty way, telling him that she had given his shoes away to the woman who cleaned their house who had no shoes of her own.

Simcha, who was still a child at the time, was traveling with his father on the train, when Rav Elchanan turned to him and said, "My new shoes are causing me distress. They have laces, and it takes a few seconds to tie the laces. If we multiply that by the number of days and years that I will wear them and tie the laces, it adds up to an enormous amount of wasted time."

For someone who used his time as wisely and purely as Rav Elchanan, the time used to do something as seemingly insignificant as tying laces was a waste of time.

The Greatest Bar Mitzvah Gift

Rav Shmuel HaLevi Wosner, author of Shailos U'Teshuvos Shevet HaLevi and rosh yeshivah of Yeshivas Chachmei Lublin, was not accustomed to visiting kevarim of tzaddikim or mekomos hakedoshim. Each day, he would go from his home to his yeshivah and back. Traveling anywhere else was avoided as much as possible.

> *Rav Wosner was once visited by his grandson, the Kosover Rebbe, Rav Shraga Feivish Hager. During the course of the conversation, his grandson asked him if he'd like to be taken to daven at various mekomos hakedoshim.*
>
> *Not wanting to engage in a lengthy back-and-forth, Rav Wosner answered, "Ein li zman! I have no time!"*
>
> *His grandson smiled at his grandfather. "What does 'ein li zman' mean? Why, the Zeide has already learned kol haTorah kulah, the entire Torah!"*
>
> *Rav Wosner, who was in his 90's, turned to his grandson and said, "It is not worth venturing out into the street unless there is a great need, for with one inappropriate sight, a person can ruin all the spiritual work and accomplishments of an entire life."*

People would often go to Rav Wosner with their bar mitzvah-age sons so he could put *tefillin* on the boys for the first time. Rav Wosner was once contacted by an American Jew who wished to bring his son to Eretz Yisrael for his *hanachas tefillin.*

"It's not worth it!" Rav Wosner told the man. "You're better off not making the trip."

The man persisted, explaining that he had promised his son that he would take him to Rav Wosner for his *hanachas tefillin.* "In fact," he told Rav Wosner, "I already booked two plane tickets, which were quite costly, and I will not get my money back if I cancel."

Rav Wosner was firm and emphatic. "Still and all, you should not come! Take those two plane tickets, place them in a picture frame, and write on it in large letters that you saved your son from being exposed to the sights and influences of the world. Then hang the frame on a wall in your home. This is the greatest gift you can give your son in honor of his bar mitzvah."

A Taste of Insight

An Uncultivated Land

When Rabbi Shmuel Bloom was sitting *shivah* for his brother, Reb Yisrael, he was visited by Rav Raphael Pelcovitz, rabbi emeritus of Congregation Knesseth Israel (the White Shul) in Far Rockaway. He told Reb Yisrael's children and family members that when Reb Yisrael arrived in Far Rockaway, he found an "*eretz lo zeruah*, an unsown land" (*Yirmiyah* 2:2). By establishing Yeshiva Darchei Torah in 1972, he was responsible for the flourishing of the community.

Rabbi Bloom asked Rav Pelcovitz, "How can you call the Far Rockaway of that time an *eretz lo zeruah*? After all, there was your White Shul and Hebrew Institute of Long Island [HILI]."

His answer was profound.

"Anyone can come into a desert and realize that it is a land that has not been planted," said Rav Pelcovitz. "It takes a wise and perceptive individual to see a land that has some vegetation and say that this land has so much more potential that right now it can be considered '*lo zeruah*,' as if it wasn't planted. This is because every additional blade of grass and certainly each new tree represent new beauty, a new shine that wasn't there before."

A Waste of Time?

When Rav Yaakov Edelstein, who was for many years the rav of Ramat HaSharon, was a *talmid* at Ponovezh Yeshivah, a group of *bachurim* who did not have a strong Torah background joined the yeshivah.

Soon after, Rav Edelstein visited the Chazon Ish, and the Chazon Ish asked Rav Edelstein to speak to the older *bachurim* in the yeshivah and convince them to learn with the weaker *bachurim*.

Rav Edelstein expressed his doubts to the Chazon Ish: "What should I say if a *bachur* tells me that he wants to use his time to learn *iyun* [in depth], and he does not want to waste it learning with such a *bachur*?"

The Chazon Ish answered, "Ask that *bachur* if he puts on *tefillin*. When he says yes, ask him why he doesn't feel that it's a waste of time, as he could be learning *iyun* during that time."

Rav Edelstein later remarked, "You see, the Chazon Ish equated putting on tefillin, which is a Biblical commandment, with learning with a weaker bachur."

Without the Desire

Rav Chanoch Henoch Karelenstein was rosh yeshivah in the town of Yerucham in southern Israel and later rosh yeshivah at Yeshivah Letze'irim Heichal HaTorah MiTzion in Yerushalayim.

A *talmid* once told Rav Chanoch that he was pained by the fact that he felt no desire to learn.

Rav Chanoch replied, "I was once visiting Rav Dovid Povarsky when a *bachur* came and told him that he had the same problem. Rav Dovid embraced the *bachur* and said to him, 'I am so envious of you. It has been 40 years since I have experienced the beautiful feeling of learning even without having a desire for it.'"

The Obligation of Yichus

From his early life, Rav Nochum Zev Dessler — son of Rav Eliyahu Eliezer Dessler, the author of *Michtav MeiEliyahu* — and scion of an illustrious lineage of Torah and *mussar*, was destined for greatness in Torah. And yet, it could have been the other way; growing up as the spiritual and biological heir to a dynasty of Torah and *mussar* could, at times, be overwhelming. Rav Nochum Zev viewed his *yichus* as an obligation. In the foreword to the *sefer* he authored, *Ilana DeChaya*, which traces his lineage to David HaMelech while detailing vignettes about his eminent forebears, Rav Nochum Zev writes: "I did not write this volume as a form of aggrandizement. On the contrary, my purpose is only to imbue future generations with their lofty responsibility."

It was this attitude that motivated his life's efforts on behalf of Torah, a lesson to us all as we look back toward our own ancestors with pride.

Test Drive

Rav Simcha Wasserman had a sixth sense in understanding and reading people and their natures. During the time he lived in Los Angeles, he was once looking to purchase a used car. He went to check out one particular vehicle and asked the owner if he could take it for a test drive.

"How do I know you're not going to steal it?" the man questioned.

Rav Wasserman responded by asking if he could use the telephone for a minute. He then called the police and reported a stolen vehicle at that very address. The police arrived, confirmed that the car he had wanted to drive was indeed stolen, and arrested the car dealer.

"How did you know?" the police asked Rav Wasserman.

"Simple," he said. "When I asked to take it for a test drive, the dealer suspected that I'd steal it. Only a thief thinks that way!"

Or, as Rav Simcha would have said to his talmidim, "Kol haposel…be'mumo posel — Whoever invalidates another is really invalidating his own shortcoming" (Kiddushin 70 a,b).

You Can Never Get It Back

Reb Shlomo Yehuda Rechnitz, noted philanthropist of Los Angeles, once received a message from his secretary that Rav Nosson Tzvi Finkel, rosh yeshivah of Yeshivas Mir Yerushalayim, needed to speak to him urgently.

Reb Shlomo Yehuda was in the middle of a meeting with some bankers who had flown in from Chicago to see him. At the time, he could not call Eretz Yisrael from his cell phone, so he rushed home and immediately phoned the rosh yeshivah. Rebbetzin Finkel picked up the phone and handed it to her husband.

"Shlomo Yehuda, how is your learning?" the rosh yeshivah asked.

"I lied," Reb Shlomo Yehuda later recalled, "and I said that it was going well, even though during those last two weeks I had been very, very busy. I told the rosh yeshivah that my secretary must have miscommunicated the message, because she said it was extremely urgent."

"'It is extremely urgent," the rosh yeshivah insisted. "Shlomo Yehuda," he continued in a stern voice, "don't forget where you come from. You're a Mirrer *talmid*. The bank will be there tomorrow. But if you miss a day of learning, you'll never get it back."

Reb Shlomo Yehuda went back into the meeting, but instead of feeling like a businessman who went to yeshivah, he felt like a yeshivahman who was doing business.

Raising Money

I heard the following story from my rebbi, Rav Shlomo Feivel Schustal.

When the Ponovezher Rav, Rav Yosef Shlomo Kahaneman, was a young rav in a small *shtetl*, he opened a yeshivah. At that point, he was not yet skilled at fund-raising and the yeshivah ran into financial trouble. The rav went to his father-in-law, Rav Aryeh Leib Rubin, the rav of Vilkomir, to seek his assistance.

Rav Aryeh Leib replied, "I will try to raise the money to cover the debts, and then we will close the yeshivah."

Rav Aryeh Leib attempted to raise the money, but he saw no success.

Afterward, Rav Yosef Shlomo went to raise money. He was tremendously successful. Not only did he cover the debt, but he raised enough funds to ensure the yeshivah's continued viability.

When his father-in-law asked him how he had done it, Rav Yosef Shlomo explained, "The *shver* went to raise money to close a yeshivah; I went to raise money to keep it open!"

Potent Words

Rav Achikam Shevach, rosh yeshivah of Yeshivas Ohr Elchanan in Teveriah, related the following story about Rav Elchanan Wasserman.

Once, Rav Elchanan and Rav Aharon Kotler met in Lithuania, and they were sitting in a room in which the wall did not reach the ceiling. Simcha, Rav Elchanan's young son, was curious to hear what his father was discussing with Rav Aharon, so he climbed up the wall to listen in.

He heard Rav Aharon discussing how Chazal teach us that anything that a *tzaddik* says is fulfilled like the decree of a king, as in the case of Yaakov Avinu, who declared that whoever stole the *terafim* (idols) of Lavan would die (*Bereishis* 31:32). Rashi tells us that because of that, Rachel Imeinu died on the road, even though Yaakov had never intended to curse his own wife. There are many other such cases in Chazal, and Rav Aharon wanted to know why this is so.

Rav Elchanan answered him, "A person's mouth is like a knife. A very sharp knife can cut even if one doesn't intend for it to cut. The mouths of our holy *Avos* and of the Tannaim were so clean and pure that they were able to 'cut' even without the intent to do so, just like an extremely sharp knife.

"The truth is," Rav Elchanan added, "that the same should be true of us, but our mouths are like rusty knives, so the things we say do not come true."

Rav Moshe Mordechai Chodosh, rosh yeshivah of Yeshivas Ohr Elchanan, commented that Rav Elchanan and Rav Aharon were actually discussing how to define the Chofetz Chaim's greatness.

When Rav Simcha told this story, he added that his father was once present at a kinnus of rabbanim where the Chofetz Chaim spoke, and someone remarked that the Chofetz Chaim had delivered the same speech the previous year. Rav Elchanan immediately objected, saying, "This year, there were 13 additional words!"

With such a clean and pure "knife," you can be sure that the Chofetz Chaim's words were fulfilled.

Give, Not Take

When he served as rosh yeshivah of Ohr Elchanan of Yerushalayim, Rav Simcha Wasserman used to daven regularly at the shul in Neve Simcha, a home for the elderly on Rechov Sorotzkin, which was near his house. Once, a well-known philanthropist was davening next to him. Rav Simcha, immersed in his *tefillos*, did not notice. Someone went over to him and pointed out the presence of the philanthropist, suggesting that perhaps Rav Simcha should speak to him about his yeshivah.

After davening, Rav Simcha told the person who had made the comment, "When I meet someone, I don't think about what I can get from him. I think about what I can give him."

Without Ulterior Motives

The late Sadigura Rebbe, Rav Avraham Yaakov Friedman, who passed away in 2013, imbued his followers with the teachings of Chassidus, while emphasizing the importance of having a positive attitude in every situation.

One year, when the first day of Rosh Hashanah fell on Shabbos and there was no *tekias shofar*, the Rebbe related that Rav Yisrael, the Baal Shem Tov, was especially joyous on a wintry day when it was impossible for him to immerse in a *mikveh*. The Gemara (*Kiddushin* 40a) states that if a person thought to do a mitzvah and was unable to do it due to forces beyond his control, Hashem considers it as if he performed the mitzvah. The Baal Shem Tov said, "If a person actually does a mitzvah, who knows if he did it without any ulterior motives? But if Hashem considers it as if one did the mitzvah, then it is considered absolutely pure of any tainted thoughts that may reduce its value."

With that, the Baal Shem Tov began dancing with joy.

The Rabbi's Notes

A small-town rav was not a very gifted speaker. Because of his weak oratory skills, he would spend months preparing his Shabbos Shuvah and Shabbos HaGadol *derashos*. At one point, the rav realized that if one of his constituents passed away, he would be stuck without an appropriate *hesped* to deliver. He began compiling *hespeidim* for each member of his *kehillah*, jotting down notes about them and their activities so that he'd be prepared if any of them died.

One day, a large blaze broke out in the town, engulfing many of the homes, including the rav's. As the locals tried to salvage their belongings, someone noticed charred pieces of paper that had come from the rav's house. Onlookers were stunned to see *hespeidim* on

Reb Chaim, Reb Shlomo, Reb Sender, and Reb Toivy. The residents of the town were enraged at the gall of the rav, who had been writing eulogies about them during their lifetimes. Without delay, they fired the rav.

> Using the above story as a mashal, Rav Yosef Shalom Elyashiv explained that, in truth, the rav was recording the actions and conduct of his people with his pen and paper. A hesped, he said, is merely a précis of one's days and years. The pen and paper of Shamayim are continuously recording our every deed, writing our "hesped" as we proceed through life, and what is written is decided by what we do.
>
> We should always imagine what our hesped would look like if the rav's paper about us would be found on the street following a conflagration.

Twenty Years of Kelm

*R*av Pesach Stein, rosh yeshivah of Telshe Yeshivah in Cleveland, explained that serenity is not something dependent on *outside circumstances. Rather, it is something that comes from within. It is a state of mind.*

Rav Eliezer (Leizer) Levin, the chief rabbi of Detroit for decades, was once presiding over a divorce proceeding. Suddenly, the irate husband pulled out a gun. While everyone in the room dove for cover, Rav Levin calmly walked over to the man. He requested that he hand over the gun and discuss the matter reasonably.

In his later years, after experiencing some pain, Rav Levin was taken to the doctor by his grandson. During the examination, the doctor told him that he was having a heart attack and should proceed to the hospital immediately. The rav slowly put on his shirt and calmly donned his frock, hat, and coat. As the seconds passed, his grandson waited tensely so they could rush to the hospital. Once in the car, the grandson asked, "Zeide, how could you be so calm at a time like this?"

Rav Levin answered: "Even in a time of danger, 20 years of working on *menuchas hanefesh* in Kelm does not fall by the wayside."

Courage is defined as "grace under pressure." How do we attain this grace? By working at it when the going is not so tough. There are uncomfortable situations that we face daily: a bounced check, property damage, a car breaking down on the highway, a missed flight. How frazzled do we get when confronted by these annoyances? Do we maintain a calm demeanor or do we totally lose ourselves?

If we handle these scenarios with a sense of calm, we prepare ourselves for greater challenges.

— *heard from Rabbi Yitzchok Tzvi Schwarz*

Why Are Children So Happy?

Rav Chaim Brim, the famed *marbitz Torah*, recounted that the Brisker Rav, Rav Yitzchak Zev Soloveitchik, was once walking with some of his *talmidim* when they passed a group of children at play. The Brisker Rav stopped and asked those around him why they thought children are generally happy and laugh easily.

A few of the young men gave voice to their thoughts. Perhaps it is because children lack maturity, which brings with it a more solemn outlook on life, one suggested. Perhaps it is because they have few responsibilities, proposed another.

The rav shook his head. Realizing that the rav wanted to teach them something, the *talmidim* stopped offering their own ideas and waited to hear what he had to say. Why are children normally in a happy and carefree state of mind?

The answer, explained the rav, is that children are happy because human beings are naturally this way. If people were born with all sorts of the varying frames of mind we find in adults — stress, worry, pessimism, discouragement, melancholy — then we would witness these emotions in children in a similar measure. The fact that normal children from stable homes are overwhelmingly happy and carefree indicates that this is a person's natural state.

As we grow older, the Brisker Rav explained, it is we who complicate matters. We erect *mechitzos*, barriers, and we bury our natural state under layers of self-imposed encumbrances, such as jealousy, desire, greed, and doubts.

Children, who have not yet made their lives complex with external baggage, are in their natural, pure state.

— heard from Rabbi Yossi Rosenberg

Adina's Lesson

I t was seemingly a *derashah* like any other their rav delivers, but several weeks afterward, the residents of the Prospect Park *kehillah* in Lakewood learned that its impact was far from ordinary.

It was the Shabbos of *Parashas Kedoshim*, and my brother, Rav Hershel Hisiger, the rav of the Prospect Park *kehillah*, highlighted the concept of *adinus* — often translated as *eidelkeit*, refinement — which Rav Eliyahu Eliezer Dessler describes in *Michtav MeiEliyahu* (Vol. 5, p. 108) as being a powerful force with which to bring *kedushah* into this world. Rav Hisiger related to his congregants how *eidelkeit* in one's day-to-day conduct and one's interactions with others will ensure that one's daily behavior brings pleasure to the Ribono Shel Olam.

Several weeks later, at a Kiddush at the Prospect Park shul in honor of the birth of his daughter, Reb Gavriel Pliver shared with his fellow *mispallelim* how he and his wife chose a name for their newborn baby.

"The rav spoke about the importance of *adinus*," he said at the time. "In order to maintain holiness, we must act with *adinus*, with *eidelkeit*. We have, therefore, chosen to name our daughter Adina.

Our hope is that with this trait of *adinus,* she will merit to bring holiness into the world."

Thus began the life of little Adina, a pure soul whose name conveyed to all the aspirations of her parents to bring holiness into a world devoid of it. With palpable joy, Rabbi and Mrs. Pliver celebrated the wonderful gift — a baby girl embraced by three doting siblings — bestowed upon them by Hashem.

Within a short time, however, Rabbi and Mrs. Pliver noticed that Adina was not growing and thriving as expected. They ultimately learned that Adina had a rare condition, one that affects just hundreds out of millions of Americans. The condition ultimately claimed the holy *neshamah* of 5½-month-old Adina during the month of Tammuz 5774.

At 3 a.m. the next morning, several dozen relatives and friends gathered for the *levayah* and *kevurah.* Despite the odd hour, the *neshamah tehorah* received an appropriate *kavod acharon.*

Those in attendance, like the residents of Prospect Park, all knew the special nature of Adina's name and the legacy that it still carries through her parents, who demonstrated their lofty aspirations from the day they named her until the day she left them.

> *It is a vital lesson in eidelkeit and avodas Hashem, along with a directive to merit the acquisition of kedushah during our earthly sojourn, which was taught years ago by Rav Dessler and applied today by a special couple in Lakewood.*

"Hari'u . . . Kol Ha'aretz"

*D*uring the times of the Beis HaMikdash, whenever a person faced a life-threatening situation and survived, he would bring a korban todah, a thanksgiving offering (Vayikra 7:12-15). Today, bereft of a Beis HaMikdash, the psalm of Mizmor LeSodah (Tehillim 100), which was recited during the actual service of the korban todah, is said in its stead.

A visitor to Rav Chaim Kanievsky asked him about the wording of this *kappitel*, which begins, *"Mizmor le'sodah hari'u laShem kol ha'aretz* — A psalm of thanksgiving, call out to Hashem, everyone on earth."

What is intended by the words *"hari'u laShem kol ha'aretz,"* that "everyone on earth" is giving thanks? The *korban todah* was brought by one who traveled on the high seas, who traveled through a desert, who was imprisoned and released, or who was sick and recovered (*Berachos* 54b, based on *Tehillim* 107). What do others, who have not experienced this miracle, have to do with the thanksgiving of the particular individual reciting this *kappitel*?

The answer, Rav Chaim said, is simple and can be understood with a brief story:

> One morning after Shacharis at a shul in Bnei Brak, one of the mispallelim covered a table with a tablecloth and began putting out an assortment of cake and schnapps. When asked what simchah he was celebrating, the mispallel explained that the day before, as he was crossing the street, he was hit by a car. Thank G-d, he emerged safe and sound. He was thus making a l'chaim to express his thanks to HaKadosh Baruch Hu.
>
> The next day after Shacharis, a different mispallel began laying out a spread of refreshments for a l'chaim.
>
> "What's the occasion?" asked the others. "Were you also hit by a car? Were you involved in that same accident?"
>
> "No," the man answered with a smile. "I am expressing thanks to the Ribono Shel Olam that for over 20 years, I have crossed that very road countless times and, baruch Hashem, I was not hit by a car even once."

This, concluded Rav Chaim, is the explanation of the words *"hari'u laShem kol ha'aretz,"* that "everyone on earth" will express thanksgiving to Hashem. One who recovered from illness or traversed the sea safely thanks Hashem for his personal good fortune. The rest of the world — *"kol ha'aretz"* — expresses heartfelt gratitude to the One Above for not being placed in that predicament in the first place.

A Taste *of* Neshamah

A Father's Love

*T*he concept of neshamah — which literally means soul — is the feeling and understanding that we weren't created to benefit ourselves, but to fulfill Hashem's Torah as well as emulate Him by showering others with kindness and care.

> Reb Avi Fishoff doesn't have a magic potion. His success in dealing with "youth-in-turmoil," those our world calls "kids-at-risk," is thanks to his expertise in language. He understands the patois of the heart and the jargon of the soul. And he doesn't talk at the youngsters and young adults he encounters. He talks to them and with them.

> Avi founded Home Sweet Home in Brooklyn to serve as a home away from home for young men who are living on the fringe. Many have long stopped observing mitzvos, and Avi befriends them and tries to lead them back to the path of Torah.

Some years ago, Avi brought some of his "street boys" into Tiferes Stam, the Flatbush *sefarim* store of the renowned *sofer*, Rabbi Heshy Pincus. Rabbi Pincus, in his unique way, often offers a crash course of sorts on the manufacture of *tefillin*, explaining to bar-mitzvah boys how their *tefillin* are made and the beauty behind this special mitzvah.

In this case, Rabbi Pincus was called upon to make his presentation to the group of boys under Avi's stewardship. One of the youth, whose dress and demeanor indicated that he had strayed far from the path of his family, showed his pair of *tefillin* to Rabbi

Pincus. It was clear, as the skilled *sofer* examined them, that there was something extraordinary about these *tefillin*.

"Where did you get these *tefillin*?" Rabbi Pincus asked the boy.

"They're from my father," the boy said.

Rabbi Pincus asked the boy what his father did for a living. From the boy's response, it was obvious that his father struggled financially.

"Can you find out who wrote these *tefillin*?" asked Rabbi Pincus.

The youth excused himself and said he would find out. Upon his return, he related that they had been written by a noted *sofer* from Yerushalayim.

Avi inquired how the boy had acquired the information so quickly.

"I called my father," the boy replied.

"You called your father?! But you haven't spoken to him in months," Avi observed.

"Your father must really love you," Rabbi Pincus interjected. "These *tefillin* were written by one of the foremost *sofrim* in the world. Very prominent people wait long periods for *tefillin* from this *sofer*. They must have cost a lot of money. Your father probably never went on vacation, but he saved $5 here and $10 there, all so that you could have these spectacular *tefillin*."

The youth was profoundly inspired and eventually returned to the path of Torah and mitzvos.

He'll Do the Rest

*M*any of the boys at Home Sweet Home engage in activities that are detrimental to them physically and spiritually. Avi works to get them back on a productive path.

One such boy, Moishy, originally from Monroe, New York, had been on the streets for three years when he was taken in by Avi. He was 17 years old at the time. About a month after he joined Avi's program, during a casual schmooze, he remarked to Avi, "You know, I have no idea where my *tefillin* are."

This comment surprised Avi, as Moishy had previously not demonstrated any interest in mitzvah observance. Avi sensed that perhaps this comment was a sign of a spiritual awakening.

"If you want your *tefillin*, they'll come to you," Avi said, not sure what possessed him to answer in this fashion.

"What do you mean by that?" Moishy asked.

"I don't know," Avi said. "But think about it: Do you want them?" Moishy said that he did not.

"When you truly want them, they will come," Avi repeated.

The conversation concluded, but it was clear that Moishy had a lot on his mind. He had verbalized a lack of interest in getting back his *tefillin*, but the look on his face and his demeanor seemed to demonstrate otherwise.

The very next day, out of the blue, he received a phone call from his grandmother.

"Hi, Babby," said Moishy, surprised. "Why are you calling?"

"Moishy," she said, "do you put on *tefillin* every day?"

Moishy confessed that he did not. "Why are you asking?" he questioned his grandmother.

"Well, last night, I had a dream. Your great-grandfather, my father, came to me in a dream and asked me, '*Farvuss leigt nisht Moishy kein tefillin*? Why doesn't Moishy put on *tefillin*?'"

Moishy hung up the phone, stunned. Was it a mere coincidence, he wondered, that just the day before he had wondered aloud about the whereabouts of his *tefillin*?

Moishy soon discovered that the "coincidences" didn't end there.

The next day, he received a phone call from one of his old apartment-mates. "Mo," the friend said, "what's up? Listen, we were just cleaning up here, and at the bottom of a closet, under a pile of dirty laundry, we found your *tefillin*. If you don't want 'em, that's fine. We'll get rid of 'em. But if you want 'em, you can pick 'em up."

The next day, Avi entered Home Sweet Home, where he encountered the most beautiful sight. There, on a ledge, sat Moishy's *tefillin*.

Moishy had been in a state of crisis when all this occurred. With the return of his tefillin, he underwent a transformation. Within two months, he closed his Facebook page. He then gave up his BlackBerry and acquired a kosher phone.

Before long, he became shomer Torah u'mitzvos. Eventually, he got married. Though he had been estranged from his parents, by the time he got married, they were again part of his life and there to schep nachas.

All Moishy needed was to demonstrate the most-minute teshukah, desire, and HaKadosh Baruch Hu set into motion a series of circumstances that brought his precious tefillin back to him. The Midrash (Shir HaShirim Rabbah 5:2) states that if we open an aperture the size of the eye of a needle in order to do teshuvah, Hashem will create openings so big that even large wagons can fit through.

He is just asking us to try, do a little bit, show our desire.
And He'll do the rest.

"Tatte, Ich Leb Noch!"

During and after World War II, Rav Moshe Yehudah Schneider, rosh yeshivah of Yeshivas Toras Emes in London, expended great effort to save hundreds of immigrant youth in England from spiritual death. Bachurim were sent by Rav Schneider to stand on street corners in London and try to draw in youngsters and convince them to attend yeshivah and embrace a Torah way of life.

One time, two brothers who attended public school were greeted by the *bachurim*, who asked if they had eaten lunch.

"Yes, we had hamburgers in school," they responded.

"Was the meat kosher?" the *bachurim* questioned.

"No," said the boys matter-of-factly, "but we brought salt from our house and sprinkled it on the meat to make it kosher." Their ignorance notwithstanding, the boys were very sincere.

When the *bachurim* told Rav Schneider about their exchange, he burst into tears. "*Yiddishe kinder* are salting *treife* meat! Can you imagine?" he said.

This episode emboldened Rav Schneider to save as many *neshamos* as he possibly could from spiritual annihilation.

Not long after, at an event in Gateshead, Rav Schneider told his audience about the two schoolboys and their effort to "*kasher*" their public school lunch. He then shared the following:

> *During World War I, a father and son were drafted into the Russian Army. The son was sent into combat, while the father was given the job of collecting the bodies of the many casualties and preparing them for burial.*
>
> *One time, the father spotted a soldier who had been shot and seriously wounded. His comrades had abandoned him, assuming he was dead. As the father lifted the soldier to have the body transported, he almost fainted when he realized that the soldier was none other than his son.*
>
> *The father placed his son's body in a wagon and, with tears streaming down his face and his body shaking from sadness, he began to push it to the collection of bodies nearby. Suddenly, he heard a whimper. He looked down and saw his son open his eyes. With his last bit of strength, the son pleaded, "Tatte, Tatte! Ratteve mich; ich leb noch! Ratteve mich; ich leb noch! Father, Father! Save me; I'm still alive! Save me; I'm still alive!"*

Rav Schneider concluded his story and addressed his listeners. "*Rabbosai*," he said, "those two public schoolboys on that London corner are placing salt on *treife* meat to make it kosher. There's a *pintele Yid* there, a spark of *Yiddishkeit* in their *neshamah* calling out to us and telling us that they are still alive. That spark is proclaiming, '*Tatte, Tatte! Ratteve mir; ich leb noch!* Save me; I'm still alive!'

"We must respond to them and answer their call!"

Rav Schneider's powerful remarks inspired the assemblage and he raised enough funds to open a boarding school to save these young boys.

> *It is our duty, too, to hear the call of those who are telling us, sometimes also in the most indirect and even ignorant fashion, that deep inside they are spiritually alive.*

Like a Cow

When Rav Shalom Schwadron was a young father, a contagious disease spread across Yerushalayim, and two of his children became infected. Not wanting his other two children to contract the illness, he took them to the home of his parents-in-law to spend the night.

On the way, Rav Shalom met his rebbi, Rav Isaac Sher, who asked him why he was taking a walk with his children at night. Rav Shalom explained that two of his children had caught the disease that was going around, and he did not want it to spread to the others, so he was bringing them to their grandparents' home.

"Aaah," replied Rav Isaac. "So the big cow is taking her young calves to a safe place so they don't get infected!"

Rav Shalom was taken aback. What had he said or done to be described in such a manner? A cow? With her calves?

Rav Isaac explained his intent: "Every act is measured by the thought behind it. If your sole intent here is based on the natural inclination of parents to protect their progeny, then you are no different from all living species that look after their young. A cow will care for its children, as will other animals. How are you different?

"As a Jew, however," continued Rav Isaac, "your act of protecting your children fulfills the mitzvah of *chesed* toward the youth of Klal Yisrael, even if they happen to be your very own flesh and blood. You should have in mind that you are fulfilling the mitzvah of *chesed*, and by doing so, you will garner mitzvah merits with every step you take."

Pain of the Divine

Rav Dovid Lubliner, a resident of Tzfas of old, was a righteous man and a tremendous *talmid chacham*. Rav Dovid had one son, an outstanding *bachur* with numerous attributes. When this son reached the age of marriage, a match was suggested between him and a daughter of Rav Mordechai Lieder, who was a respected Slonimer Chassid from the city of Teveriah.

In short order, the *shidduch* was finalized and the wedding date was set. It was a beautiful *shidduch*, with an exceptional *chassan* and an equally virtuous *kallah*, both from G-d-fearing families steeped in Torah.

In honor of the *aufruf*, Rav Mordechai and his family traveled to Tzfas to spend Shabbos with their future *mechutan*, Rav Dovid, and his family. Numerous guests descended upon Tzfas for the weekend to take part in the *simchah*.

As Shabbos began, torrential rains poured down on Tzfas. The ancient city was flooded with water, and many of the old and dilapidated residences were not strong enough to withstand the deluge. Some homes were completely destroyed, while others filled with water, as the rainstorm wreaked havoc on the lives of the locals.

The *chassan,* who was in one of these homes, had nowhere to go when the roof of the house caved in, landing directly on his head and killing him on the spot.

News of the tragedy spread. The city was in shock. The heartbreak was indescribable.

However, to the amazement of all, upon being informed of the tragic passing of his only son, Rav Dovid remained composed. In fact, rather than falling into a state of despair and mourning, he engaged in the weekly Shabbos rituals, davening, singing *zemiros*, and eating the *seudos*, as if nothing had happened.

At one point, he even turned to the father of the *kallah*, Rav Mordechai, and said, "I don't have another son — but *mechutanim* we can remain! Let us maintain a relationship of fondness and friendship forever." Rav Mordechai and everyone else present were speechless. They had never seen such deep-seated faith, fortitude, and righteousness.

Upon the conclusion of Shabbos, right after Havdalah was recited, Rav Dovid fell to the ground and passed out. The entire Shabbos, he had maintained his resilience with unbelievable strength. After reviving Rav Dovid, those around him asked: What occurred after Shabbos ended?

Rav Dovid explained, "On Shabbos, I knew that it is forbidden to mourn. And of course, we all know that *'Kol de'avid Rachmana le'tav — Everything that the Merciful One does is for the good'* (Berachos 60b). Thus, this difficult decree was certainly designed by Hashem for our good, and nothing bad could result from it. However, as Shabbos departed and I began to contemplate the depth of the loss of my only son on the Shabbos of his *aufruf,* and in such a brutal fashion, the pain I felt was extremely severe!

"As I pondered this misfortune, I arrived at the conclusion that surely the *Shechinah* is in great pain over this calamity. As the Gemara [*Sanhedrin* 46a] says, when a person suffers for his sins, the *Shechinah* cries out, *'Kalani mei'roshi kalani mei'zro'i — I am burdened by My head, I am burdened by My arm.'* The *Shechinah*, as it were, feels the 'weight' of Its head and arm due to the punishment meted to the wicked for their transgressions. In this case, who caused Hashem such pain? Surely it was me, myself. My *aveiros* brought about all this sorrow and the resulting pain to the Divine Presence. When I came to this realization, it was too much to bear and I collapsed."

> *This holy Jew somehow found the strength to deal with the pain of his only son's catastrophic death. But the cognizance that his perceived weaknesses had caused the Shechinah anguish was too much for him to endure.*

Getting the Heart Used to Good

*R*av Moshe Dov Rose, a master mechanech and one of Rav Shlomo Wolbe's most notable talmidim (from the time that Rav Wolbe was still the mashgiach in Yeshivas Be'er Yaakov), was 16 years old when he first arrived at Be'er Yaakov in 5725/1965.

He related, "Someone once came to the mashgiach and asked for some *chizuk* in abstaining from *lashon hara*. Those of us who overheard the exchange were interested in hearing what the mashgiach would say. Would he suggest that the man conduct a *taanis dibbur*? Would he recommend davening for success in that area?

"He made no such suggestion. Instead, he told the questioner, 'Do a *chesed* three times a day.'

"Everything the mashgiach said was the product of thought and depth, and this piece of advice was no different. Why does a person speak *lashon hara*? Because he has evil in his heart, and that evil flows from the heart to all the other limbs, so the mouth, too, is evil. But if a person's heart becomes a good heart, then everything changes. And how is the heart turned around?

"A person's heart is affected by his deeds. When we do good deeds, our hearts grow accustomed to doing what is right, and then our tongues become good, as well."

"Al Yimna Atzmo Min Harachamim"

When Rav Moshe Tuvia Lieff, today the rav of Agudas Yisrael Bais Binyomin in Brooklyn, was a *bachur* at the Mirrer Yeshivah in Brooklyn, there was a group of outstanding *Chassidishe yungerleit* who were members of the yeshivah's kollel. One of the *yungerleit*, a Klausenberger Chassid, was a tremendous *masmid*; he would learn from morning until evening without interruption, taking only a brief break for lunch.

At one point, the *yungerman* began to miss *seder* regularly. This was uncharacteristic of this *ben Torah* and *masmid*, so the rosh kollel, Rav Eliezer Ginsburg, approached him. "You are an outstanding *yungerman*," said Rav Ginsburg. "What's going on?"

The *yungerman* explained: "I have cancer. Once or twice a month, I must go for chemotherapy treatments. These treatments are very debilitating and I have no strength afterward, so I am forced to stay home."

Shaken by the news, Rav Ginsburg and the other members of the yeshivah davened for the *yungerman*'s recovery, but his condition worsened and eventually he was hospitalized. Rav Ginsburg went to visit the *yungerman*, who was hooked up to various machines, his body racked with pain. During the course of their conversation, the *yungerman* suddenly turned serious.

"You know that *bachur* in yeshivah who sits on my bench?" he asked Rav Ginsburg. "He's a nice boy. Why don't we find him a *shidduch*? We must try to marry him off."

With raised eyebrows, Rav Ginsburg glanced at his surroundings and then at the many machines filling the room. He said to the *yungerman*, "Your life is flashing in front of you; you are in a very precarious situation! Get a little better and then we'll worry about *shidduchim*."

The *yungerman* was unconvinced and he shared a thought that he had heard from the Klausenberger Rebbe, Rav Yekusiel Yehudah Halberstam, whose *Chumash shiur* he regularly attended. He quoted the well-known Gemara in *Maseches Berachos* (10a), which relates that Chizkiyahu told Yeshayahu, "*Kach mekublani mi'beis avi abba: Afilu cherev chadah munachas al tzavaro shel adam al yimna atzmo min harachamim* — I received the following teaching from the house of my father's father: Even if a sharp sword is resting on a person's neck, he should not refrain from praying for mercy."

"The Rebbe explained that '*al yimna atzmo min harachamim*' doesn't just mean not to give up on Hashem having *rachmanus* on you and to keep on davening. It also means that no matter what your situation in life is, '*al yimna atzmo min harachamim*,' don't stop doing merciful things! Don't stop worrying about others!

"So what's with that *bachur*? We need a *shidduch* for him."

Three days later, the *yungerman* was *niftar*.

> But his message is still with us. "Al yimna atzmo min harachamim." We must never stop demonstrating rachmanus, no matter how dire our own circumstances.

Another Second of Relief

One year prior to his untimely *petirah*, the Kopycznitzer Rebbe, Rav Moshe Mordechai Heschel, underwent what was then considered experimental open-heart surgery.

Shortly before the Rebbe left New York to travel to the Mayo Clinic in Rochester, Minnesota, one of his close Chassidim told him of a young girl, a distant cousin of his from Eretz Yisrael, who was scheduled for difficult surgery at the clinic at the same time as the Rebbe.

This Chassid traveled to the clinic with the Rebbe and was there shortly after the Rebbe awoke from the anesthesia. The Rebbe was still very weak and was barely able to speak. Nonetheless, he asked his Chassid to take out his checkbook and write a check to the family of the girl.

The Chassid wrote out the check and the Rebbe signed it. The Chassid wanted to wait until the Rebbe dozed off again before delivering the check, but the Rebbe requested that he bring it to the girl's family immediately.

"But the bank is closed now in any case, so there is no reason to rush," said the Chassid. "I would rather sit with the Rebbe a little longer."

"Go now," responded the Rebbe, "and let them have some *ruyigkeit* [relief] a minute earlier."

The Rebbe's kindness didn't end there. When the young girl was released from the hospital, her father went to take care of his bill. The cashier smiled and said, "Your account is clear. The rabbi took care of it last week."

"I Haven't Sold a Policy"

While he was convalescing from open-heart surgery, the Kopycznitzer Rebbe heard that the son of a Chassid intended to enroll in a coed high school. Despite his poor health, the Rebbe traveled to the summer camp the youngster was attending. He sat on a bench with his arm around the boy's shoulder and confided, "I've been inactive for two months now. I haven't sold a single policy in all this time."

"Policy?"

"Yes. Helping people do what they really know is right — that's my 'business' and the kind of 'insurance policies' I 'sell' in order to merit Heavenly mercy and blessing. So, we know the type of genuine Torah school you should be attending next year. Won't you help me merit Heavenly mercy?"

The boy agreed to attend a yeshivah and ultimately became an ehrliche and respected communal activist.

A Taste of Compassion

The Important Phone Call

One Erev Shabbos in the winter, Rabbi Dov Brezak, noted *mechanech* in Yerushalayim, traveled to the home of Rav Chaim and Rebbetzin Batsheva Kanievsky in Bnei Brak to receive advice and a blessing. While he was speaking to Rebbetzin Kanievsky, she received an "important" phone call. Over the phone, the rebbetzin repeated a strange set of phrases again and again: "No, nothing will happen to you. Not today and not tomorrow. Not here and not anywhere. To others it may have happened, but to you it won't happen. Nothing will happen to you. Everything will be fine."

This went on for over a quarter of an hour, with the rebbetzin listening and then repeating: "It happened to others, but it won't happen to you. Not here and not anywhere. Not today and not tomorrow…"

When she hung up, Rabbi Brezak asked the rebbetzin about the strange bits of conversation he had just overheard. She explained that a woman was very nervous and frightened by dreams. Each time she called, the rebbetzin would listen to her and tell her that everything will be fine and that she has nothing to fear. The woman would not be reassured until the rebbetzin went through the whole litany of comforting phrases again and again.

Then the rebbetzin concluded her explanation with a remark that left Rabbi Brezak awestruck: "When I speak to her," she told me, "it usually helps for a few hours."

This means that this woman called the rebbetzin often, and each time the rebbetzin would go through the entire ritual of listening and responding, just to make the woman feel good for a few hours. As Rabbi Brezak witnessed, the rebbetzin did this even on busy Fridays, when she was involved in cooking for Shabbos and had a house full of people, many of whom were waiting to speak to her.

It wasn't just the rebbetzin's listening ear and soothing words that showed her greatness. It was the caring that she demonstrated to this woman, by helping her with all her heart.

Not One Word of Reproof

Shortly after World War II, in one of the displaced persons camps, an irreligious young man was brought to the Klausenberger Rebbe, Rav Yekusiel Yehudah Halberstam.

"I heard that before the war, you were the top *bachur* in the Munkatcher Yeshivah," the Rebbe said to him. "What happened to you?"

"I saw that the best were burned and only the *pesoles* [chaff] remained," the former *yeshivah bachur* replied.

"You are so right," the Rebbe answered him. "The best were burned and only the *pesoles* remained."

Then the Rebbe, who had lost his wife and 11 children during the war, burst out crying. The two sobbed together for over half an hour.

Eventually, the young man returned to full religious observance. Of his return, he said, "Had the Rebbe given me one word of *tochachah*, reproof, I would have walked out and never returned.

"But he just cried with me."

How to Give Tzedakah

Rav Tzvi Hirsch of Liska, known as Rav Hershele Liska and also commonly referred to as the Ach Pri Tevuah after the *sefer* he authored, was once asked by his Chassidim to spend a Shabbos in the city of Munkatch. As was the custom, people flocked to where he was staying to give him *kvittlach* and receive *berachos*. Among the many people who came was an individual with a pitiful story to tell.

The man's daughter had already been engaged for two years, but no wedding date had been set, as the dowry he had promised was beyond his means. It was impossible for him to fulfill his promise, and this was delaying the marriage of his daughter.

"How much are you missing?" Rav Hershele asked him. "How much do you need?"

The man responded, "I need 100 *ranish*," a tremendous amount of money at that time.

Rav Hershele immediately gathered the full sum from the money that was lying on his table and handed it to the needy individual.

Standing at the side and observing this episode was a prominent gentleman, who asked Rav Hershele, "Why did the Rebbe find it necessary to personally solve this person's financial problem?"

"I would like to tell you a story," the Rebbe responded:

> *I used to be a melamed, in a time when poverty was rampant. One year, I developed a strong desire to travel to Belz for Shavuos, to bask in the holiness of Rav Shalom Rokeach, the Sar Shalom of Belz. However, I did not have the necessary funds required for travel, so I began my journey by foot. When I arrived in Lemberg, my feet were horribly swollen, and I went to the local shul to rest. I noticed a group of Chassidim with several carriages being pulled by horses. They were from Munkatch and were on their way to Belz, using this stopover to replace the horses that were weary from their long journey.*
>
> *One person stood out as their leader. I approached him and asked if he would allow me to travel with them to Belz. He responded that I would need to pay 60 gratzer. I pleaded with him, explaining that I did not have even one gratzer to my name. I showed him my swollen feet so he would see how much I had suffered up until that point in my strong desire to spend Shavuos in Belz. He told me to go around and collect the 60 gratzer, as there were still two hours left until the group was to depart*

on their journey to Belz. But if I did not come up with the money, he warned, I would not be able to join the group.

Seeing that I had no choice if I wanted to fulfill my desire to spend Shavuos in Belz, I went out to collect the 60 gratzer. It was customary in those days to ask for charity either in the form of money or for material to exchange for money. When I walked into the first store, I was asked, "Money or material?" and I replied "Material," thinking that it would be easier to accumulate 60 gratzer utilizing this method. And so I was given a feather. In the second store, I was given a button, and in the third, a needle. By the time I came to the fourth store, I possessed a feather, a button, and a needle... and one hour had already passed. When I realized that at this rate, there was no way I would reach my goal before the group left to Belz, I broke down and cried. The fourth storekeeper had pity on me and gave me the full 60 gratzer for my journey. I was overjoyed.

I paid my share and was on my way to Belz for Shavuos.

"At that time," concluded Rav Hershele, "I took it upon myself that whenever I am approached by a poor person and I have the means to help him, I will contribute the entire amount and not send him to collect from others."

As Rav Hershele finished his story, he turned the person who raised the question and said, "I learned this lesson from you. I recognize you even though you don't recognize me. You were the person who taught me to give *tzedakah* in the entire amount — as you were that very storekeeper!"

— *heard from Pinchos Ben Tzvi*

Zorei'a Tzedakos

Rav Yitzchak Meir Heschel, the first Kopycznitzer Rebbe, passed away in 1936. Before his *petirah*, he borrowed very large sums of money to distribute to *tzedakah*, leaving significant debts. When his successor, Rav Avrohom Yehoshua Heschel, traveled to visit the Kopycznitzer Chassidim in Galicia, his *gabbaim* were hoping that the money the Rebbe would receive during the trip would pay off the debts.

During his visit to Tarnopol, a large number of Chassidim came to seek blessings and guidance. Soon, the table the Rebbe was sitting at was piled high with *kvittlach*, banknotes, and coins.

Suddenly, a poverty-stricken couple entered the room, and the Rebbe asked all those present to please step out. After the couple left, Reb Moshe Gelbtuch and the other *gabbaim* returned to find only the *kvittlach* on the table; the Rebbe had given the couple all the money he had received.

Reb Moshe, who had exerted much effort to ensure that the Rebbe's visit would be successful financially, couldn't restrain himself from respectfully reminding the Rebbe about the large debts and asking what happened to all the cash.

The Rebbe, with emotion in his voice, quoted the words from *Birchos Krias Shema*: "*Zorei'a tzedakos matzmiach yeshuos*," and translated the words in his own way: "If one plants *tzedakah*, *yeshuos* will sprout."

Then he explained, "If you want me to be a *poel yeshuos*, I have to be a *zorei'a tzedakos*."

"I Can Cry"

At 2 o' clock one morning, there was incessant knocking at the entrance of the home of Rav Shlomo Zalman Auerbach, in the Shaarei Chesed neighborhood of Yerushalayim. Rav Shlomo Zalman opened the door to find a couple standing there. He ushered them inside and asked how he could be of help. From the look on their faces, it was obvious that they were in great pain.

The two took turns describing their predicament: They were a chassan and a kallah, and a beis din in Yerushalayim had just determined that they could not get married, because there was strong doubt regarding the purity of the kallah's lineage.

They pleaded with Rav Shlomo Zalman for help. "Is there anything you can do for us?" they begged.

The great tzaddik looked at them lovingly. "I'm not sure," he said. "Halachah is halachah. What can I do?"

He thought for a moment.

"Then again, there is something I can do for you. Ich ken veinen. I can cry for you."

Rav Shlomo Zalman began to cry. He cried profusely, causing alarm to his family members who were still awake, as they wondered what was troubling their great father.

He then gave the engaged couple a berachah, wishing them the best.

The next day, after returning home from delivering his shiur at Kol Torah, Rav Shlomo Zalman heard a knock at his door. There, once again, stood the young couple. The chassan spoke up.

"We came to tell the rav some good news. A firsthand witness from Brazil has come forward and testified that the question that was raised regarding my kallah's lineage was completely unfounded," he said. "The beis din has ruled that her yichus is 100 percent kosher and that we may marry."

The mesader kiddushin at the wedding was none other than Rav Shlomo Zalman.

We often hear of tzaros or difficult nisyonos in the form of parnassah, shidduchim, illness, chinuch habanim, or the many other challenges facing members of Klal Yisrael. Yet even when we feel that we cannot be of assistance or we do not know what we should be saying or doing, there is something we can do: We can cry.

— *heard from Rav Moshe Tuvia Lieff*

About Face

Rav Aharon Schechter, rosh yeshivah of Yeshivas Rabbeinu Chaim Berlin, was once heading home on a Shabbos afternoon after Minchah. As he made his way down a Flatbush street accompanied by a small group, he encountered three Jewish boys smoking cigarettes. Rav Aharon, still surrounded by his coterie, continued for another block or so when suddenly he turned around.

It was clear that Rav Aharon preferred to walk alone this time, as he headed back to the boys he had just passed. He approached them by himself, so as not to embarrass them, and with a fatherly smile he told them, "Boys, *ich hub eich leeb*! [I love you!] Please come by and discuss anything you want. My doors are open to you 24 hours a day."

With that, the rosh yeshivah said goodbye and headed home. One week later, one of the boys showed up at the door of the rosh yeshivah's office. Rav Aharon proceeded to spend much time with this boy he did not know.

Rav Schechter demonstrated one approach of conveying the beauty of Shabbos, utilizing the most meaningful words a troubled youth will ever hear: "I love you."

The Power of a Hug

In May 2011, Dr. Itzhak Brook, a pediatric infectious disease doctor at Georgetown University in Washington, D.C., penned a most touching article in the Los Angeles Times. I was so impressed by what he wrote that I reached out to him and let him know what an impression his words made on me. I asked him if I may share his story here and he graciously acquiesced.

Hypopharyngeal cancer, cancer of the lower part of the pharynx (throat).

Words no one ever wants to hear.

Dr. Itzhak Brook had discovered his illness somewhat differently than the average person finds out about such things. As a doctor, he had access to his hospital's laboratory results. After undergoing testing, he looked up his name in the pathology laboratory logbook.

What he saw shook him up.

"Mildly differentiated squamous cell carcinoma."

There it was, black on white.

How was it possible? Could it be an error?

Deep down, Dr. Brook knew that it wasn't. But just to be sure, the good doctor went to view the biopsy specimens under the microscope himself.

There was no denying it. The diagnosis was correct.

Dr. Brook knew that his life would never be the same. He had always felt impregnable and impervious to illness. Now his entire world was filled with unpredictability and apprehension.

Overtaken by despondency and incredulity, Dr. Brook walked slowly from the laboratory to his internist's office. He stammered as he broke the news.

The internist didn't say a word. Instead, he slowly stood up and walked over to Dr. Brook. He then gave Dr. Brook a warm, caring embrace.

It was a hug that Dr. Brook has not forgotten.

He felt so good knowing that the internist cared for him beyond their professional connection. That hug encouraged Dr. Brook like nothing else could. It made him feel that he was in the company of people who genuinely recognized his anguish and distress, who felt his personal tragedy. And at that moment, that meant more to him than a thousand words of support or elaborate explanations.

It was the potency of a concerned, human touch. Dr. Brook now knew that he was not alone in his battle to overcome his illness. His doctor would fight it with him.

It was the first time that Dr. Brook had ever been hugged by a medical caregiver. In fact, never had Dr. Brook himself hugged any of his own patients, believing instead in maintaining a professional distance. At that moment, however, he realized that there are times in the medical field when the power of an embrace is so much more powerful than anything else a doctor or professional can provide.

In order to have his cancer removed, Dr. Brooks underwent a total laryngectomy, in which his entire larynx was removed.

The ensuing period was draining, physically and emotionally. Dr. Brook had great difficulty speaking and contended with myriad medical complications.

But he always remembered that hug.

Months of seemingly impossible challenges were made tolerable by the knowledge that his doctor would care for him and help him in any way he could. That emotional support, thoughtfulness, and sensitivity assisted Dr. Brook in surmounting many of the hurdles he faced as a laryngectomee (one who has undergone a laryngectomy). In fact, they played a crucial role in his ultimate recovery.

Dr. Brook was dealt a most daunting test that rendered speaking arduous and laborious. But he discovered a different manner of expression that, he says, is so much more effective.

He had experienced the impact of a heartfelt hug.

Sympathy in Spring Valley

On Friday, July 11, 2014, a 20-month-old boy, Dominic Mero, died after being run over by a vehicle in the Lottie Gardens parking lot in Spring Valley, New York.

The family did not have the money to pay for the burial, so a fund-raising effort was undertaken at a local deli on Rose Avenue in Spring Valley, where a bucket for donations was placed. This heartbreaking situation was exacerbated when the pail of money — containing approximately $300 — was stolen. A 17-year-old was later arrested and charged with petty larceny for making off with the cash.

In stepped Yossi Gestetner, founder of the Orthodox Jewish Public Affairs Council (OJPAC), as well as Rockland County Legislator Aron Wieder, and Benny Polatseck.

These three Orthodox Jews met Jacqueline Jones, the neighbor who had put out the bucket, and then the boy's father, uncle, and other relatives, who were completely overwhelmed; they couldn't believe that people would show up to try to help them. They were in such dire straits that the father had planned to sell his car to pay the funeral home.

By that Tuesday night, Polatseck had set up a website to raise funds for the Mero family, and Gestetner worked to get the word out and garner media attention. Within 24 hours, a large sum had been raised.

They were hoping to raise perhaps $1,000, but the funds came in from all over. Aside from a large contribution from Kansas, the rest of the donations were modest $5, $10, and $20 contributions from all over the world, particularly from many Jewish people in Brooklyn, Monsey, and elsewhere.

About 24 hours later, after the wake for the child in Queens, where they had handed the family a certified check for $2,250 to cover the funeral and burial, the Gestetner, Wieder, and Polatseck trio were on their way back to Monsey.

Onlookers at the wake had been surprised to see three *Chassidishe* men walking in, but they soon learned of the altruism and kindliness of these Orthodox Jews.

"The boy's uncle asked me how he can one day repay us for what we had done," related Wieder. "I told him, 'If you ever find someone in distress, even if he is not from your community, help him.'

" 'That's how you'll repay us.' "

Back Support

*R*av Menachem Manis Mandel, the founding menahel of Yeshiva of Brooklyn, treated every person, young and old, Jew and non-Jew, with the utmost respect.

A physically handicapped girl who was attending Yeshiva of Brooklyn was transported to school each day by a minibus, which was fitted with a lift that accommodated her wheelchair. Every day, someone in the school building had to sign a slip for the bus driver, attesting to the fact that the girl had arrived safely.

Rav Mandel was standing outside one morning waiting for the school buses as he always did, when the minibus pulled in. The bus driver, Anthony, asked Rav Mandel if he could sign the slip. Rav Mandel looked around for something to lean on in order to sign his name. When Anthony offered him his own back for support, Rav Mandel politely refused.

"G-d created you in His image," said Rav Mandel. "It would not be honorable to use your back as a support. G-d has much more respect for you than that."

A Taste of Warmth

What Do You See?

Rav Aryeh Levin, menahel of the Eitz Chaim Yeshivah of Yerushalayim, once stood with his son at a window overlooking the yard where students were playing during their break.

"What do you see?" asked Rav Aryeh.

"I see that the skinny boy over there looks shy," said his son. "The boy next to him is very outgoing, almost aggressive. And the boy in the middle seems to get along with everyone. Why? What do you see?"

Rav Aryeh shook his head.

"The skinny boy looks like he hasn't had a good meal in days. The boy on the left is wearing torn shoes, and the boy running near them is not wearing a coat. He probably doesn't own one. Here is what I'll do: I'll invite the skinny one to eat lunch with me, and I'll *farher* the other two so they can 'earn' a reward of shoes and a coat respectively."

Rav Aryeh gave each boy a test with questions he knew they would be able to answer. He then sent a note to each boy's father informing him of the reward the boys had "earned."

Rav Aryeh's talmidim saw firsthand how he was tuned in to their specific needs and that he took action to fill in the blanks in their lives.

Spontaneous Dance

A young man who was a member of a certain Chassidic dynasty encountered various issues in connection with his upcoming marriage. Upon hearing of his difficulties, the boy's Rebbe realized that there was only one man who could deal with them properly. He called the Kopycznitzer Rebbe, Rav Moshe Mordechai Heschel, and asked him to speak to the young man.

When the young man entered the room, Rav Moshe Mordechai saw that he was depressed. He stretched out his hand, offered him a hearty mazel tov, and then, to relieve the depression, said, "I am sorry I wasn't present at your engagement party. Let us have a short dance right here, so I will be able to perform the mitzvah of being *mesamei'ach* a *chassan*."

In short order, the two were humming a *niggun* and spinning around the room in a joyous dance.

It was not long before the young man acknowledged that he had found a person who, in one second, could change a person's whole outlook.

And, a short time later, the Rebbe was present at the young man's wedding, which turned out to be a time of great simchah for all involved.

Breakfast First

It was the first day in a new school for Moshe. As he waited for the subway that was to take him to school, Moshe was feeling anxious. What would the new yeshivah be like? How would the boys treat him? Would his new principal be kind or scary?

After waiting a short while, Moshe heard that the train was delayed, and his anxiety only grew. He tried to calm himself down by closing his eyes and taking deep breaths, but he was still very impatient as he continued to wait for the subway.

Finally, after what seemed like an eternity, the train arrived and he got on, still feeling edgy. Imagine coming late on his first day in a new school! What was the principal going to tell him? Would he be reprimanded? How would Moshe explain his tardiness on the very first day?

At long last, the train pulled into his stop and Moshe dismounted and headed directly toward Yeshiva Torah Vodaath. When he reached the building, he entered its doors and made his way to the stairwell that led to the classrooms. But then, his greatest fear was realized; he tensed up and his faced turned red as he saw the principal, Rav Dovid Bender, looking down at him from the top of the staircase.

"I…I…I know I'm late," stammered Moshe, "but…but my train was delayed. I am so sorry. I'll make sure it doesn't happen again."

Rav Bender walked down the steps toward Moshe. Putting his arm around the new student, he said, "If your train was late and you just arrived, then you must have missed breakfast, as well. Come with me."

Rav Bender took Moshe to his office, where he gave him a bowl of cornflakes with milk, and kept him company as he ate. Only then did he escort him to his new class.

Reb Moshe/Moe Marx, a veteran Wall Street executive, later told Rav Dovid's son, Rav Yaakov Bender, that this episode was the single most-significant incident in his school years, profoundly impacting him and the life he later led.

Fueled With Love

In the city of the Chida, Rav Chaim Yosef David Azulai, lived a 10-year-old boy and his widowed mother, who were penniless. They had no bread to eat or even water to drink. The child wanted very badly to bring home some food for his mother and himself to eat, so despite his young age and dreadful appearance, he headed out to look for a job. He turned to the various craftsmen of the city and offered his services.

By performing odd jobs of all kinds, the boy managed to bring home money with which to provide the most basic sustenance for himself and his mother. They were surviving, but barely.

One day, the child entered a large factory. Like he had done so many times before, he offered to perform any job, big or small. "It doesn't matter what it is," said the boy, "as long as it is work."

The owner of the factory was an arrogant and cocky fellow. Peering at the vulnerable child, garbed in clothes that were torn and tattered, he said, "I just thought of the most perfect idea. It is a very important job." The man smirked, but his sarcasm was completely lost on the sincere, well-meaning— and desperate — lad. "If you do this job correctly, I will pay you 1,000 *gilden*."

"I am ready," replied the boy.

The factory owner proceeded to explain the nature of the job. "Not far from here, right outside the city, is a river. With the onset of night, enter the river, and remain standing there until dawn. I will be coming to check on you from time to time to ensure that the task is being carried out properly. Then come to me and I'll give you 1,000 *gilden*."

The factory workers who had gathered around broke into peals of laughter. The boy, however, didn't get the joke. With childlike innocence, he asked the employer if they could sign a contract verifying their arrangement.

"Definitely," replied the pompous factory owner, who went to his elegant desk, pulled out a sheet of parchment, and wrote out a contract documenting their deal: The boy would stand in the river all night, and in return he'd receive the sum of 1,000 *gilden*.

The child returned home and, with great joy, told his mother about the "job" he had accepted.

"It's a great opportunity," he told his mother. "I will earn in one night a huge fortune — more than I ordinarily earn in several years!"

His mother was not happy. "This idea is extremely dangerous," she said. "Staying in the frozen river on a cold night like this is a *sakanah*. Even just to stand in the cold streets is brutal. How can you remain in a freezing river all night?"

The child was unperturbed. "There is no choice," he said. "It's an opportunity that does not come along every day."

The mother was beside herself, but her son was unrelenting. So, as day turned to night, she and her son headed to the river. Her eyes filled with tears. How had she allowed her son to get caught up with this nonsensical idea?

She tried one more time, and cried to her son, "Your father passed away, leaving me with absolutely nothing but you. How can I allow you to subject yourself to this dangerous endeavor?"

Her cries went unheeded. The child insisted on going ahead, desiring to put an end to their desperation and starvation. With one night of supreme sacrifice, he'd earn enough money to support both of them for a long time.

They arrived at the river and he jumped right in.

The anxious mother did not leave her son for a moment. Her body shook with fright, as words of prayer passed through her lips that Hashem protect her precious son. She spoke to her son, trying to cheer him up and telling him to stay focused so that he does not inadvertently drift into the depths of the river.

As the hours passed, the temperature dropped and the howling winds blew fiercely. The river was no longer calm, and the stormy weather didn't allow the young boy a clear view of his mother. Still, he heard her cries, reminding him to stay strong, to remain vigilant, and that it would soon be morning.

With the frigid temperatures reaching unbearable lows, the mother gathered some twigs and lit a fire on the riverbank, hoping that it would provide some warmth for her son. Her efforts, as well intentioned as they were, were futile. Her little flame was no match for the freezing water.

Throughout the night, the factory owner visited the river. He could not believe his eyes. There, to his astonishment, was the 10-year-old boy, in the freezing water. He turned to go home in disgust. He had been bested by a determined youngster.

The boy stood bravely and boldly until dawn, when his mother drew him out of the water. He was wet to the bone and shaking from head to toe. His devoted mother immediately wrapped him in multiple layers of clothing and blankets, took him straight home, and placed him next to the fireplace. She served him some tea and did what she could to restore his equilibrium. With time, color returned to his face and his breathing was normal again. Once he began to feel better, he also began to smile. He had done the impossible.

The next day, the boy and his mother went to the office of the wealthy factory owner to collect the promised payment. The owner laughed in their faces.

"1,000 *gilden*? For what?" he shouted.

The boy and his mother looked at each other and then at the man. "What are you talking about? Here is the contract that you signed," she said, pulling out the document.

"Not quite," mocked the man and then said to the mother, "During the course of the night, as I did my inspections to determine if your son was immersed in the river as we had discussed, I noticed that you violated our agreement."

"What?!" cried the boy and his mother.

"Yes, indeed. I saw you," he said, pointing to the mother, "lighting a fire next to the river to warm your son as he stood in the water. Your son, therefore, did not fulfill our agreement, as he was required to stand in the cold river all night. Instead, he stood in a river that was being warmed by your fire. He is thus not eligible to receive my payment."

The boy and his mother could not believe what they were hearing. They called the man to a *din Torah* in the *beis din* of the Chida. Upon being apprised of the story, the Chida summoned the man.

The Chida greeted him with great respect, inviting him inside. The man sat down next to the Chida, who excused himself as he approached his stove and placed a kettle at the side of a burning flame, explaining that he was preparing water for tea for his esteemed guest. The Chida then returned to the man and began conversing with him. "As the water is heated for our tea, we can talk."

The Chida began speaking to the man about a variety of topics. The great *tzaddik* was deep in conversation and appeared to have forgotten about the tea. The man gently reminded the Chida about the water he had placed on the stove. "The rav may not have realized that he forgot to put the kettle on the actual fire," he said, pointing to the stove. "The way it is now, sitting adjacent to the flame, the water won't get hot."

The Chida smiled. "If only your ears would hear the words your mouth has just uttered!" he said. "When the fire is burning beside the water, the water will never become hot. Now you certainly understand why you have been summoned here. As you well know, a small fire on a riverbank cannot possibly warm the river. The water in the river remains as cold and as frozen as before."

The man was caught off guard.

"You may not enter the city shul until you pay every penny agreed to in the contract with the young boy!" commanded the Chida.

The man realized that he had better pay up. He immediately pulled out 1,000 *gilden* and handed it to the boy and his mother.

After the parties had left, the Chida turned to his *talmidim* and shared a lesson from this story.

"There is no question that the tiny fire could not warm the frozen river waters. But there is also no question that the young boy's heart must have been warmed upon seeing the concern of his mother and her devotion to him. The fire didn't warm him physically, but it warmed him in other ways. Were it not for the encouragement and reinforcement of his mother, the boy could never have pulled through. It was the great love of a mother that helped him accomplish the impossible."

Even if you cannot help your friend physically or materially, you can encourage him with a good word and expressions of support. Even from a distance, one can do wonders by opening his heart and sharing his concern.

Equally Loved

*R*av Nachman Bulman was a visionary and a dreamer. One of his dreams was to build up Eretz Yisrael. Toward that goal, he established Kiryat Nachliel, an English-speaking community in the northern town of Migdal Ha'emek. While the community did not prove to be economically viable, the people who lived there during the 14 years it lasted remember with longing the inspiration it engendered and the sense of many diverse Jews becoming united in one great enterprise.

One of the residents of Kiryat Nachliel, Yaakov Yisrael, was visited by his mother shortly after he had joined the community. She was scheduled to arrive Friday morning after a long, multitransfer flight from California. But there was a delay. By the time she got all her things and was ready for the 90-minute ride from the airport, there was only about that amount of time left until *hadlakas neiros*. But once she arrived, she was in for a treat; this Shabbos would be special, for she and her son had been invited to attend the Friday-night *seudah* at the home of the rav, Rav Bulman.

At the *seudah*, though she hadn't slept for about a day and a half, Yaakov Yisrael's mother tried to be at her social best. Polite exchanges ensued and Rav Bulman soon picked up that she was a woman of high intellect and culture. Around soup time, he threw out a question meant to be a springboard for a philosophical discussion:

"A man has two children. One labors diligently, always trying to do every little thing his father wants, but often doesn't do the job right. The other sometimes tries, and usually does a very nice job, but at times he is lazy and neglectful. Whom do you think the father loves more?"

In her fatigued state, Yaakov Yisrael's mother took the path of least resistance. She answered, quite perfunctorily, "Oh, well, he loves the one who tries hardest, of course."

Rav Bulman glanced at her for a moment in surprise. Then he said compassionately, "Ah, I see. You must be tired!"

Despite her tiredness, her curiosity was piqued. She smiled and asked, "So what's the answer?"

"All right," Rav Bulman said, smiling slyly. "The father loves them equally! They're both his children! The only question is which of them may not feel the love…"

> *Like so many others blessed to be impacted by Rav Bulman's influence, this woman saw the depth of his greatness and his understanding of human nature through the prism of Torah.*
>
> *And she never forgot this lesson: A parent's love for every child is without limits. In that vein, Hashem, too, loves each of His precious children equally. We may not feel the love because of our own shortcomings. We may even have to work to sense His fondness. But we must know that it is there.*
>
> *He loves you and me, and all of us, equally.*

Forty Years of Kaddish

Rav Gamliel Rabinovich, rosh yeshivah of Yeshivah Shaar HaShamayim, recalled the time he was davening with his father, Rav Levi Rabinovich, in shul and his father began saying *Kaddish Yasom*. Knowing that his father didn't have *yahrtzeit* for either of his parents that day, Rav Gamliel asked him why he was reciting *Kaddish*.

"Over 40 years ago," Rav Levi responded, "a certain *bachur* passed away. Not having married, he left behind no progeny and thus no one to say *Kaddish* for him. I made note of the *bachur*'s name and have been saying *Kaddish* every year on his *yahrtzeit*."

Rav Levi didn't know the bachur or have any connection to him, but the reality of his circumstance and his lack of family greatly moved him. Thus, without anyone knowing, he made sure to say Kaddish on the yahrtzeit for over 40 years.

It was only his son's prodding that led to the revelation of this chesed shel emes.

It's Worth It

Rav Yechiel Michel Feinstein, rosh yeshivah of Yeshivah Bais Yehudah in Bnei Brak, was known for his refinement, warmth, and sensitivity.

He once went to the tailor who had made his frock and asked to have it altered. "The frock is heavy," Rav Michel, as he was known, told the tailor.

But then, worried that he had insulted the hardworking tailor, he quickly corrected himself and said, "It's heavy on me. It's very good for younger men, but I am elderly and for me it's heavy."

The following story illustrates the warmth and compassion

Rav Michel displayed to strangers, as well, and his intentions behind his actions.

A penniless man entered Yeshivah Bais Yehudah to collect money. Rav Michel wished to help the impoverished fellow, but he had no money on him, so he approached a *yungerman* seated nearby and asked if he could borrow some money to give to the collector. The *yungerman* replied that he didn't have any money on him. Another *yungerman* was approached by the elderly rosh yeshivah, but he also didn't have any money to lend. Rav Michel made his way from one *yungerman* to the next, seeking to borrow some money to help the poor man.

Finally, Rav Michel found a *yungerman* who had some money to give him, but by then the man had exited the *beis midrash*. Rav Michel asked one of the *yungerleit* to kindly hurry to the steps of the yeshivah leading to the street so he could catch up to the collector and give him the money.

The man was deeply moved. He reentered the *beis midrash* and headed to the front, where he walked toward Rav Michel. He bent down and whispered in Rav Michel's ear, "Reb Michel, you are a good man. You are a very good man. Thank you. But be aware that someone who is so good suffers in the end."

Rav Michel smiled and wished the man well.

After the man left, Rav Michel turned to the *yungerman* sitting next to him and said, "The *pasuk* in *Koheles* (1:18) states, '*V'yosif daas, yosif machov* — For with much wisdom comes much grief.' The Kotzker Rebbe, Rav Menachem Mendel Morgenstern, remarked that yes, it is true that the greater one's comprehension, the greater pain one suffers. But it is still worthwhile to enhance one's understanding.

"I also say," concluded Rav Michel, "that the pained words that the man expressed may be true, but it is still worthwhile to be a good person and then become even better."

A Taste of Tefillah

The Tefillah of the Tzibbur

*T*hough all tefillos have an impact in Heaven, there is no doubt
that the tefillah said with a minyan has special power.

A rosh yeshivah in Eretz Yisrael was frustrated that one of his
talmidim, Shmuel, was having an exceedingly difficult time learning. No matter how hard he tried and no matter how much his
rebbeim worked with him, Shmuel seemed to make no progress. It
was as if his brain were sealed, not allowing the words of Torah to
enter. The rosh yeshivah was at a loss, not sure what to do to help
his *talmid*. He sent Shmuel to present his dilemma to Rav Chaim
Kanievsky.

"Daven and Hashem will help you," Rav Chaim said.

"But I daven every day," Shmuel said. "I daven, and I cry, and
I plead while saying the *berachah* of *Atah Chonein* [the blessing of
wisdom] to merit *hatzlachah* in my Torah learning. And yet I struggle."

"Accept upon yourself to be extremely vigilant about davening
b'tzibbur and you will see a *yeshuah, b'ezras Hashem*," Rav Chaim
responded.

Shmuel accepted upon himself to daven every *tefillah* with a *minyan*, no matter what.

One evening, after having kept to this *kabbalah* for a while,
Shmuel was sitting in his yeshivah, when he fell asleep on his

shtender, exhausted. At 2 a.m., he awoke and realized that he hadn't yet davened Maariv. Recalling his *kabbalah*, he was intent on finding a *minyan*, but where would he be able to at such an hour?

Shmuel quickly ran to the famed Zichron Moshe shul in Yerushalayim, hoping that there'd be a *minyan* there. Unfortunately, there wasn't. It wasn't until over an hour later that he was able, just barely, to gather 10 men to form a *minyan*. As he davened *Shemoneh Esrei*, the floodgates opened and he shed copious tears, begging Hashem to allow him to comprehend the beautiful words of Torah that his peers seemed to grasp and remember so easily.

After davening, Shmuel remained in the shul until morning and davened Shacharis *k'vasikin*. He then returned to his yeshivah and immediately sat down to learn. Strangely, despite going on limited sleep, he felt rejuvenated. As he began reading the words of the Gemara, he felt a sense of clarity and comprehension he had never experienced before.

"*Shor she'nagach es haparah* — If an ox gored a cow; *v'nimtza ubarah b'tzidah* — and the cow's fetus was found at its side; *meshaleim chatzi nezek la'parah u'revia nezek la'vlad* — the owner of the ox pays half damages for the cow and a quarter damages for the calf…" (*Bava Kamma* 46a).

Wow! said Shmuel to himself. *How simple! How sweet!*

He continued learning, word after word, line after line. Never before had he experienced anything like this.

"*…zu divrei Sumchus d'amar mamon hamutal b'safeik cholkin* — this is the opinion of Sumchus who maintains that money that lies in doubt is divided" (ibid.).

On and on he went. Shmuel felt like he had been given a new lease on life. No longer was his mind shut off from the words of Torah.

Weeks passed, and then months. Shmuel saw remarkable *aliyah* in his *limud haTorah*. Ultimately, he even published a *kuntres* of his *chiddushim* on some of the most complex *sugyos* he had learned.

When the *bachur*'s turnaround was subsequently described to Rav Chaim, he responded, "This is surely possible, as Chazal (*Devarim Rabbah* 2:12) say that the *tefillah* of the *tzibbur* does not return unanswered."

Prayer Answered

On Lag BaOmer 5775, following the day's festivities, a bus was on its way back from Meron to Bnei Brak when the driver decided to stop for a brief break for the passengers. He was about to pull into a parking lot, but he noticed that there was no room to park and the line of buses waiting to get in was quite long. The driver presented his passengers with a choice: Either they could wait in line at that lot, which would take over an hour, or they could continue driving to Bnei Brak.

The passengers responded unanimously that they'd prefer to continue on to Bnei Brak without stopping at that point.

As the trip progressed, the passengers realized that the time of *shekiah* was approaching, so they asked the driver if he could pull over to the side of the road where they would daven Minchah. The driver agreed, but he told them that they would soon be exiting Highway 6, and he would be able to pull over more easily over there. After a few minutes, the bus got off Highway 6, the driver found a place to pull over, and the passengers disembarked to daven Minchah.

Just as they began the *tefillah*, an Israeli soldier showed up and joined their *minyan*. When davening was over, the passengers greeted the soldier and asked him where he was coming from. It seemed to be an unusual place for the soldier to find himself, they pointed out, as that location was not close to any community.

"I am a *baal teshuvah*," he related. "This past Rosh Hashanah, I made a *kabbalah* to daven every *tefillah* with a *minyan*, and, *baruch Hashem*, I have been able to keep to my commitment. I have been on duty in the South, and today, my commander informed me that I can go home for Shabbos. I found a driver who agreed to take me this far. When I got out of the car, though, I realized that it was almost sunset and I had not yet davened Minchah. But I was in the middle of nowhere. Where would I get a *minyan* here? I davened to HaKadosh Baruch Hu with all my might, stating that I so badly wish to daven with a *minyan*. Suddenly, I saw a bus pulling over.

To my surprise, your group got off and gathered to daven Minchah. I couldn't believe it!"

One of the passengers pointed out that Hashem could have arranged for the soldier's ride to take him all the way to a destination that had a shul, rather than arranging for a full bus of people to stop at a seemingly random location.

Sometimes, though, when a person has a pure desire to serve Hashem, He will reveal His Providence more openly.

Daven With Hislahavus

*T*he Chazon Ish had a shul in his home in central Bnei Brak, where he would daven with a small minyan of talmidei chachamim and yerei Shamayim.

On Erev Shabbos, the Chazon Ish's custom was to daven at the time of Minchah Gedolah, forming a *minyan* for Minchah early in the afternoon. This proved difficult at times, because getting a *minyan* together at that point was no easy task, with people busy running errands and preparing for Shabbos; Bnei Brak of those days was a much smaller city, with fewer residents.

Every Friday, several of the *mispallelim* in the Chazon Ish's *minyan* would stand outside his home and try to recruit men to join them for Minchah. One time, one of the *mispallelim* called in a Chassid, who was honored to join the *minyan* of the *gadol hador*. The Chassid began to put on his *gartel* as he waited for Minchah to begin.

The Chazon Ish noticed the Chassid who had joined the *minyan*. Appreciatively yet apologetically, the Chazon Ish turned to him and said, "I didn't mean for them to call you to complete the *minyan*; I don't want to deprive you of the flavor and *geshmak* of a *tefillas* Minchah davened with *hislahavus*, after immersing in the *mikveh* and donning your beautiful Shabbos attire, topped off by your *shtreimel*. I don't want to prevent you from davening Minchah after all your regular Erev Shabbos preparations have been completed.

"Please," continued the Chazon Ish, "go on and continue your preparations for Shabbos Kodesh. Then, when the time for Minchah arrives in your regular *kehillah*, you'll be able to conduct yourself as you are accustomed, beginning with *Hodu* [*Perek* 107 in *Tehillim*, which is said by those who daven *Nusach Sefard*], followed by a warm, deeply felt davening. As for us, we will *b'ezras Hashem* find another person to complete our *minyan*."

The Chassid departed, following the Chazon Ish's directive. He was a bit disappointed about not being able to daven with the great gaon, but he was moved by the sensitivity of the Chazon Ish and the respect that was shown for the Chassid's own hanhagos and minhagim.

One Minchah

R av Nechemiah Becker was an outstanding mechanech, who *taught tinokos shel beis rabban at the Kamenitzer Cheder in Yerushalayim for decades.*

Shortly after Rav Nechemiah's wife gave birth to their first child, a girl, Mrs. Becker became very ill. The doctor, an expert in his field, said that in light of the dangers involved, emergency surgery must be performed. However, the procedure would render Mrs. Becker unable to have any additional children; the Beckers' newborn daughter would be their only child.

Rav Nechemiah instructed the doctor to proceed with the surgery, but at the last moment, he asked the doctor to hold off. "I wish to ask the Chazon Ish for his advice before we go ahead," explained Rav Nechemiah.

With that, he traveled from Yerushalayim, where he resided,

to Bnei Brak, to meet with the great *tzaddik*. At that time, in the mid-1900's, the trip from Yerushalayim to Bnei Brak took several hours.

Rav Nechemiah arrived in Bnei Brak to find the Chazon Ish preparing to daven Minchah. Seeing the urgent look on Reb Nechemiah's face, the Chazon Ish asked him what was troubling him. After Rav Nechemiah shared his predicament, the Chazon Ish replied, "What's the question? It's a matter of *pikuach nefesh*. Listen to the doctor's recommendation and have the procedure done."

As Rav Nechemiah turned to leave, the Chazon Ish asked him if he had davened Minchah yet. When he said no, the Chazon Ish told him, "Come. Daven with us."

After the *tefillah* concluded, Rav Nechemiah again turned to leave, but he was stopped by the Chazon Ish once more. "Please," said the Chazon Ish, "tell me the details of the issue again."

Rav Nechemiah repeated the particulars of his wife's condition and the medical question involved. The Chazon Ish's response was confounding. "Go home in peace," he told Rav Nechemiah. "There's no need to have the surgery performed. Everything will be all right."

Rav Nechemiah stood there open mouthed. Before turning to leave, he asked the Chazon Ish the obvious question: Why had he first advised him to proceed with the surgery, and then guided him in the opposite fashion? "Didn't the rav say that it is *pikuach nefesh*?" asked Rav Nechemiah.

"That," answered the Chazon Ish, "was before Minchah. Now, when I am telling you otherwise, it is after Minchah."

Rav Nechemiah returned to Yerushalayim with the Chazon Ish's words ringing in his ears:

That was before Minchah. Now it is after Minchah.

When he returned to the hospital, he instructed the doctors not to operate on his wife. The doctors protested, explaining that his wife's life was in danger. Rav Nechemiah responded that the Chazon Ish had told him that the surgery should not be performed.

Several days later, as Mrs. Becker recovered, it was discovered that she had previously contracted an infection. Had the surgery been performed, it could have been deadly.

Mrs. Becker ultimately recovered and gave birth to an additional nine children.

The family would relate this story from time to time, contemplating the words of the Chazon Ish: That was before Minchah. Now it is after Minchah.

Look what prayer can accomplish. With one tefillah, especially that of a tzaddik, a person's destiny can be transformed.

Tefillah can turn a time of potential tragedy into a time of blessing and salvation.

Morning to Night

The administration of Yeshivas Givat Shaul once asked their founder and mashgiach, Rav Shlomo Wolbe, to daven Minchah with them not only during the winter, as he had always done, but during the summer as well. Rav Wolbe turned down their request. "I prefer to daven earlier in the day, at the time of Minchah Gedolah, the earliest time possible to daven Minchah," he explained.

Minchah in the yeshivah was late in the day during the summer months, but the yeshivah administration did not relent. They explained that if the mashgiach were to attend their Minchah at 7 o' clock in the evening and then stay for Maariv, the *bachurim* would have some time to approach him in his private room and speak with him, which would certainly be beneficial.

"Still, I prefer to daven Minchah Gedolah," Rav Wolbe replied.

"Perhaps the mashgiach can daven earlier and then come for our Minchah anyway, without davening with us," they persisted.

"*Chas v'shalom!*" was Rav Wolbe's reaction. "How can I be in a yeshivah without abiding by the *sedarim* of the yeshivah?"

The yeshivah administrators were at a loss. Rav Wolbe was unwilling to wait until the end of the day to daven Minchah, yet he refused to come to the yeshivah for Minchah once he had davened earlier in the day. They sent someone to speak with him to determine the reason for his reluctance to daven with them.

After some discussion, Rav Wolbe finally revealed his reason: "I simply can't go from 7 in the morning until 7 at night without speaking to Hashem!"

Saying Tehillim

"*S*o what do you say?" *is a common refrain after a communal tragedy.*

Following the Yom Kippur War, the Beis Yisrael of Ger, Rav Yisrael Alter, was visited by numerous people from all over the world. He abhorred discussions and questions about the political and military situation. To all such queries, he had one answer: "We must pray."

Once, an American rabbi asked him, "What do you say about the current situation?"

The Rebbe replied, "I say *Tehillim.*"

Prayer Preparation

*T*oward the end of Rav Avrohom Pam's life, it became too difficult for him to climb the stairs to the second floor of his home where his bedroom was located. The family therefore added a room on the ground floor, right off the kitchen. This entailed building a wall where there had previously been a window in the kitchen facing the backyard.

One morning, one of Rav Pam's grandsons noticed his grandmother, Rebbetzin Pam, in the kitchen with her *siddur* in hand, just staring at the wall.

"Bubby, what are you doing?" he asked her.

"Until now," she responded, "before I davened Shacharis, I would stare out the window, looking at the trees and the beautiful world that Hashem made. By thinking about Hashem's wonders, I was able to properly address Hashem and daven to Him. Now that the window is no longer here, how can I start davening just by staring at a blank wall?"

Psalms for Success

*I*n 1935, when in his early 20's, Rav Michel Yehudah Lefkowitz arrived in the Chevron Yeshivah in Yerushalayim. He later described some of his experiences during his first week in yeshivah.

On Motza'ei Shabbos, following an uplifting Shabbos, Michel Yehudah saw a *talmid* of the yeshivah approach the *amud* in the *beis midrash* and begin leading the *bachurim* in reciting *Tehillim*, saying each of the *pesukim* with great fervor.

Seeing the intensity with which the *Tehillim* was being said, Michel Yehudah wondered if someone was seriously ill.

He approached one *bachur* and asked, "Who's sick? Who needs a *refuah*?"

The *bachur* looked at him strangely. "Sick? No one's sick."

"So why is the yeshivah saying *Tehillim*?" asked Michel Yehudah.

"We gather every Motza'ei Shabbos to say *Tehillim* for *hatzlachah* in our learning during the coming week," said the *bachur* simply.

For the rest of his life, Rav Michel Yehudah would recall the fervor and passion of the weekly Tehillim in Chevron.

A Tear for Our Children

A man once approached the Brisker Rav and admitted that he was covetous of the fact that the rav merited such exceptional children, truly outstanding individuals, while many of their peers had fallen prey to outside influences.

The Brisker Rav did not respond, but listened to his remarks silently. After the man left, he turned to his son, Rav Refoel, and said, "They talk about the success of my *chinuch* and how my children turned out, but do they know of the many, many tears that I shed while I rocked each of my children when they were just infants in their cribs? Do they know of the *tefillos* that I davened to the Ribono Shel Olam and the many *kapitlach* of *Tehillim* that were said amid tears, as I begged Him to ensure that my children follow the *derech haTorah*?"

Twin Tests

*E*zer Mizion, a health support organization in Israel, erected a guesthouse called the Oranit right near Beilinson Hospital in Petach Tikvah. The guesthouse is intended for cancer patients from across the country who are scheduled for treatments and need a place to sleep. Many families spend the whole week there during treatment, while some just go for overnight stays. While there, the patients have access to the Donald Berman Rehabilitation Center, an activity center that provides many forms of psychological therapy, plus fun times to brighten faces that almost forgot how to smile. The patients also receive support from the staff at the Center as well as from the other families who are experiencing the same difficult challenges.

One day, Natan, a traditional Jew from Dimona, arrived at Ezer Mizion's guest home. He was the father of twin boys, one of whom had cancer. The child had already undergone two rounds of treatment and now had an appointment for a third round. Natan arrived with his son the night before the scheduled treatment. He put his child to sleep and then took a walk around the building.

On one of the floors, Natan noticed a shul. Even though he was not religious, he decided to enter. The shul was almost completely dark. Only the *ner tamid* flickered, shedding a shadowy light.

Natan sat down and opened a volume of *Tehillim*. The darkness around him and the feeling of solitude in his sorrow opened his heart. He began reading the *kapitlach* slowly, and he felt as if every word of David HaMelech was written specifically for him: "Hashem, my G-d, I cried out to You and You healed me. Hashem, You have raised up my soul from the depths, You have preserved me from falling into the pit" (*Tehillim* 30:3-4).

Before long, the tears came in a torrent. There was no one there to feel embarrassed in front of; nobody saw. The hours slipped by, as Natan sat and cried and shook up his soul. He knew — he really knew — that all is in Hashem's power. He understood that if his child is sick, it is meant to be, and as painful as it is, it is ultimately good. And he understood that chemo and all the rest are simply Hashem's tools, and He can create a cure at any moment.

When he was finished, he felt a sense of relief. He was not alone. Hashem was holding his hand. He got up, left the shul, and went to sleep.

In the morning, Natan went with his son for the next treatment. But first, the child had to undergo a routine examination, which took about an hour, to assess his condition. When it was over, Natan went to the doctor for the results.

"Something did not come out right," the doctor said, shaking his head as he perused the results. "They have to perform the test in a better position. Tell them to do it while he is on his back."

After another hour, Natan was in the doctor's office with the new results.

"Again it did not come out good," the doctor mumbled. "The child must have moved around. Go back again for another test. This time, ask them to take the picture from the side."

The third time, there was also a problem. In the end, the doctor got up and went over to the office of the doctor who was performing the test, to discuss the situation. Outside, Natan and his son waited impatiently. Would they ever manage to do the test properly? Suddenly, the door swung open. The doctor motioned for them to come in.

"We are having some kind of a problem," he said a bit uncomfortably. "We can't seem to locate the disease. We checked your son's medical file and noticed that he is one of twins. Did you perhaps confuse the two and bring the healthy child?"

For the man of science, whose world stops and ends with what can be proven, there could be no other answer.

Only the maamin, the believer, knows the power of prayer from the depths of one's heart.

A Taste *of* Integrity

No False Pretenses

One Motza'ei Shabbos in the late 1930's, a *melaveh malkah* was held in a shul near Yeshiva Torah Vodaath, to benefit Rav Elchanan Wasserman's yeshivah in Baranovich.

The rav of the shul rose and began extolling the merits of Rav Elchanan's yeshivah in Baranovich, saying, "This yeshivah has 300 *bachurim*."

Rav Elchanan, who had come to America to raise funds for the yeshivah, pounded on the table and corrected him. "296!" he bellowed.

The rav of the *shul* continued, "And it has a budget of $10,000 per year."

Once again, Rav Elchanan banged on the table and said, "$9,900!"

— *heard from Rabbi Ahron Dovid Lebovics (as heard from Rav Yitzchok Karpf)*

The Late-Night Visit

The Bnei Brak printing house was bustling with activity, workers walking to and fro, tending to the many projects at hand. Reb Lipa Friedman, the owner of the business, cheerfully oversaw the operation. *Baruch Hashem*, he mused, his shop was kept busy publishing the volumes of Torah thoughts from some of Eretz Yis-rael's finest *talmidei chachamim*. It was often stressful, as deadlines loomed and last-minute corrections were required, but it was a ful-filling field of work.

One day, as he walked around the printing house, Reb Lipa no-ticed that the flurry of activity suddenly stopped. A special visi-tor had arrived and all the workers stood in awe. As soon as he realized who was there, Reb Lipa walked over to the person and invited him in.

It was Rav Elazar Menachem Man Shach, rosh yeshivah of Yeshi-vas Ponovezh.

"*Shalom aleichem*, Rosh Yeshivah," Reb Lipa said with a smile. "How can we be of help?"

Rav Shach explained that he had just finished writing his lat-est volume of *chiddushim* based on the works of the Rambam and wished to publish it. "Reb Lipa," said Rav Shach, "there are ap-proximately so-and-so many pages in this volume. Please tell me how much it would cost to publish the *sefer* so I can determine if I can afford it."

Reb Lipa thought to himself, *How much would it cost? Why, I would print the sefer of the great rosh yeshivah for free!*

But Reb Lipa knew that Rav Shach insisted on paying the full price to publish his *sefarim* and would never even agree to a discount, let alone have it printed for free. So Reb Lipa made a quick calculation and quoted a price. Rav Shach listened and then thanked Reb Lipa for his time before leaving the shop.

That night, Reb Lipa told his children about the *chashuve* visitor at his printing press earlier that day. Several hours later, as he was getting ready to retire for the night, Reb Lipa heard a knock on his door. When he opened it, he was surprised to see Rav Shach him-self standing there.

After inviting the Rav into his home, Reb Lipa asked, "Rosh Yeshivah, what brings you out so late at night? Is everything all right? Why did the rosh yeshivah trouble himself to walk all the way here?"

Rav Shach explained, "Reb Lipa, tonight, as I was making a *chesh-bon hanefesh*, one thing troubled me. Today, after you quoted a price for publishing my *sefer*, I left your shop without assuring you that I planned to give you the business. Perhaps you thought that I had come to price-shop and compare your rates with the prices of other printing businesses, and that I may not have you print the *sefer*. *Chas v'chalilah*! I don't want you to think that way for a moment. Doing so is not proper and I would never consider acting that way.

"My manuscript is not 100 percent complete, and that is why I didn't finalize with you. But I couldn't let the night pass without assuring you that you have my business. As the Torah tells us (*Bamidbar* 32:22), '*Vi'h'yisem neki'im meiHashem u'miYisrael* — You shall appear vindicated from Hashem and from Yisrael.' "

Reb Lipa was floored. "For that the Rosh Yeshivah schlepped all the way to my home at night?" he wondered aloud.

Rav Shach repeated: "Again, Reb Lipa, as soon as I am ready to publish the *sefer*, I will do so with you! I will publish it only at your business. Please, don't worry."

Not Entitled

During the week, Rav Shlomo Wolbe would get a ride home from Yeshivas Givat Shaul, where he served as mashgiach, with his close *talmid*, Rav Bentzion Kugler, the menahel of Talmud Torah Chavos Daas (which was also founded by Rav Wolbe). From the window of his house, Rav Wolbe's neighbor, Rabbi Tzvi Yaakovson, often saw the mashgiach emerge from Rav Kugler's car and then hail a taxi.

Reb Tzvi once asked him the reason for this practice. After extensive questioning, Rav Wolbe finally admitted, "I take a taxi to Har Nof after Rav Bentzion drives me home."

Rav Wolbe would get out of Rav Kugler's car and enter his building, pretending to make his way to his apartment. Only after his benefactor had left would he emerge from the building and hail a taxi to take him to his actual destination.

"But why?" Reb Tzvi questioned. "Rav Kugler wouldn't mind taking you to Har Nof himself. It's only a little bit farther. He simply doesn't know that you want to go there!"

"True," the mashgiach said, "but Rav Bentzion drives me home from my job at the yeshivah because the yeshivah has to see to it that I have a way home. I am not entitled to ask the yeshivah to provide transportation for my own purposes."

One Ambition

I f a person lives with the sense that he has a mission to accomplish even in the context of his business dealings, he can be capable of performing extraordinary acts of kiddush Hashem. The following story, told to me by Rabbi Shraga Freedman, who heard it from Rav Avrohom Chaim Feuer, is a case in point.

After years of intense negotiations, the parties involved in a very lucrative transaction on the West Coast were about to conclude the deal, and the buyers and sellers gathered in a conference room to work out the final details. One of the major investors was Mr. Gershon Kamin (name changed) of New York, a man whose participation was critical to the deal and who stood to earn a fortune at its successful conclusion.

During the final discussions, Gershon became very disturbed by one of the attorneys working for the other side. The man was simply unable to refrain from using vulgar language; every other word he uttered was an expletive of some sort. Gershon politely asked the lawyer to refrain from using profanities, and the man promised to do his best. But the use of such language was apparently deeply ingrained in him, and the lawyer continued to slip. Finally, Gershon grew incensed and warned the lawyer, "If you utter even one more profanity, the deal is off!" It did not take long for the lawyer to inadvertently make use of another offensive word, and Gershon stood up and stalked out of the room, scuttling the entire deal.

Larry Fisher (name changed), another religious Jew who was present at the proceedings, was shocked by Gershon's abrupt departure. Larry was aware of the years of hard work that had gone into the deal. Where had Gershon derived the inner strength to make such a sacrifice? Larry lived with this question for several years, until he happened to hear a lecture from a noted rav that delivered the answer.

> *The rav told a story about a man named Gershon who had been learning at the Telshe Yeshivah in Cleveland, Ohio, decades earlier. As a bachur, he had demonstrated great promise, and he seemed to have a stellar future in the beis midrash. But Gershon's parents wanted him to pursue a career, and with much reluctance, he agreed to leave the yeshivah to acquire a secular degree.*
>
> *On his last day in the yeshivah, Gershon was learning diligently in the beis midrash when he was summoned to the office of the rosh yeshivah, Rav Chaim Mordechai (Mottel) Katz, for a farewell conversation. Gershon was certain that the rosh yeshivah would remind him to maintain his learning sedarim or to continue to daven with a minyan when he entered the business world. But Rav Mottel had something else in mind.*
>
> *"Gershon," he said, "you are about to leave the shelter of the yeshivah's walls and venture into the outside world, where every step you take will be a test. You must always have one ambition, one concern above all else: to sanctify Hashem's Name. Remember that everything you do will be either a kiddush Hashem or a chillul Hashem, and choose accordingly!"*
>
> *Gershon took the rosh yeshivah's words to heart, and that principle became the guiding light of his career.*

After the lecture, Larry approached the rav and asked, "By any chance, was the boy in your story Gershon Kamin?"

Dumbfounded, the rav exclaimed, "How did you know that?"

"Because I saw with my own eyes just what kind of impact the rosh yeshivah's message had on him," Larry replied.

"You Really Meant It?"

Rabbi Shmuel Bloom related this story, which he heard from his rebbi, Rav Yaakov Yitzchak Ruderman, rosh yeshivah of Yeshivas Ner Yisroel in Baltimore.

Rav Ruderman was once called upon to dissuade a middle-aged Holocaust survivor from marrying a non-Jewish woman. The rosh yeshivah spent over an hour and used every argument in his arsenal to try to convince him what a mistake it would be to marry out of his faith. But it was no use. The man had made up his mind and was adamant.

As the man was ready to leave, he opened his wallet and took out a $100 bill to give to Rav Ruderman for his time. Rav Ruderman refused the money and told him that he receives a salary as rosh yeshivah of Yeshivas Ner Yisroel and doesn't accept other remuneration.

"You mean you really meant it? You really meant everything you told me?" the man asked. "Then let's sit down and discuss this again."

They spoke for another hour and the man finally relented.

What I Must Do

My father merited to study under Rav Tuvia Goldstein, rosh yeshivah of Yeshiva Emek Halachah during the last few years of the rosh yeshivah's life. Rav Tuvia's honesty and integrity were beyond compare. My father shared the following story, which demonstrates just how honest he was:

Rav Tuvia once asked someone to go to a local store to purchase something on his behalf. Upon returning, the man handed Rav Tuvia the change. Rav Tuvia noticed that he had not paid tax on the item and questioned him about it.

"The storeowner doesn't pay his taxes to the government anyway," the man explained. "There's no purpose in paying it to him."

Rav Tuvia was very disappointed.

"My obligation of '*dina de'malchusa dina* — the law of the land is the law' is to pay the tax," he explained. "What happens afterward, and whether the storeowner does what he's supposed to do, has no bearing on my obligation. I must do what I have to do."

He had the man go back and pay the proper tax.

An Amazing Rabbi

Peter, the owner of a tile company in New Jersey, shared the following incident:

"A few years ago, Talmudical Yeshiva of Philadelphia hired my company to redo the floors in their study hall. We gave them a price, and when they agreed to it, we ordered the sand and tiles we needed and began the job.

"After we finished, the yeshivah paid the sum we had agreed upon, but before I left, one of the rabbis came over to me and handed me a check for another $400. When I asked him what it was for, he explained, 'Rabbi Shmuel Kamenetsky, the dean, noticed that you ordered additional sand while you were in the middle of the job. He realized that you initially miscalculated the amount you would need, and that the job ended up costing you more than expected. He made some calls to find out how much the extra sand cost you, and he is giving you this extra money to cover it. He insists that you accept it.' "

Peter was genuinely moved. "Never in my life have I received money for something when I didn't ask for it," he said with feeling. "What an amazing rabbi!"

— *heard from Rabbi Shraga Freedman*

Land Deed

*R*eb Chaim Nosson Glick was a baal habayis in Shaarei Chesed, Yerushalayim. At his shivah, his sons related a story that showed the example that their grandfather, Reb Yitzchak, had set for his son and grandchildren, too.

In 1936, a friend of Mr. Yitzchak Glick, a contractor by trade, came to him with a dilemma along with a business proposition. Because of problems with Arab workers, all construction had come to a halt and he had no source of income. He did, though, have a piece of property near Kever Shmuel HaNavi. He asked Mr. Glick if he would purchase that property from him.

Mr. Glick asked for a day to consider the offer. The next day, he informed his friend that he had decided to make the purchase, and the two agreed upon a suitable price. Mr. Glick then gave him the cash, and his friend gave him the deed.

In 1948, the area became a part of Jordan and lost nearly all its value. However, in 1967, this land once again became a part of Israel, and its value skyrocketed.

Mr. Glick informed the children of his friend, who by then had passed away, that their father had a piece of property near Kever Shmuel HaNavi. "As far as we can remember," they responded, "you purchased that property from him many years ago."

"No," responded Mr. Glick, "I never intended to purchase the land. If you check in the land record office, you'll see that I never recorded the deed. It is still in your father's name. Your father was a respected businessman who had always earned his own living. There was no way that he would accept charity. This was my way of giving him the money that he needed."

The children, however, would not accept the land as theirs. Eventually, both parties agreed to a compromise: The children would return the original amount that Mr. Glick had paid, and the increase in value would go to them. When they brought the money to Mr. Glick, he asked them to give it to one of their family members who found himself in a difficult financial situation.

When Rav Shlomo Zalman Auerbach heard this story, he commented, "In my lifetime, I have known many geonim. But such a gaon in chesed I never knew."

— heard from Rabbi Shmuel Bloom

The Power of Honesty

Shalom Goldberg (name changed) once needed to have an important package shipped from his home in Flatbush and failed to make it to the post office before it closed on Friday. On Sunday, when the post office is normally closed, he happened to drive past and noticed that the gates outside were open and a worker was loading packages onto a truck. Shalom pulled up and asked the man if the office was open. The worker answered in the negative. "This is only for Amazon. They have a special arrangement for Sunday deliveries," he explained.

"Would it be possible for you to do a favor for me and accept this package anyway?" Shalom asked politely. "It's very important."

The worker looked at Shalom, his gaze coming to rest on his yarmulke. To Shalom's surprise, the worker asked if he knew Reb Abish Brodt, the well-known *askan, baal chesed,* and *baal menagen*.

"Of course," Shalom replied. "Everyone knows him!"

"In that case, I will do you the favor," the worker decided. "I worked for Abish and his family for 17 years, and it was an incredible experience, one that I will not soon forget. They were the most honest and kind employers I ever had."

After praising Reb Abish effusively, the non-Jewish postal worker suddenly launched into a heartfelt rendition of Rav Shmuel Brazil's famous *niggun* for *Modeh Ani,* which is sung by Reb Abish.

— heard from Rabbi Shraga Freedman

A Taste *of* The Omnipresent

The Ultimate Power

*E*ven as we face challenges and obstacles, we must remember that
an Omnipresent Force is constantly at our side.

Yosef turned the knob to the front door of his Bnei Brak apartment, ready to enter and share the news with his wife. Then he
stopped. Tears began falling from his eyes as he contemplated his
predicament. *Parnassah* had never been easy, as he barely managed
to eke out a meager living from the modest grocery store he oper-
ated in the city. But news that a Jew would be opening a competing
establishment on the very block of his *makolet* was devastating. To
make matters worse, the new store was being opened by a mafia-
type mogul whom no one dared to challenge.

Yosef dug deep within himself, to his reservoirs of *emunah* and
bitachon, in order to remind himself that *parnassah* comes from
Above, regardless of what others do. But this *nisayon* seemed too
great to bear. To exacerbate matters, how would he break the news
to his wife that their already paltry earnings may disappear altogether once the new establishment made its presence felt among
the local populace?

After finally discussing the situation with his wife, Yosef contacted the *beis din* of Rav Shmuel HaLevi Wosner. He explained the
circumstances to the *beis din* and the seemingly clear violation of
hasagas gevul set to be committed by the owner of the new store on
the same block as his.

The *beis din* listened to Yosef's story, wrote up a
sent it to the new storeowner, summoning him to b

A week passed with no response from the storeo
tomary, the *beis din* sent the man a second *hazman*
the summons was ignored, so a third *hazmanah* wa

Meanwhile, Yosef was consumed with fear of the
was he, a poor little storeowner, to try to battle the macho new kid
on the block, who had the wherewithal to withstand the competition
and do whatever was necessary — and then some — to ensure the
success of the new business? Still, Yosef hoped that the storeowner
would come to *beis din* already so that the matter could be settled.

When the third *hazmanah* was ignored, the *beis din* was in a
quandary. How should they proceed? It was midweek when the
beis din's members approached Rav Wosner and explained the
circumstances to him.

Rav Wosner was unfazed and his response was brief but sharp.

"In this world, we have *dinei adam,* judgments rendered by man,
and *dinei Shamayim,* judgments rendered by Heaven," said Rav
Wosner. "This fellow is obviously ignoring *dinei adam,* so we'll
leave it in the hands of *dinei Shamayim.*"

That Monday was the new storeowner's *levayah.*

*The above story elicits varied responses. Some people mar-
vel at the "ruach hakodesh" of Rav Wosner. Others say he performed a neis. All agree that the man's death was no random
occurrence.*

*Beyond the seemingly supernatural aspect of the story, there
is an elementary lesson conveyed by Rav Wosner, who expressed
the very real authority of the Ribono Shel Olam in this world.
We are used to living with the concept of "olam k'minhago no-
heig — the world follows its natural order," which often camou-
flages the fact that nothing is happenstance. Yet a person cannot
just wreak havoc on someone else's life or act with abandon and
not expect repercussions.*

Sometimes it takes a lifetime for Heaven to render j
and sometimes, as in the above case, it takes mere days
er things turn out, there is a Supreme Power controll
nuance of creation.

A Taste of The Omni

The Man in the Dream

As a member of Kollel Avreichim in Toronto, Rabbi Yosef Binyamin Simon had a regular *seder* with a young *baal teshuvah*, Avrohom. One day, as they began to learn, Reb Yosef Binyamin noticed that Avrohom seemed rather preoccupied and distressed, and he asked him if something was bothering him. Avrohom replied that he hadn't slept well the night before because he had had a very strange dream. Reb Yosef Binyamin asked Avrohom to relate the dream.

"There was an older man with a white beard who was totally unfamiliar to me," said Avrohom. "He didn't look like anyone I had ever seen, and he said to me, 'Avrohom, I am very pleased with the way you have turned your life around. Keep up the good work. Hashem is very happy with your new way of life.' Then I asked him who he was, and he said something like Rabbi Eli, Eliyahu, Lop…eeon, eeone… something like that."

"Rav Eliyahu Lopian?" asked Reb Yosef Binyamin. "Was that his name?"

"Yes, yes! That was definitely it! How did you guess?" Avrohom asked excitedly.

"Why, Rav Eliyahu Lopian was a great rabbi," explained Reb Yosef Binyamin. "In fact, scholars study his *sefarim* in this very kollel. Would you like to see a picture of him? I think one of the *sefarim* he authored has his picture at the front of the volume."

"I'd love to," replied Avrohom eagerly.

Reb Yosef Binyamin got the *sefer,* turned to the page that had Rav Lopian's picture on it, and showed it to Avrohom.

"That's him; that's the man I saw in my dream. He looked exactly like that!" exclaimed Avrohom.

Reb Yosef Binyamin was astounded. How could someone dream about a person he had never met or even heard of? It was really a mystery.

Several days later, the two met again for their *seder*. This time, Avrohom had more exciting news for Binyamin. He had spoken to his mother and told her the fascinating story of his dream. He had also shared with her how Reb Yosef Binyamin helped him figure out who he had seen in his dream, and that it was a famous rabbi who lived in England many years ago named Rav Eliyahu Lopian.

Much to his surprise, his mother was familiar with Rav Lopian. Avrohom was born in England and his family had lived there for many years before that. His mother remembered that although her family was not religious, there was one rabbi whom her parents respected very much. Not only that, but they had given considerable donations to his yeshivah. That rabbi was none other than Rav Eliyahu Lopian.

When he heard this, Reb Yosef Binyamin concluded that in the merit of the charity that Avrohom's grandparents had contributed to Rav Lopian's yeshivah, he must have watched over their grandchild, Avrohom, from Heaven, and appeared to him in a dream to further encourage him in his religious lifestyle.

Avrohom was very moved by all this. His wife was due to give birth any day, and so he asked her, "If you give birth to a boy, would you mind if we named him Eliyahu, after the great rabbi who seems to be watching over us?" His wife was understandably a bit spooked by this whole story and refused.

The day before the baby's *bris*, however, Avrohom's older son came home from his day school very excited because he had won a prize; his teacher gave out pictures of great rabbis to the children when they were especially good. The picture he was holding in his hand? A photo of Rav Eliyahu Lopian.

Avrohom's wife conceded that it was obviously meant to be and they named their new son Eliyahu.

Every so often, the veil between the physical and the spiritual is lifted, and we are able to catch a glimpse of another dimension.

— heard from Mrs. Leah Eisgrau

Like a Father

*W*hen speaking about emunah, Rav Yisrael Brog, rosh yeshivah of Yeshiva Tiferes Avigdor in Cleveland, Ohio, explained that believing in Hashem and His power to do anything at any
time is not an external skill that we are meant to acquire. Rather, Klal
Yisrael is a nation of maaminim bnei maaminim (believers, the sons of
believers), and this capability is in our genes.

> The challenge, he said, is to bring this koach to the fore and
> to be aware of what is going on inside our neshamos. For at all
> times, the guf pulls us to the physical world, away from the spir-
> itual dimension and from a personal connection to HaKadosh
> Baruch Hu.

Rav Brog received a phone call from a distraught woman, Mrs.
Rivka Lerner, who had moved to Eretz Yisrael when she had gotten
married and now lived in Kiryat Sefer.

"My husband and I decided to dedicate our lives to HaKadosh
Baruch Hu," Mrs. Lerner said. "Neither of us had any family to de-
pend on, surely not for financial support, but we settled in Kiryat
Sefer and my husband threw himself into serious learning."

The couple grew together in their *Yiddishkeit* and had four children.

"At some point," Rivka continued, "our expenses exceeded our
income and we began to accumulate debt. Our debt grew and grew,
until we had accumulated *chovos* of over $15,000. I decided that we
cannot go on like this, so I took various steps to pay the debt down.
I stopped serving meat and chicken at home, and we found other
ways to save money. But the debt did not go away."

Mrs. Lerner then looked into various job options and did something that she would never have imagined doing: She began hiring
herself out to friends and neighbors to clean their homes.

"I started with some houses a few blocks away, but as my name
got out, people from all over started calling me. I was very humiliated. Here I was, a proud American girl, whose circumstances
had forced her to do what had previously been unthinkable. But I

wished to support my husband and family, so I did it."

Thanks to her self-sacrifice, Mrs. Lerner managed to reduce her family's debt to $8,000. But it had gotten too difficult for her to continue working in this fashion. Broken and frustrated, she placed a call to Rav Brog for his guidance and *chizuk*. As she continued her story, she reiterated, "I can't take it anymore," and she began to cry.

Waiting a few moments, Rav Brog gently asked her, "So what is your *shailah*?"

"My question," said Mrs. Lerner between sobs, "is whether we should sell the apartment we purchased when we came to Eretz Yisrael. It has since gone up in price. We figured out that we can move to another *frum* neighborhood, and after all our moving expenses and related payments, we would end up with $10,000. Should we sell our apartment and move?"

"Is your husband learning well where he is?" asked Rav Brog.

"Yes," said Mrs. Lerner. "He is learning very well."

"Does he have a *chaburah*?"

"Yes."

"Then don't do it."

"But what about our debt?" asked Mrs. Lerner.

"Why don't you ask your father?" responded Rav Brog.

"My father? I don't have a father."

"How long have you not had a father?" asked Rav Brog.

"I don't remember my father," said Mrs. Lerner. "I never had a father."

"So why don't you ask your Father?" questioned Rav Brog.

Mrs. Lerner was confused. "I just said that I don't have a father."

Rav Brog made it clear that he meant what he had said. "Are you not aware of the fact that there is a special relationship between HaKadosh Baruch Hu and *yesomim*?" he asked. "It says that HaKadosh Baruch Hu is the '*Avi yesomim* — Father of orphans' (*Tehillim* 68:6). He is there for you and for others like you."

"But I don't know how to address that Father," said Mrs. Lerner. "I never related to a father. I only know how to relate to a mother."

Rav Brog proceeded to describe to Mrs. Lerner what a father is. "Imagine that you discovered that you were a child of a well-known *baal tzedakah* and philanthropist. He is a wealthy magnate who has money coming out of his ears. Would you understand what it means to have a father?

"I want you to know that you do have a Father Who has all the money in the world, Who loves you more than anything else in the world. You are a child who is dedicating her life for one thing and one thing only: Hashem. You are not living for yourself; you and your husband are living for Hashem, and you are raising your family with *tznius* and with *frumkeit*. You are in a position to do wonders."

Mrs. Lerner digested what Rav Brog was saying as he continued: "Why don't you ask Hashem for what you need? Do you understand that by hiring yourself out you have been humiliating Hashem, as well? Can you imagine if I was the philanthropist and I heard that my daughter is now cleaning homes in Kiryat Sefer because she needed $15,000? I would be furious! 'What? You, my daughter, are cleaning homes? I have plenty of money. Why didn't you ask me for the money?' And you'd respond, 'I don't like to ask. I don't know how to ask.'

"Stop crying to Hashem as you have been doing," advised Rav Brog. "I want you to daven with a totally different perspective. Go into a room and think about the fact that you have a Father Who is the *Kol Yachol*. He is the Al-mighty. He has all the money in His hand. For Him to give you $8,000 is not *stam* a *shmeck taback*. It's nothing! But you've got to believe that you have that Father. You've got to believe that He wants to help you. It's going to involve work. It's a whole new relationship. You have this Father you never knew about. I know you are *frum*. I know you daven to Him. But you have never davened to Hashem like He is your Father.

"People go to the government offices seeking assistance and programs. They look for what's available. While dealing with the bureaucracy, they hope the people are nice to them as they go from office to office and jump through hoops. That's not a father. That's the government. You are talking to Hashem like you talk to the government. By doing so, you are losing out tremendously.

"Don't ever clean a house again," Rav Brog said in summation, "and don't move, because doing so will diminish your husband's *aliyah* in Torah and your family's *aliyah*. You are in a good place, you have friends, your husband is learning well, and you are doing mitzvos."

Mrs. Lerner thanked Rav Brog and said goodbye.

Several weeks later, Rav Brog came home to find a garbled message on his answering machine. He knew that it was from the woman from Kiryat Sefer who had called him earlier, but he didn't know her number. He hoped that she would call him back, which she did the very next day.

"I am calling to tell you that I am holding a large check in my hand," said the woman.

"Really?" said Rav Brog. "Can you tell me how it happened? How did your Father give it you?"

"I thought extensively about what you said, and I davened like you told me," she said, "and this is what happened." Then she shared the following story:

> A while back, my mother filed taxes for me in America and she fudged some of the numbers. She tried to get creative and imaginative, hoping that it would make me money, but after she did so, all I got back was $3,000. I went to my rav in Kiryat Sefer and asked if I am permitted to keep this money.
>
> "Absolutely not," he said. "It is not honest money."
>
> I explained how desperate I was and the debt I was facing. This check, I said, would bring my debt down to $5,000.
>
> But the rav wouldn't budge. He said that it was obtained dishonestly and is not my money.
>
> I decided to return the money. I told my mother to send back the check and to re-file the tax form honestly, with all the details as they are.
>
> My mother said, "But you won't get more than $1,000 that way."
>
> I said, "Ma, I'm going to get what's coming to me."
>
> My mother filed the return properly, and within a short period of time, the IRS contacted us to let us know that I am entitled to a larger refund and would be receiving a check shortly.

The amount of the check? $8,000.

Gadol Yih'yeh

Rav Yonason Abraham, dayan on the London Beth Din and rav of Kehillas Toras Chaim, began his career in rabbanus as rav of the Caulfield Hebrew Congregation in Melbourne, Australia. There he delivered a Gemara shiur on Wednesday afternoons to retirees, mostly Holocaust survivors, one of whom was Reb Shmuel Bennett. Reb Shmuel was a journalist by profession, and he authored a Yiddish supplement for the local Jewish weekly newspaper. He gave Rav Abraham a book containing many of the interesting interviews he had conducted over the years. In it was an interview with a gentleman named Boris Green, who at the time was in his late 70's and resided in Richmond, a suburb of Melbourne.

Boris was born in 1913 in Disna, Byelorussia, about 150 miles east of Vilna. He came from a family of watchmakers and had been taught this skill by his father, Yechiel. When the Russians invaded the area in 1939, Boris was inducted into the Russian Army and rose in rank until he was second-in-command at a supply base in Bialystok. War broke out on the Russian front on June 22, 1941, and he was among the few people in his unit to survive.

He trekked along, all alone, for a month until coming to a town called Vileika. He and his brother Fima later joined the Soviet partisan unit of Colonel Feodor Markov. Boris's technical skills proved useful and lifesaving to him and his brother, as he became the radio operator for the command post.

During this time, Boris and other Jewish partisans risked their lives to keep the Jewish families who were hiding in the forests alive, by providing them with food and clothing. Due to the inherent anti-Semitism in the Russian and Polish partisan groups, Boris and his peers were encouraged to start their own all-Jewish *otriad*, or partisan group, which they called Nekamah. This unit was reinforced by fighters from the Vilna Ghetto and eventually became a significant fighting force: saving other Jews, disrupting German supply lines, hampering the German advance, and conquering military positions.

Many members of this group of about 500 people had families — wives and children—who were burdens and drains on Nekamah's resources. Yet Boris wouldn't let any of them go, doing everything in his power to ensure their safety and survival.

When the Germans rolled in with huge forces and combed the entire area, the other partisan groups fled, without warning Boris and his faction. With great courage, Boris led his group to an island in Lake Naroch, a spot in the swamp-infested lake that they named "America," because it was a safe haven, which the Germans hadn't reached.

In this manner, this simple watchmaker kept alive hundreds of men, women, and children, some of whose descendants he later had contact with in Melbourne.

After the war, Boris worked in a senior position in the Byelorussian military government's postal department, using his rank to forge documents, which allowed Russian Jews to escape the Soviet Union for Poland in the guise of repatriating Polish Jews. When the scheme was discovered, he fled to Western Poland, and then moved on to France, eventually moving to Australia, where he settled in 1949, spending the rest of his life as a watchmaker.

Some years after reading about his life story, Rav Abraham met Boris at a Holocaust memorial in Melbourne. Rav Abraham asked him where he had gotten the determination and confidence to lead the partisans, to attack the Germans, and to take responsibility for hundreds of men, women, and children.

Boris, a soft-spoken, quiet man, turned serious. "*Ich heist nit Boris Green*. My name is not Boris Green," he told Rav Abraham. "*Ich heist Baruch Greineman*. My name is really Baruch Greineman, and I am a relative of the Chazon Ish. When I was a young boy, I was a wild child. But the Chazon Ish wrote me a letter, and at the end of the letter he wrote the words [said at a *bris*]: '*Zeh hakatan gadol yih'yeh* — May this little one become great.' You don't know how many times I was so close to death, but because of the Chazon Ish's *berachah*, I am here."

Baruch/Boris passed away on March 30, 2008, at the age of 95, leaving behind his wife, Chana, and three sons and grand-

children, as well as thousands of people whose very lives are owed to words of encouragement from the Chazon Ish — words we would do well to remember as we seek to raise the youth of our own generation.

They are ketanim, little ones, and they are still growing, and it can be slow and painful. But they can, and will, become gedolim, leaders, and paragons of virtue, of whom we will be immensely proud.

The Matzah Miracle

*T*ales abound of the miracles and unusual happenings related to the 2014 Gaza War in Israel. Here is one story:

In the summer of 2014, a group of Bnei Brak residents traveled to Kibbutz Sufa, which is located in the northwestern Negev on the border with southern Gaza, not far from Egypt, to harvest wheat for matzah for Pesach 5775/2015. Rabbi Aharon Samet, owner of the Samet *tzitzis* factory, was the mashgiach of the harvest operation for the Badatz (the Beis Din Tzedek of the Eidah HaChareidis).

"Since we were preparing for the upcoming year of *Shemittah*, we were harvesting wheat for two years," Rabbi Samet later related. "We looked across the entire country for wheat sown later in the season. In Kibbutz Sufa, we discovered a field sown in mid-January, which is very unusual. There were 2,000 acres of wheat. It was just what we needed.

"As we harvested the wheat, undercover and regular military police kept coming to check on us. The Gaza air campaign was already underway and we saw the smoke clouds over Gaza. We heard the sirens wailing as we harvested the wheat and brought it to the trucks, which were transferring it to a plant where all foreign matter would be removed prior to the milling process."

Two days later, at 4:30 a.m., 13 terrorists infiltrated Israel from

Gaza, emerging from an underground tunnel that had been dug right into the fields of Kibbutz Sufa. The Hamas terrorists had planned to kidnap or kill Israelis in the Kibbutz Sufa area. However, IDF field intelligence units monitoring the border area detected them immediately and notified authorities, who reacted with an air strike on the cell. The terrorists, who were taken by surprise, quickly retreated to the tunnel. The tunnel exit was blown up seconds after the terrorists moved underground. Weapons left behind by the terrorists included a number of rocket-propelled-grenade launchers and AK-45 assault rifles.

How did the terrorists mess up so badly?

They had been counting on hiding in the massive Kibbutz Sufa wheat field upon exiting the tunnel. Thus, they were confounded when they discovered that their camouflage — the wheat that had been cut for matzos — had disappeared.

As Providence guided the wheat-cutting group to the wheat field of Kibbutz Sufa, no one knew that, at the same time, an operation that would save numerous lives was being carried out.

Reward for Becoming Frum?

Shortly after becoming a *baal teshuvah*, a promising *bachur* was killed in a car accident. The boy's rebbeim wished to be *menachem avel* his parents, but they did not know what to say to comfort them. They visited Rav Chaim Kanievsky and asked, "What do we answer the parents when they say to us, 'Is this the reward for becoming *frum*?' "

Rav Chaim responded, "Tell them that the *bachur* was supposed to pass away earlier, but Hashem had *rachmanus* and allowed him to remain alive so that he could become a full-fledged *baal teshuvah*." Upon hearing Rav Chaim's response, the rebbeim were unsure and very hesitant to offer such an answer, as it seemed provocative and insensitive.

Soon after they entered the *shivah* house, the mother, as expected, began ranting, "Look what happens when you become religious!"

Yet, as soon as one of the rebbeim shared Rav Chaim's answer, she suddenly stopped her tirade and told them, "Over a year ago, our son decided to keep Shabbos. That Friday evening, his friends came to pick him up for a trip. It was an inner struggle for him, as he really wanted to go with them. He said to himself, *Maybe I'll just begin keeping Shabbos next week.* But in the end, he remained steadfast in his commitment and did not go along.

"The van his friends traveled in got into a terrible accident, and every single passenger died. Except our son, who stayed home."

The Hand of Providence

*H*ashem doesn't take His focus off of us for even a second. He knows what we need and when we will need it, and He plans our salvation way before we even know we have a problem.

Rabbi and Mrs. Mordechai Sultan spent the summer of 2015 in a rented home in Lakewood. At 3:30 a.m. on Motza'ei Tishah B'Av, Rabbi Sultan woke up with pains in his chest. He and his wife weren't sure if he was experiencing indigestion or if his discomfort was something to be concerned about, so they decided to call Hatzolah just to be on the safe side. Since they were not in their hometown, they did not know the phone number for the local Hatzolah. However, when Mrs. Sultan approached the telephone, there, staring right at her, was the name "Hatzolah" next to a speed-dial button. She quickly called and asked Hatzolah to come.

"You need not put on your sirens," she told the dispatcher, "because it is not an absolute emergency. We don't want to wake anyone up."

Rabbi Sultan went downstairs to wait for Hatzolah. Less than 30 seconds after the call was placed, Hatzolah paramedics arrived at the home. The Hatzolah paramedics had brought along a LifePak 12 cardiac defibrillator/monitor, which they first used to monitor the activities of Rabbi Sultan's heart. Rabbi Sultan suddenly remarked that he's really not feeling well and he immediately began having a seizure. The paramedics looked at the LifePak and saw that he was in cardiac arrest.

Rabbi Sultan seemed to have died in their hands.

The Hatzolah volunteers began shocking Rabbi Sultan's heart. Within 30 seconds, he was speaking and asking the paramedics what had just occurred.

Rabbi Sultan had suffered one of the most severe heart attacks, which occurs when the main artery running down the front of the heart is totally blocked or has a critical blockage right at the beginning of the vessel. The medical term for this is a proximal LAD (left anterior descending) lesion. It is also called the widow-maker, since as far as heart attacks go, this is a catastrophic one, which can lead to sudden death.

Later, a doctor explained, "When a heart attack occurs, the electric current of the heart is dimmed and machines can bring it back to life. In this case, however, the lights were not just dimmed, but totally out, and the only way for them to go back on was if Hashem turned the switch on."

Which apparently He did.

It was an open miracle.

Hatzolah had arrived at the crucial moment, shocking Rabbi Sultan just as he was suffering the heart attack. Hatzolah paramedics later attested that rarely are they able to revive a person suffering that type of heart attack, since it is difficult to detect. In fact, the symptoms Rabbi Sultan was suffering were not those of a heart attack. It was only due to that special device, the LifePak 12 cardiac monitor, that they quickly detected it and were able to immediately shock him back to life. The device is generally not carried in a Hatzolah vehicle, which is usually only equipped with a conventional defibrillator.

Earlier that day, on Tishah B'Av, Mrs. Sultan had been inspired by a Chofetz Chaim Heritage Foundation presentation she had watched. She decided to put into practice the lessons she had heard about giving in and being forgiving. At 1:30 a.m., two hours before her husband suffered the heart attack, Mrs. Sultan received a text message that upset her and could have caused *machlokes*. She was immediately *mevater* and did not allow the message to disturb her. She later observed that perhaps by having that text message sent to her, Hashem had given her the opportunity to earn the merit she needed to save her husband.

The Sultan family called the Chofetz Chaim Heritage Foundation to thank the organization for the *chizuk* they received and to relate the story of Rabbi Sultan's salvation. The person who answered the call responded, "There's much more to this story than you even know. Do you know how the Hatzolah volunteer was able to be at your house so quickly at 3:30 a.m., and why he had the LifePak with him?" The representative went on to tell the rest of the story:

> *On Tishah B'Av morning, her brother-in-law, a Lakewood Hatzolah member, received a call from a relative. His son, who was in a sleep-away camp in the Catskills, hadn't been feeling well for a few days and was awfully weak. The doctor at the local Catskills clinic said that he had an infection affecting his heart, and he wanted to transfer him to a hospital close by. The parents asked for the diagnosis of the clinic to be sent to the family's doctor, Dr. Reuven Shanik, who said the condition was serious and advised that the boy be brought to Children's Hospital of Philadelphia (CHOP) instead.*
>
> *The clinic refused to transport the boy, as there was a hospital in closer proximity, so a crew from Lakewood's Hatzolah drove the three hours to upstate New York, picked up the boy, and then embarked on the four-hour trip to Philadelphia. In light of the child's symptoms and nature, the Hatzolah crew had taken along advanced life-support equipment, including a LifePak 12 cardiac defibrillator/monitor.*
>
> *After a full day and half the night of traveling — from Lakewood to the Catskills and then to Philadelphia — the Hatzolah vehicle was finally on its way back to Lakewood. The other para-*

medics reminded the exhausted driver not to miss his exit on the Garden State Parkway. Despite the reminders, though, the driver passed two exits for Lakewood and was forced to take the exit up in Freehold, which was 15 minutes out of the way.

As the ambulance pulled into Lakewood, Hatzolah received a call.

"My husband is complaining that he has chest pains. He's very nervous," said the caller. Rather than hauling other Hatzolah members out of bed to take the call, the exhausted crew decided to answer it themselves, as they were only a few blocks away.

The paramedics arrived within half a minute, with an ambulance containing the very device that would ultimately save Rabbi Sultan's life.

But there is more:

After the incident, Mrs. Sultan thanked the owner of the Lakewood house for putting the number of Hatzolah on speed-dial and displaying it so prominently.

The woman responded, "You'll never believe this, but that was our old phone. We had purchased a new phone system for our house and had planned to buy a second one for our residence in the Catskills. However, I didn't get a chance to purchase the second one, so we just took the new one with us to the Catskills and put the old one back in the house. The new one does not have Hatzolah's number on speed-dial."

Hashem had been laying the plans— down to the minutest detail — for Rabbi Sultan's miraculous salvation.

Prayer for the Waiter

R abbi Yoel Gold, rav of Congregation Bais Naftoli in Los Angeles, California, related the following story about his uncle and aunt, Simon and Betsy of Beverly Hills:

During the summer of 2015, Simon and Betsy traveled to Israel. While there, they went to eat at a restaurant in Herzliya. They were initially seated on the lower level of the restaurant, but Betsy asked the waiter if they could be moved upstairs, so that they could enjoy the view from there.

Once upstairs, a different waiter came over and told them about the night's specials. They *kibbitzed* a bit and the jovial waiter left them to mull over the menu, but not before telling them, "By the way, if you need anything, my name is Barak."

Betsy's eyes opened wide.

"We must find out what that waiter's mother's name is," she told her husband.

Simon called back the waiter. "Hey, Barak," he asked, "what is your mother's name?"

"It is Orna," said the surprised waiter.

"Did you say Orna?" asked Betsy, making sure she heard correctly.

"Yes," confirmed the waiter. "Why do you ask?"

Betsy couldn't contain herself. "Did you by any chance fight in the Gaza War, Operation Protective Edge, last summer?" she asked.

"Yes, I did," said Barak. "How do you know?"

"I've got your name on my kitchen cabinet at home!" said Betsy, who explained that during the war, she'd called a hotline that provided names of Israeli soldiers to daven for.

The name she received was *Barak ben Orna.*

Betsy told Barak that just two weeks prior, she had walked into her kitchen and seen his name on her kitchen cabinet. She began davening for him, as she'd been doing for many months, and while doing so, she said to Hashem, "I don't even know if he's alive. It would be nice to meet him and to see how he's doing."

"Betsy prayed for me to come back home safe and I came back home safe," remarked Barak. "When you realize that someone is praying for you, it warms the heart."

A short while later, Barak sent Betsy an email in which he related that the day after they met, he began putting on tefillin, something he had not done in years.

In his words, "I felt that our meeting was a sign from G-d."

Rabbi Gold pointed out that in a world of seven billion people, it is sometimes hard to imagine that the Creator is looking after each and every one of us and orchestrating every event in our lives.

But He most certainly is.

A Call From Upstairs

Rav Shimon of Yaroslav lived to a ripe old age. When asked in what *zechus* he was granted longevity, he told his disciples, "I have always been careful not to analyze or ponder the decisions of the Ribono Shel Olam. I have not questioned His ways or complained about His judgments."

"But what is the connection between accepting Hashem's decisions and meriting long life?" he was asked.

"It's very simple," he replied. "People often wonder why others have it better than they do. Why, they wonder, do others have a more fruitful or easier *parnassah*, outstanding children, or better social standing? Why do others have health, wealth, and peace of mind? People wonder why they have it so much worse than their friends. When a person poses questions about the ways of Hashem, complaining and acting resentful about his lot in life, Heaven responds, 'You are bitter about the ways of Providence? If so, please come and stand before the Heavenly Court, where you will see that everything in this world is carried out with integrity and justice.'

"And so," continued Rav Shimon, "the person is taken from this world so that he can be given a firsthand explanation of every detail of his life, thus allowing him to understand why things are the way they are. He then comprehends that '*HaTzur tamim pa'alo ki chol d'rachav mishpat, Keil emunah v'ein avel tzaddik v'yashar Hu* — The Rock, perfect is His work, for all His paths are justice; a G-d of faith without iniquity, righteous and fair is He' (*Devarim* 32:4).

"But I've never complained," said Rav Shimon. "I've never pondered Hashem's verdicts, so there's no need for me to be invited Upstairs to be told what the truth is. I know that everything is right and just. I have had no objections, so I've been allowed to remain here."

A believing Jew knows that everything Hashem does is for a reason, and even when it is difficult to see the good in a given situation, he trusts in our Heavenly Father.

Not only is this the correct mindset, but, according to Rav Shimon of Yaroslav, it may also serve as a source of merit for arichas yamim.

A Taste of Faith

Ah Mamme's Emunah

Reb Leib and Mrs. Yocheved Fishman survived the travails of World War II. Persecuted but not broken, they married in a DP camp in Berlin in 1948. Seeking to rebuild their lives on a new continent, they first stopped in Detroit and Syracuse before making their way to New York City in the early 1950's.

More than anything else, the Fishmans wished to establish a family and to raise children with the values and *hashkafos* that they had brought from the *alter heim*. They waited five years, but were not blessed with children.

Then in 1953, Mrs. Fishman was devastated to learn that she had contracted cancer. She went to numerous doctors, and they all agreed that she needed a very specific surgery, one which would render her incapable of bearing children.

"If you don't have the surgery," the doctors said, "you will die."

She asked if she would be able to have a child before the procedure is performed.

"If you do," she was told, "you will die in childbirth. Your body won't be able to handle it. You must undergo this procedure for your very life."

Mrs. Fishman would hear none of it. She refused to undergo the procedure, explaining, *"Ich hub nisht durch gemacht di milchamah nisht tzu hubben kinder* — I did not survive the war not to have children." After all she had undergone, she was determined to continue her family's chain.

She and her husband asked every Rebbe, rav, and *tzaddik* they encountered for *eitzos* and *berachos*. The rabbanim all gave heartfelt *berachos*, but none of them felt capable of advising her not to go ahead with the operation.

"Zei hubben mir nisht farshtanen — They didn't understand me," she would say again and again. *"Ich hub nisht durch gemacht di milchamah nisht tzu hubben kinder* — I did not survive the war not to have children."

And so, Mrs. Fishman and her husband, without the luxury of owning a car, took buses and trains from doctor to doctor, never giving up hope of salvation. Once, after a tiring day spent riding public transit and consulting with doctors in Manhattan, Reb Leib noticed that the hour was late and he had to daven Minchah. He entered a small shul and joined the *minyan*. Following Minchah, he remained in the *beis midrash*, where the unassuming and humble rav delivered a Mishnayos *shiur* before a *minyan* for Maariv was held.

After davening, Reb Leib rejoined his wife, who was waiting for him outside. When Mrs. Fishman asked her husband if he had sought out the rav of the *beis midrash* and asked for a *berachah*, he said that he did not. "He's a rav of a small shul," explained Reb Leib. "They barely had a *minyan*."

"No matter!" insisted Mrs. Fishman. "We went to all the Rebbes. We went to the rabbanim we know. I want a *berachah* from every rav who can give one."

Mrs. Fishman then entered the *beis midrash* along with her husband, where they met with the rav and described their predicament. The rav listened with great sensitivity to their tale of woe. He told the Fishmans not to worry, instructing them not to have the procedure done. Then he added, "And you will be *zocheh* to *banim talmidei chachamim*, children who are Torah scholars."

Mrs. Fishman was significantly uplifted by the rav's *berachah*.

"Der rav hut mir farshtanen — This rav understood me," she remarked.

Approximately 10 months later, the Fishmans celebrated the birth of their *bechor*, Berish. Their joy was indescribable. The birth was not a simple one, and Mrs. Fishman's precarious health required close supervision throughout the pregnancy, but she persevered.

Shortly after the baby's birth, one of the surgeons whom the

Fishmans had consulted saw them pushing a baby carriage. In all seriousness, he commented, "Nice. So you adopted a child." He couldn't believe that they had merited a child of their own. Medically, it seemed an impossibility.

The Fishmans told him that no, they had not adopted a child.

"So are you babysitting for a nephew?" he persisted.

No, they responded. This beautiful baby was their own, a gift from Heaven.

The surgeon was flabbergasted. "Well," he said in a defeated tone, "you were fortunate to have a miracle baby. Now have the surgery, as your illness is still wreaking havoc on your body."

To the doctor's vexation, Mrs. Fishman shook her head.

"No," she said, "the rabbi who gave us a *berachah* said that we would have '*banim*,' meaning children, in the plural. If that's what he said, there's no way I can have a doctor perform an operation that will prevent me from having another child."

Approximately four years later, she did indeed merit a second child, who was named Dovid.

> *That second miracle child is Rav Dovid Fishman, today rosh yeshivah of Yeshiva Kesser Torah in Monsey, New York.*
>
> *For years, Reb Leib and Yocheved Fishman kept this story under wraps, not sharing it even with their own children. Shortly before Rav Dovid Fishman's marriage, his mother related the story of the births of her two children.*
>
> *A crucial detail had been omitted, however. "Who," Rav Fishman asked his mother, "was the rav who granted you the berachah of 'banim talmidei chachamim'? Who was the tzaddik who advised you and encouraged you so many years earlier in that small Manhattan shul?"*
>
> *Mrs. Fishman admitted that she didn't remember. "He was ah kleiner rav, a short rabbi," she recalled.*
>
> *Reb Leib described where they had been and where the beis midrash of this particular rav had been located.*
>
> *Before long, it emerged that the "kleiner rav" who had given his havtachah that the Fishmans would have "banim" was none other than Rav Moshe Feinstein, rosh yeshivah of Mesivtha Tifereth Jerusalem, and the great posek and gadol hador.*

Final Words

One of the most heart-wrenching jobs a rabbi performs is visiting the sick in the hospital. Rabbi Emanuel Feldman, who was for many years a rabbi in Atlanta, Georgia, often visited patients in local hospitals to encourage them and to pray for their recovery.

Mrs. Mary Lichtman was suffering from cancer, and the disease had spread to her lungs and her throat. Rabbi Feldman visited Mary the day before her larynx was to be surgically removed. It was Mrs. Lichtman's last day on earth with the power of speech; without her larynx, speaking would be impossible.

When Rabbi Feldman entered the hospital room, Mrs. Lichtman was surrounded by close family members who had gathered to show their love and support. Mrs. Lichtman appeared to be in good spirits. Soon, the family members withdrew and left Rabbi Feldman to speak with the ailing woman. Mrs. Lichtman became very upset; she could no longer hold in her emotions.

Rabbi Feldman tried to assure her that all would be well, but to no avail. He then suggested that perhaps she would feel a little better if she prayed to Hashem. Mrs. Lichtman said that she did not know any prayers. It was her final day with the gift of speech, but, unbelievably, she did not know how to pray.

Rabbi Feldman suggested that the two say *Krias Shema* together. He slowly directed Mrs. Lichtman, word for word, in reciting, "*Shema Yisrael Hashem Elokeinu Hashem Echad* — Hear, O Israel: Hashem is our G-d, Hashem is the One and Only" (*Devarim* 6:4).

> The only Hebrew words Mrs. Lichtman uttered are perhaps the most important in the entire Torah.
>
> Shema is one of the most significant verses in the Torah because it defines the Jewish nation: We are a nation who believes that Hashem is the Master of the Universe.
>
> Every Jew eventually comes to recognize Hashem's unity and His mastery over the whole world.

Before World War II, the mayor of Kosznitz was Joseph Gonchor, an assimilated Jew who had married a non-Jew. Mayor Gonchor was not on very good terms with the local Jewish population. When the dreaded war finally reached Kosznitz, the Germans rounded up all the Jews, including Gonchor, and on the day after Rosh Hashanah 5704 (1943), the Germans burned down the Kosznitzer shul.

Mayor Gonchor was taken in for interrogation, and soon, all the Jews were forced to gather in the town square. A car then drove up with the mayor inside, and the Germans led the mayor to the square. A large fire was prepared and the Nazis brought out a Sefer Torah.

With all the Jews present, the Germans told the Jewish mayor, "Throw this Sefer Torah into the fire or we will throw you into the fire." The mayor hesitated. His non-Jewish wife pleaded with him to give in to the Germans and throw the Sefer Torah into the pyre.

The mayor thought for just a moment and then proclaimed for all to hear, "My grandparents and great-grandparents sacrificed their lives to uphold this Torah, and I should now throw it into the fire?"

The Germans took the Jewish mayor, wrapped the Sefer Torah around his body, and then set the Sefer Torah on fire. As the flames grew, the heretofore assimilated Jewish mayor cried out, "*Shema Yisrael Hashem Elokeinu Hashem Echad!*"

The deceased mayor's non-Jewish wife later produced a letter that her husband had written shortly before he was put to death. In it, he wrote:

> *I left my religion because of my need to make a living and to advance my profession. But as much as I tried to forget my origins, I could not. My girsa de'yankusa, the Torah that I learned as a child, remained with me and followed me; it was not willing to leave me alone.*
>
> *Regrettably, I did not live my life as a Jew, but I beg You, Almighty G-d, let the Torah that I learned as a child protect me so that at least I will die as a Jew.*
>
> *— heard from Reb Matisyahu Wolfberg*

Responding to Tragedy

In October 2014, Chaya Zissel Braun passed away from wounds she sustained when a terrorist drove a vehicle into a crowd at the Ammunition Hill station of the Jerusalem light rail.

The morning before this tragedy, Chaya Zissel was a typical infant in Yerushalayim. She traveled with her parents to the Kosel, where they davened for her, for themselves, and for a successful new *z'man* in her father's yeshivah. That afternoon, she was still simply Chaya Zissel. In the evening, because of a murderous terrorist who had set his vicious sights on Jewish lives — even those of innocent babies who had barely tasted life — she became Chaya Zissel, *aleha hashalom*.

As soon as news of the terror attack began to circulate, the inhabitants of Yerushalayim waited with bated breath for news of her fate. When it was learned that she had succumbed to the *Malach HaMavess*, a collective cry escaped from the mouths of Jews everywhere. Hundreds made their way to the Shamgar Funeral Home that night. Little Chaya Zissel lay on a stretcher before the *maspidim*, barely taking up a quarter of its surface.

Her father stared at her, trembling but maintaining his composure. Soon it was his turn to speak and he struggled to overcome his pain. Only once, when he mentioned his wife, did his voice break, as he cried, "How will Mommy go on?"

He described their visit to the Kosel, all their prayers and hopes, and how they were filled with gratitude for this child — but now Hashem had taken her away. As he spoke, tears streamed from the eyes of all those in attendance.

Those who attended the funeral were at a loss: What was there to say to a young father, a refined *avreich*, who had suddenly lost his only child? How could anyone comfort her bereaved mother?

Standing in Shamgar and listening to the weeping young father, Rabbi Tzvi Yaakovson, a *Yated Ne'eman* correspondent, remembered a different incident.

His nephew and niece had once lost an infant. Their child had been pulling on a plastic tablecloth and had become entangled in it, suffocating to death. It was a bitter tragedy, accompanied by terrible feelings of guilt. The levayah took place in the middle of the night and Reb Tzvi himself placed the small body in the grave in the children's section of Har HaZeisim. The graves in that section of the cemetery are not even marked. There are no tombstones and the parents do not know exactly where their child is buried. This was the ruling that was given by rabbanim in order to spare the parents from repeatedly experiencing the pain of bereavement.

A few days after Chaya Zissel's petirah, Reb Tzvi, on his way to the shivah house, passed through Be'er Yaakov, where he davened Maariv in the yeshivah in which Rav Moshe Dovid Lefkowitz serves as the mashgiach. After davening, Reb Tzvi approached him and asked him for advice: "What can I say to a young couple who lost a 3-month-old baby?"

Rav Lefkowitz looked at Reb Tzvi and replied, "Tell them what I said to Rav Avraham Genechovsky, the Tchebiner rosh yeshivah, when he lost a young child of his own."

Reb Tzvi was surprised. "I didn't know that Rav Genechovsky lost a child," he exclaimed.

"He did," the mashgiach confirmed. "The child passed away from the dreaded disease. And I told him what my own father said when I lost a son."

Once again, Reb Tzvi was taken aback. "I didn't know about that either."

The mashgiach was surprised. "You didn't know? My son drowned at the beach in Tel Aviv. It was an awful story. It seemed like all of Bnei Brak was at the levayah."

"And what did your father say?" Reb Tzvi pressed.

"He told me what the Chazon Ish, Rav Avraham Yeshayah Karelitz, had said to him when his daughter passed away."

Once again, Reb Tzvi was shocked. The mashgiach's father was Rav Michel Yehudah Lefkowitz, rosh yeshivah of Yeshivas Ponovezh L'Tzeirim. Reb Tzvi had never known that he, too, had lost a child.

"You didn't know?" the mashgiach exclaimed. "I had a little sister. Once, my father made a pot of soup, and when he picked up the pot, my sister came up behind him quietly and tugged on his trousers from behind. He was so startled that the boiling soup spilled on her; she passed away from the burns. It was a horrible tragedy. My father was broken by it."

"And what did the Chazon Ish tell him?" Reb Tzvi asked. By this point, he was barely able to hear about any more tragedies.

Rav Moshe Dovid replied, "The Chazon Ish commanded my father not to become absorbed by the tragedy, not to allow it to overwhelm him. He told him that he must return immediately to the yeshivah and resume delivering his shiurim. My father asked the Chazon Ish if he should seek some form of kapparah; perhaps he should consider himself an accidental murderer. The Chazon Ish looked at him and waved his hand dismissively. It was as if he was saying, 'Don't speak nonsense.' Then he added, 'Go back to being immersed in learning.'"

Hashem gave the Braun family a precious gift and Hashem took it back all too soon. But they taught us all a lesson in refinement, in faith, and in accepting the Divine judgment.

And the Chazon Ish taught us all how to respond when tragic occurrences threaten to overtake us.

Strength in the Midst of Tragedy

Rav Yitzchak Zilberstein, rav of the Ramat Elchanan neighborhood in Bnei Brak, related the following story:

A *talmid chacham* lost his married daughter in a tragic car accident, which took place as the entire family was returning from an *upsherin* in Meron. The taxi driver who had been at the wheel went to visit the family during the *shivah*, beside himself with remorse and grief.

The bereaved father himself consoled the driver and declared, "Do you think that we blame you for the accident? Absolutely not!

It was a *gezeirah* from Hashem because of our *aveiros*, and we do not hold it against you in the slightest. To prove that to you, I am hereby hiring you to take us on another trip to Meron immediately after the conclusion of the *shivah*."

These words, spoken to an irreligious taxi driver out of the depths of a father's grief, created a lasting kiddush Hashem.

The Agreement

Two men, Reb Yehudah and Rav Avraham, approached Rav Nosson Nota Shapira, rav of Krakow and author of the *Megaleh Amukos* and *Ranav Ofanim*, to conduct a *din Torah*. Reb Yehudah was one of the wealthiest men of the city, while Rav Avraham was a respected *talmid chacham* who spent his days occupied in Torah learning. Reb Yehudah was taking Rav Avraham to a *din Torah*.

"I am here because Rav Avraham has reneged on an agreement we made," explained Reb Yehudah to the Megaleh Amukos, as Rav Shapira was known.

"What was your agreement?" asked the rav.

"Rav Avraham used to go to the market for several hours each day to sell baked goods and thus earn money to support his family," explained Reb Yehudah. "Once Rav Avraham had sold enough of his products to make it through that day, he would leave the market and return to the *beis midrash*, where he would learn until late at night.

"When I saw this, I was very bothered. I felt that it was unbecoming for such a great and righteous Torah scholar to be engaged in the mundane activity of selling items at the market. I approached Rav Avraham and made the following offer: I would pay him a salary to cover his living expenses, and he would sit and learn Torah undisturbed the entire day. As soon as he agreed to this arrangement, I gave him the money he needed and he engaged in full-time *limud haTorah*."

"So what's the problem?" asked the Megaleh Amukos.

"A few days ago, I noticed that Rav Avraham had returned to the market, selling his wares for a few hours each day. When I asked him about this, he said that unfortunately he has to cancel our agreement and he can no longer take money from me. I refused to accept this. I told him that an agreement is an agreement.

"But still Rav Avraham refuses to budge. I can't change his mind. Because we are at an impasse, I have been forced to bring Rav Avraham here for a *din Torah*."

The Megaleh Amukos turned to Rav Avraham. "Why have you backed out of your agreement? Reb Yehudah was supporting you and you were learning Torah in peace. What was wrong?"

"Initially, I felt the same way," Rav Avraham responded. "I figured that I'd be able to learn with *menuchas hanefesh*, undisturbed, while my expenses would be covered. It sounded ideal, so I agreed. However, after a while, I noticed that I was experiencing a loss in a different area. Until now, when I had to engage in selling items in the market and earning a *parnassah*, I felt appreciation to the Ribono Shel Olam for providing my sustenance. Each evening, when I prepared the dough for the items I would sell the next day, I would utter a *tefillah* to the Ribono Shel Olam, asking Him to ensure that the dough would rise properly and that it would then bake nicely. In the morning, I would beseech Hashem to bless me with success in the market, so that all the items would be sold at a good price and in a short amount of time. As I was busy earning a *parnassah*, I had the Ribono Shel Olam constantly on my mind, asking Him for success every step of the way. I saw His Hand in every penny I earned and was cognizant of His limitless kindness and the need for me to express my gratitude to Him.

"From the day that I agreed to the arrangement with Reb Yehudah, however, I no longer had that feeling. Reb Yehudah, a kind and magnanimous man, provided me and my family with all that we needed, generously and sensitively. We had everything! I no longer sensed that I was reliant on the Ribono Shel Olam for every single need. I didn't feel the same urgency to daven, and certainly not with such intensity and sense of dependence.

"It is for this reason," concluded Rav Avraham, "that I determined that our entire arrangement was a *mekach ta'us*! Our agreement had been finalized under false pretenses, because it distanced me from the true Provider of all *parnassah*, rather than bringing me closer to Him. Since I do not feel beholden to Hashem as much as I used to, and I am not constantly turning to Him in prayer to provide for me and family as the One Who is '*nosein lechem l'chol bassar* —gives nourishment to all flesh' (*Tehillim* 136:25), I have to pull out of our deal."

> *At a certain juncture, the Megaleh Amukos announced that he was leaving the city of Krakow, and his students held a farewell seudah in his honor. When he got up to speak, he told his listeners that he had changed his mind. He related this story and explained that if a city can produce such elevated people, then it is the place where he wants to reside.*

Every Child a Sefer Torah

*I*n the following story, we see how, no matter the circumstances, Yidden never lose their deep-seated faith and belief in the eternity of Klal Yisrael.

Rav Mendel Alter, brother of Rav Avraham Mordechai, the Imrei Emes of Gur, was murdered in the Treblinka extermination camp, along with his *kehillah*. On his way to the gas chambers, he noticed a bundle on the ground. Stooping to investigate, he discovered that beneath the rags was a baby. Tenderly, he picked up the child and turned to his flock.

"*Rabbosai*," he cried emotionally, "when the Nazis came into my home to arrest me, they started beating me up. As soon as they noticed the *aron kodesh* in my house, they turned away from me, ripped the *aron kodesh* open, and began attacking the Sefer Torah instead, spearing it with bayonets and stomping with uncontrolled hatred on the holy scroll.

"The Torah is why they hate us and the Torah is why they will never win. This child I am holding, although he himself may not survive, represents the future of Klal Yisrael, the guarantors of To-rah for the generations."

Here, he paused and caressed the baby in his arms. "I will now do *hagbahah* with this *leibedige* Sefer Torah!"

Lovingly, he raised the child in the air, and with great feeling cried out the words recited when the Torah is lifted before the congregation: *"Ve'zos haTorah asher sam Moshe lifnei Bnei Yisra-el* — This is the Torah that Moshe placed before the Children of Israel" (*Devarim* 4:44). All the Jews around him repeated these words.

Thus fortified, Rav Mendel led his flock to martyrdom.

Paid in Full

It was a few hours before *hadlakas neiros* on Erev Yom Tov, and Reb Gershon was completing his last-minute shopping. The Israeli supermarket was bustling, as shoppers feverishly collected the items they needed. The checkout line was long, but for the most part the customers waited patiently, drinking in the pre-Yom Tov atmosphere.

It was Reb Gershon's turn at the register when his phone rang. It was his wife, who told him that she had forgotten to write several items on the shopping list. Reb Gershon asked the cashier if he could run to grab those last few things. The cashier didn't mind, but the shoppers in line were less accommodating. As Reb Gershon ran to get one item and then another, the frustration of the shoppers behind him was unmistakable. When he finally returned, Reb Gershon apologized, muttering something about his wife, but no one was interested in explanations.

One of the shoppers, Natan, let Reb Gershon have it. "What kind of business is this?" he hollered for all to hear. "Don't you have respect for other people's time? Don't you see all these people waiting? Do you think you're the only one shopping for the *chag*?"

Reb Gershon's face turned all shades of crimson, but he kept quiet as he bagged his order and then waited by the side for a few minutes. When it was Natan's turn to pay, he felt horrible about how he had publicly lashed out against Reb Gershon, justified or not. Seeking to make amends, he approached Reb Gershon and asked his forgiveness. He then went over to the cashier and told him that he would be paying for Reb Gershon's entire order.

As he left the store several minutes later, Natan encountered Reb Gershon, who was on his phone, crying. Reb Gershon hung up and turned around to find himself face-to-face with the man who had humiliated him. He tried, unsuccessfully, to hide his tears.

"Again, I am really sorry," said Natan, assuming that Reb Gershon was still not placated. "I regret having shamed you. What I did was wrong, no matter the circumstances."

"No, no," R' Gershon mustered. "Don't worry. I am not upset at you. These aren't tears of sadness. They are tears of relief!" He wiped his eyes.

"You see," he explained, "when I left my home today to buy some necessities for Yom Tov, I had not a *shekel* in my pocket. My wife and I didn't know what to do. In the end, my wife told me to go shopping while she took a *Tehillim* in hand and began beseeching the Ribono Shel Olam for salvation. 'Go out and buy what we need,' she told me. 'Hashem will surely help.'

"When it was almost my turn to have my groceries rung up, my wife called and I asked her what I should do, since I had no money to pay for the items in my cart. She told me to get several additional items that she had forgotten and added that she would continue davening. 'Hashem will help!' she promised. With her *emunah* and *bitachon* empowering me, I had my groceries scanned by the cashier and told him that I would pay him shortly; that is why I was standing on the side when you came along and told me that you would pay for my entire order.

"When you came outside and saw me crying while on the phone, I was speaking to my wife, telling her how you had come to my rescue. My wife and I were expressing our amazement at the power of genuine faith and belief in the One Above."

Moved by what he had just heard, Natan promptly took out

his checkbook and wrote out a generous check to further help Reb Gershon and his family.

The Ticket

At the conclusion of the Birchos HaShachar, we say: "Baruch Atah Hashem Hagomel chassadim tovim l'amo Yisrael — Blessed are You, Hashem, Who bestows beneficent kindnesses upon His people Israel."

What is meant by the term chassadim tovim? Are there chassadim, kindnesses, that are not beneficent, that are not good?

The Tiferes Shlomo (Moadim, Shaar HaTefillah: "Hagomel chassadim tovim…") explains that sometimes the Ribono Shel Olam sends trials and tribulations, which will ultimately lead to salvation and blessing. However, the kindness behind these acts is not revealed to the world until later on. Therefore, during the period of pain or challenge, the one who is undergoing the suffering cannot understand the chassadim, for only Hashem knows and comprehends the mercy behind the difficulty one is enduring.

And so we say, "gomel chassadim tovim le'amo Yisrael," for we want kindnesses that are good in the eyes of His people, Klal Yisrael — chassadim that are good in both hidden and revealed ways.

Reb Chaim'ke, who was known by many for his wealth and philanthropy, went to speak to Rav Levi Yitzchak of Berditchev privately and began to unburden himself. Reb Chaim'ke described the downward spiral of his finances, sharing with Rav Levi Yitzchak how his once successful business had crumbled, leaving him penniless. Every effort he had made to get back on his feet failed. He had begun to borrow money to cover his losses, but these loans just left him with mounting debt.

"To add to all this," cried Reb Chaim'ke, "I have several daughters of marriageable age, but I don't have a penny with which to marry them off. Very soon, my situation will become known to one and all, my creditors will come after me, and my disgrace will become public. I will be forced to declare bankruptcy and will face the ire of my creditors. I may even have to flee my town, and my daughters will have no hope of ever getting married."

The man sobbed to Rav Levi Yitzchak, begging him for help.

Rav Levi Yitzchak waited for Reb Chaim'ke to calm down somewhat, and then he looked at the *kvittel* Reb Chaim'ke had placed before him and sat in quiet contemplation. Suddenly, he lifted his head and said, "Please go to the offices of the lottery and purchase a lottery ticket. And may Hashem be with you."

Reb Chaim'ke accepted the directive of Rav Levi Yitzchak without any question. He departed from the Berditchever and went directly to the closest lottery stand and purchased a ticket, fully convinced that he was a step closer to his salvation.

Reb Chaim'ke began his trip home, and as night fell, he found a local inn, where he planned to spend the night before continuing on his way at dawn.

About an hour later, a *poritz* arrived at the same inn. This *poritz* was a lottery enthusiast. Despite the many parcels of land he owned and the vast wealth he had amassed, he was addicted to the lottery, selecting his numbers carefully and buying tickets for every drawing. In fact, he had just bought a ticket for the lottery that was to take place the very next day.

After retiring for the night, the *poritz* fell into a deep sleep. He dreamed that in that very inn, there was a Jew who was going to win the upcoming lottery. The *poritz* woke up and dismissed the dream as nonsense. *It's all claptrap,* he tried to convince himself. He closed his eyes and went back to sleep.

Once again, the *poritz* had a dream, and again he was told that a Jew in that very inn was going to be the lucky winner. He awoke, tried to ignore the dream, and went back to sleep. But again he had the same dream.

After this happened several times, he awoke fully. As much as he tried to dismiss the dream, he could not shake it off. He got up, dressed, and summoned his servants, ordering them to check every room in the inn. "If you find a Jew, wake him up and bring him to me immediately!"

The servants began an urgent search, rushing from room to room looking for the Jew. Soon, they found the man they were looking for. They woke him up and ordered him to follow them.

Upon being awakened, Reb Chaim'ke was scared out of his wits. Perhaps one of his creditors had sent some hoodlums to get him to pay up his debt. Or maybe these were some bored souls looking to torment a lonely Jew. Either way, he was worried.

He asked the men surrounding him what was going on. "What do you want from me? Where are you taking me?" In response, the men commanded him to remain silent and dragged him to another part of the inn.

Reb Chaim'ke entered the room of the *poritz*, who was sitting and waiting impatiently. The *poritz* said to Reb Chaim'ke, "Forgive me for my obtrusiveness, but are you by any chance in possession of a ticket for the upcoming lottery?"

Reb Chaim'ke tensed up. He did have a ticket, the very one that Rav Levi Yitzchak had told him to purchase. But why did this interest the *poritz*?

Fearing the *poritz*, he replied that he had purchased a lottery ticket. "Why does this concern you, though?" Reb Chaim'ke asked. "And why at this late hour? There are thousands upon thousands of such tickets sold all over."

The *poritz* wouldn't reveal what was driving him. Instead, he got straight to the point. "Listen here," he said. "I have a business proposal for you. I also bought a lottery ticket. Let's make an exchange. You give me your ticket and I'll give you my ticket, and for doing this, I will pay you 100 rubles! With that money, you can buy many tickets for the lottery. All you need to do is hand me yours."

The *poritz* sensed that Reb Chaim'ke wasn't convinced, so he continued his sales pitch. "Chances are that you won't win the lottery anyway," he said, "so what difference does it make to you? Here, I am offering you 100 rubles, right here and right now! You surely know what people say: 'A bird in the hand is worth two in the bush.' Do this. It's a no-brainer."

Reb Chaim'ke pretended to ponder the offer for a few minutes, but instead of thinking about the proposal, all he could think of were the words of Rav Levi Yitzchak, who had directed him to buy the very ticket the *poritz* was trying to get him to give up. He couldn't fathom letting go of his precious ticket. In his eyes, this wasn't just any ticket. It was his ticket to salvation.

"I bought this ticket," Reb Chaim'ke finally said, "and I will not sell it."

"I'll give you 200 rubles!" said the *poritz*.

"No!" said Reb Chaimke.

"500!"

"No way!"

"1,000 rubles!"

"No! There's nothing to talk about!" insisted Reb Chaim'ke.

The *poritz* kept raising his offer, but as he did so, Reb Chaim'ke became even more stubborn in his refusal to part with his ticket. Reb Chaim'ke felt in his heart of hearts that he was holding the winning ticket. Thus, this ticket he was guarding was worth millions. There was no way he would sell it.

And so, the *poritz's* offers of 5,000 rubles and then 10,000 were rebuffed. Reb Chaim'ke made it clear that he was not selling, period. This caused the *poritz* to grow even more agitated. Realizing that the Jew wouldn't let go of his ticket peacefully, the *poritz* lunged at Reb Chaim'ke, threw him to the ground, and began to wrestle with him, trying to get the elusive ticket. Joining the *poritz* were his bodyguards, who were more than happy to take part in the scuffle, beating the Jew viciously as they grabbed the lottery ticket from him.

Reb Chaim'ke lay on the floor in excruciating pain. The burly henchmen of the *poritz* deposited him in the hallway of the inn, and as they did so, they threw at him the *poritz's* lottery ticket, which he had promised Reb Chaim'ke in exchange.

Chortling at the pathetic site of the moaning Jew, the *poritz* and his thugs left Reb Chaim'ke, who shed bitter tears as he dragged himself back to his room. His physical agony was compounded by the realization that his salvation had been stolen from his hands. Was it not enough, he wondered, that he was financially broke? Was it not enough that he was being hounded by creditors?

This was like a mean trick. He had managed to receive the blessing of Rav Levi Yitzchak. He was finally going to be extricated from his financial quagmire, and yet here he was, utterly humiliated, robbed of any and all hope. He kept crying until he fell asleep.

He awoke in the morning to find that the *poritz* and his entourage had already left. Despondent, he pulled himself together and headed out, making his way to the local lottery stand. There, to his astonishment, he discovered that the winning numbers matched the ticket he was now holding — the ticket that the *poritz's* men had thrown at him after stealing his own ticket.

Reb Chaim'ke won a fortune of money and, after paying off his debts, rebuilt his business and saw great success.

He returned to Berditchev to tell Rav Levi Yitzchak what had occurred and to thank him for his *berachah*, which had come to fruition, albeit in an unexpected way.

Rav Levi Yitzchak smiled knowingly. "While you were lying on the ground, beaten and bruised and in a state of despair, you had no idea that what was taking place was actually paving the road to your salvation. You perceived yourself as being at the lowest point possible. There seemed to be no hope. And yet, HaKadosh Baruch Hu was orchestrating the events that would ultimately lead to great wealth."

> *Sometimes the most difficult challenges are actually the very sources of blessing and salvation.*

The Seudah

Though Dovid and Chaya Katz were married for many years, they had not been blessed with children. The emptiness in their lives was painful, but they remained optimistic, believing that they would soon parent a child. Like so many others, they were assisted by Bonei Olam, the international organization led by Rabbi Shlomo Bochner, which assists couples who wish to establish families.

Doctor after doctor told the Katzes that there was no hope, but they persisted, constantly seeking out additional professionals who could be of assistance. In time, Dovid and Chaya were introduced to an expert physician in the field, Dr. Gavin A. McAllister; he was their last hope. With concern written all over his face, Dr. McAllister carefully studied their case. After reviewing the records of the many treatments that had not been successful, he realized that his chances of success were slim, as well. As he scheduled a day of treatments, he told the Katzes that the odds were stacked against them, but that he would do whatever he could to help.

The day of treatments arrived. Armed with prayers, along with the knowledge that the *yeshuah* would come only from the Ribono Shel Olam, the Katzes met with Dr. McAllister.

A few weeks later, Dr. McAllister contacted the Katzes, and they traveled to meet him. A lump formed in his throat as Dr. McAllister informed Dovid and Chaya that the treatments had failed. There was nothing more he could do.

The doctor was shocked by Chaya's response. "Did you try your best?" she asked him.

"What do you mean? Of course I did. I always try my best," said Dr. McAllister, chagrined by the question.

"I understand," said Chaya. And then she repeated, "But did you really try your very best?"

Dr. McAllister looked at his patient as if she were not all there. "Absolutely. I tried my best," he said.

With that, the meeting was over. There was a thick silence in the car as Dovid and Chaya made their way home. The doctor's diagnosis had been said with finality. Until now, there had always been hope — the thought that somewhere, someway, someone would be able to help.

Now, it was all over.

Shortly after arriving home that night, Dovid went out to daven Maariv. He hoped that by the time he returned, his wife would be sleeping. It had been a painful day and he didn't want to talk. What was there to say?

When Maariv was over, Dovid returned home, still feeling weighed down by the depressing events of the day. But when he opened the door, he was surprised to find the house well lit. He was doubly surprised to see the dining-room table set beautifully, as if for a Shabbos or Yom Tov meal. He did a double take, thinking that perhaps he had walked into his neighbor's house by mistake, but then quickly realized that it was indeed his own home.

Had his wife gone crazy? Why in the world was the table set, with china, Shabbos cutlery, cloth napkins, and crystal stemware? And what was that delicious aroma wafting into the dining area from the kitchen?

As he shook his head in bewilderment, Chaya walked into the room.

"Is everything O.K.?" Dovid asked. "What's going on?"

Chaya seemed relaxed and composed as she replied, "Dovid, we went through a difficult *nisayon*. Today, I asked the doctor if he tried everything. He said he did. I asked him if he tried his very best. He said he did. So we know that we have done all we can. Everything that has happened has been orchestrated by Hashem, Who gave us a *nisayon*. And we passed the *nisayon*.

"Come, let us express our gratitude for all that we have. Let us celebrate that we were *zocheh* to endure this test and emerge with our faith intact."

Inspired by his wife's attitude, Dovid joined her at the table.

Early the next morning, the phone rang in the Katz home. It was a nurse calling from Dr. McAllister's office. "Overnight, we reviewed our findings," she related, "and it seems that what we told you yesterday may not be accurate. There may be something else we can do to help you. Come back as soon as you can."

Dovid and Chaya dressed in a hurry and flew out the door. They headed right back to Dr. McAllister's office and followed the doctor's directives.

About a year later, Rabbi Bochner received a phone call from Dovid and Chaya, calling to inform him of a miracle. They were the proud parents of a healthy baby boy.

In the world of psychology, there is a concept called "radical acceptance," which means accepting reality as it is, and realizing that life can be worth living even with painful experiences.

This special couple showed that it is possible to rise above anguish and heartbreak with courage and valor, reacting with deep faith and trust in the One Above.

A Taste of Clarity

Me'ein Olam Haba

"And Hashem blessed Avraham with everything [ba'kol]" (Bereishis 24:1). The Gemara (Bava Basra 17a) learns from here that Avraham merited "me'ein Olam Haba — an inkling of the World to Come." Likewise, says the Gemara, Yitzchak (based on the word mi'kol: ibid. 27:33) and Yaakov (kol: ibid. 33:11) merited this otherworldly pleasure, which we request every time we recite Bircas HaMazon and say the words "ba'kol mi'kol kol — in everything, from everything, with everything."

What is me'ein Olam Haba? Is it something ethereal? Astral?

Not at all. It's right here, in front of us, as a young Rav Yaakov Galinsky learned firsthand from a non-Jew.

In his later years, Rav Yaakov Galinsky lived in Eretz Yisrael and was the rosh yeshivah of Yeshivas Chadera and a famous *maggid*. In 1939, though, he was learning in Yeshivas Novaradok in Bialystok, in northeastern Poland. War was imminent, and the Jews were already feeling vulnerable. Yaakov was unusually short and looked very young, so when his rosh yeshivah, Rav Avraham Jofen, needed a courier who would not attract undue attention to make a delivery for the yeshivah to Warsaw, Yaakov was chosen.

When Yaakov arrived at the train station, the clerk informed him that all the seats in both third class and second class were taken. A first-class seat was available, but the price was so much higher that he could afford only the fare to the very first stop, which was far from Warsaw. *Nu*, if the travel to one station was all he could afford, so be it.

Yaakov entered the first-class car. What soft, elegant seats! What fancy decor! In addition, the train had recently been equipped with the latest convenience: a radio with headphones, free for anyone's use. One fellow traveler, a distinguished-looking non-Jew sitting opposite him, had already donned his headphones and closed his eyes, and was listening rapturously to some radio station he had found on the dial.

The train car filled up, the doors closed, the whistle blew, and the train slowly pulled out of the station. A few minutes later, someone came in from the next car and announced, "There's a peasant over here playing folk tunes on his accordion!" Hungry for a little entertainment and eager to forget the impending war, nearly everyone jumped out of his seat and headed next door. Soon the car was empty, except for Yaakov and the distinguished non-Jew, who was still listening intently to whatever was on that radio.

The conductor stuck his head into the car. Spying only two passengers, he said loudly, "You're missing some great music over here!"

Yaakov said nothing.

But the non-Jew, noticing the conductor, pulled off his headphones and politely inquired, "What did you say?"

The conductor explained the goings-on in the next car.

Pursing his lips, the non-Jew snorted, "I am listening to a concert by the Paris Symphony Orchestra. Do you expect me to turn it off and run to hear some peasant with his bellows and folk tunes?"

Planting the headphones firmly back on his head, he soon fell back into his reverie.

Suddenly, the train stopped. There was an accident ahead. Since the tracks needed repair work, the train had to return to its original station. Yaakov hopped off, went straight back to yeshivah and found Rav Jofen, who exclaimed, "You went there and came back already?"

"No," Yaakov explained, "the train had to turn back. However, I heard a *mussar shmuess* from a non-Jew, and for that alone, the trip was worth it!"

Noting Rav Jofen's surprise, Yaakov told him of the non-Jew's flat-out refusal to listen to the peasant's folk music.

"That peasant is like this world, with its crude, fake, but tempting entertainment," said Rav Galinsky. "Our pleasure in a life of Torah may not be so immediate. To attain it, we have to close ourselves out from this world and 'tune in' to the world of Torah. Still, there is no comparison, as the ecstasy we can acquire is, indeed, me'ein Olam Haba."

— heard from Rabbi Raphael Waldman

Living Halachah

In 2001, Rav Chaim Kanievsky suffered a stroke and his hands were paralyzed for a few days. As he emerged from the paralysis, the physical therapist at Mayanei HaYeshua Hospital wanted to determine if power had returned to Rav Chaim's hands. He handed Rav Chaim a pen and a sheet of paper and asked him to write something. Rav Chaim took the pen and jotted down the words, *"Yekum purkan min shemaya,"* from the very beginning of the *tefillah* we say each Shabbos before Mussaf.

The therapist was gratified to see that Rav Chaim could write, but he was somewhat surprised, a sentiment he shared with his distinguished patient. "I have been doing this job for decades," he said to Rav Chaim. "Without exception, each person I have ever asked to write something — and we're talking about thousands of people — has immediately written his name. Why did the rav choose to write the words *'Yekum purkan'*? Why not sign your name like everyone else?"

Rav Chaim responded simply: "It's a *befeirishe din*, a halachah brought in *Choshen Mishpat* [69:2] and in the Gemara in *Maseches Kesubos* [21a], that one should not write his signature on a blank paper. Otherwise, perhaps a dishonest person will find the paper and then write on it whatever he wants above the signature, such as that the undersigned owes him a sum of money."

It's a halachah. Period. End of story.

What the Halachah Demands

*T*he following story was related by Rav Yaakov Edelstein.

The Chazon Ish and the Brisker Rav led a battle to save Jewish children by ensuring that they receive a Torah education.

As such, bachurim from Yeshivas Ponovezh in Bnei Brak, known as the p'eylim, worked with their mashgiach, Rav Eliyahu Eliezer Dessler, to save immigrant children from the secular establishment, who wanted to see them grow up unaware of the beauty of their Jewish roots.

Each year, during the two-week period designated for school registration, Rav Dessler instructed dozens of *bachurim* to go out to the immigrant camps during their night *seder* and offer the parents a Torah education for their children. The Brisker Rav ruled that the *bachurim* were even allowed to go bareheaded, so they would not be recognized as yeshivah *bachurim* and would be allowed into the camps.

One time, registration took place during a period of extremely cold weather, and the *bachurim* found out that the directors of the absorption camps were giving out warm clothes and blankets only to parents who registered their children for secular schools. This presented a difficult *nisayon* for the parents.

Therefore, before heading out to the camps, the *bachurim* went from house to house to collect warm clothing for the immigrants. They managed to amass a large quantity of clothes, but were concerned that some of the winter coats contained *shaatnez*. The question arose: Should these coats be checked for *shaatnez*, a process that would take a few days and would mean that the *p'eylim* may miss the brief window for school registration? Or should the garments be given to the immigrants immediately, as is, along with a warning that they may contain *shaatnez*?

The question was brought to the Chazon Ish, who ruled that the coats should be checked for *shaatnez* before being given to the immigrants. He explained, "When we do what the halachah demands, no damage or harm will come as a result!"

The Zechus to Give

Someone once asked the Chazon Ish to explain why, when a person approaches someone to support Torah, the response is often, "Come back tomorrow." Does the person believe that tomorrow he's going to become wealthy?

The Chazon Ish replied, "It means that the person needs another three *tefillos* to have the *zechus* to give money for *hachzakas Torah*. That's why you have to return the next day."

Worried About Reward

A money-forging press was once discovered near Pressburg, and the police arrested a number of communal leaders, eventually stipulating that they would be freed only if the local rav swore to their innocence. Since halachah discourages making oaths, the rav was terrified to do so, even though he knew without a doubt that the community leaders were innocent. He went to ask the Chasam Sofer, Rav Moshe Schreiber Sofer, the rav in Pressburg, what to do.

Drawing himself up to his full height, the Chasam Sofer proclaimed, "Jews have been thrown into jail for weeks on end, and families have been left with no source of livelihood — and you're worrying about your *Olam Haba*?

"Believe me, my dear friend, in Hashem's eyes, freeing a Jew from a dungeon is far more important than your eternal reward."

Doing the Best We Can

After World War II the Klausenberger Rebbe once asked a wealthy patron for a donation to help build a yeshivah.

"Rebbe," the man said sincerely, "I will do the best I can."

The Rebbe wasn't satisfied with this response.

"Let me share a memory with you," responded the Rebbe. "When I became a leader in my *shtetl*, I was given a *gabbai*. Everywhere I went, my *gabbai* went with me. He carried my *tallis zekel* and held my coat. I wasn't allowed to carry anything myself."

The Rebbe paused, becoming emotional as he went on. "When I was in the concentration camp, the Nazis forced me to carry rocks weighing 50 kilos [over 110 pounds]. I, who had never carried my own *tallis zekel*, found out the hard way what I was able to do."

"A person doesn't know what he can accomplish," concluded the Rebbe. "Sometimes he must be put in a trying situation to reveal what his best truly is."

We like to believe that we try our hardest, expending as much energy as we can. But are we being truly honest with ourselves?

It takes an honest look in the mirror, and sometimes a challenging circumstance, to reveal just how much we can accomplish and what our best truly is.

Not Yours or Mine

Chaim was a promising student. Already from the time he was in fourth grade, he showed amazing potential. In the early 1960's, there weren't too many boys with his *hasmadah* or abilities in Detroit, and his rebbeim and teachers predicted a great future for him. "If he stays in yeshivah past elementary school, the sky's the limit," they all agreed.

Unfortunately, his father did not agree. One winter day, he showed up at the school and demanded to take his son home. "I've had enough of your religious stuff," he fumed. "I'm sending my son to public school, where he'll grow up to be an all-American boy. I want him to attend college and have all the opportunities this country has to offer. He may become a doctor, a lawyer, whatever he wants!"

"Calm down," said the boy's rebbi, Rav Avraham Abba Freedman, a gentle smile camouflaging the fierce determination that was his trademark. "Give him another year or so. He's doing so well here. We have a fantastic secular program, as well."

The father relented, and allowed his son to remain until he graduated elementary school. By then, young Chaim was committed to a Torah lifestyle and determined to continue his education in a yeshivah high school. Rabbi Freedman arranged for Chaim to travel to a prominent yeshivah in New York, where he quickly became a rising star. The father gnashed his teeth in frustration, but he was outnumbered two to one.

There was, however, the matter of his younger brother; Josh, who also demonstrated great promise, was two grades below Chaim and far more impressionable. With him, his father was determined to have his way. "I'm gonna show you!" he raged at Rav Avraham Abba. "You won't steal both my children!"

He removed Josh from yeshivah and sent him to public school. The poor child cried for days, refusing to get onto the school bus. Finally, his father relented. Then, after several more years in yeshivah in Detroit, Josh stealthily followed his younger brother to New York.

The father stormed into Rav Freedman's classroom and began to holler. "First one kid and then the other! How can you do this to me, Rabbi? I thought that you'd take one kid and leave the other for me. But now you steal both?!"

Rav Avraham Abba smiled patiently and waited until the man had run out of steam. Then he slowly explained. "Wait a minute, sir. You're mistaken. There is no 'yours' and no 'mine.' These boys don't belong to either of us. They are Hashem's children and, as such, are entitled to a yeshivah education."

The elder son went on to become a prominent rosh kollel, while his younger brother became a successful mechanech in a well-known yeshivah.

Free of Personal Bias

*T*he Chasam Sofer was officially appointed rav of Pressburg in *Tishrei 5567/1806, and he occupied that position for 33 years. Within a short time of his appointment, he became regarded as the rav of the entire Diaspora, receiving questions from all over the world. Meanwhile, his yeshivah continued to expand, spreading Torah to thousands of talmidim.*

On one occasion, the Chasam Sofer was asked a question involving an *agunah* whom many rabbanim had allowed to remarry.

"According to strict halachah," said the Chasam Sofer, "I cannot argue with them. But my heart tells me that her husband is still alive."

The woman accepted the Chasam Sofer's opinion and, sure enough, her husband returned not long after.

His son, Rav Shimon Sofer, known as the Michtav Sofer, once asked the Chasam Sofer how he managed to answer halachic questions with hardly more than a quick review of the related issues.

"It is true," replied the Chasam Sofer, "that halachic decisions normally require deep analysis. Nevertheless, in every generation, Hashem designates a person who holds the keys to all hidden things, and this individual, who has no prejudice, partiality, or predisposition, is endowed with special *siyata d'Shmaya*."

It was with immense humility that the Chasam Sofer continued, feeling compelled to explain his ability to promptly answer the knotty *shailos* that came his way.

"With great effort, I have prepared myself to be ready to solve halachic problems and I have, *baruch Hashem*, freed myself from all personal bias. Therefore, it is not possible that I will err in a ruling. At the most, I will err in my choice of proofs. Perhaps how I reached my conclusion could be questioned. But my final decision is granted Heavenly blessing."

The Greater Feat

On Rosh Hashanah 5700/1939, the Nazi army was approaching and the tension had the *talmidim* of Yeshivas Kamenitz on edge. Some of them began devising all sorts of impulsive schemes to escape the advancing enemy.

At that time, the rosh yeshivah, Rav Reuven Grozovsky, delivered a *shmuess* about *Akeidas Yitzchak*. "There is a well-known question: Why isn't the *Akeidah* named for Avraham? It was basically his test. The Midrash tells us (*Yalkut Shimoni, Vayeira* 101) that the actual binding was Yitzchak's idea, as a restraint against forcibly resisting his father's sacrificial knife. Hence the name *Akeidas Yitzchak*. But wasn't Avraham's task of wielding the knife the more difficult one? Shouldn't this have been memorialized in the name of this incident?"

Rav Reuven explained: "The Torah gives greater recognition to Yitzchak's attention and meticulousness, which he applied in order to avoid a wrongful action, than it does to Avraham's heroic act, which did not require the same careful thought."

A deep, transformative lesson.

Enough for Both of Us

Prior to assuming the mantle of leadership, the Kopycznitzer Rebbe, Rav Moshe Mordechai Heschel, worked as a broker in the diamond district on Manhattan's 47th Street, where his acts of chesed were well known. The Skverer Rebbe, Rav Yaakov Yosef Twersky, once remarked, "Rav Moishele [as he was known] purifies 47th Street."

A young *mechanech* hoped to devote afternoons to earning a few extra dollars in the diamond market and approached friends and relatives for leads. Most responded, "Best wishes, but you don't expect me to give away customers, do you?"

When the man confided in Rav Moshe Mordechai, he immediately produced his entire list of clients and contacts. The man was flabbergasted. A "list" is a diamond dealer's most precious and carefully guarded secret.

"How can I possibly take this?" the man asked. "You are practically giving me your entire *parnassah*!"

"Do not worry," was the response. "Our *parnassah* is in the hands of the Ribono Shel Olam, and He has enough for both of us."

Help in the World to Come

During World War I, the Germans occupied Lithuania for four years, causing rampant starvation. At the time, Rav Eliyahu (Elya) Lopian, a prominent leader of the *mussar* movement, was relatively young, but already a father to nine children. Several of his children were learning in the yeshivah in Telshe, so the minimal amount of food he had was sent as food parcels to his *yeshivah bachurim*.

One day, his neighbor came to visit and said to Rebbetzin Lopian, "I don't understand. You're blessed with so many children. Can't some of them get jobs and bring in some sustenance for the household?"

She answered, "In this world, I don't need my children to help me. I have the Ribono Shel Olam to rely upon to provide for my family. But in the World to Come, that is where I will need real help from my children. And that is why I cannot afford to take them away from their true occupation of learning Torah."

Me Versus Us

*T*he following story was told to Rav Yisrael Perlow of Stolin by
an elderly Chassid, who would share tales about Rav Yisrael's
grandfather, Rav Aharon, the Beis Aharon of Karlin. It was retold by
Rav Yisrael Grossman, rosh yeshivah of Yeshivas Pinsk-Karlin.

One year, winter arrived early, along with its inclement weather.
Starting from Rosh Hashanah, the winds raged and a heavy snow
fell, covering the streets of Karlin in white. Preparations for Succos
were hampered due to the weather. Most people were unable to
construct a *succah*, and even those who had built *succos* had to con-
tend with the snowfall that now covered their humble huts. Others who had retractable roofs, which could be opened each year to
allow the use of an indoor *succah*, were in no better shape, as the
roofs could not be opened due to the snow that was piled on top.

The Chassid — who, in his later years, told the story to Rav Yisrael — tried everything he could to enable the Beis Aharon to fulfill
the mitzvah of *succah*. To that end, he went to the roof of the Rebbe's home and, despite the bitter cold, began to work laboriously,
clearing the mounds of snow that had fallen on top of the area of
the roof that would normally be opened for the Rebbe's *succah*. For
hours on Erev Succos, the Chassid shoveled and shoveled, ignoring
the pain and aches in his bones and the howling winds that made
the freezing temperatures feel even colder. Finally, he had cleared
enough space. He proceeded to open the roof and then went about
laying *s'chach* on the opening and setting up the *succah*.

The Rebbe was informed that thanks to the devotion of his Chassid, he'd be able to fulfill the mitzvah of *succah*. The Rebbe went to
see for himself and stood almost in disbelief, looking at the *succah*
and the *s'chach* like they had fallen from the sky. His joy knew no
bounds.

He turned to his Chassid and said, "I would like to grant you a
gift in appreciation for your *chesed*, and the choice is up to you. Either I can bless you to join me in Gan Eden, where you will be '*imi*

b'mechitzasi — with me, inside my partition' (based on *Berachos* 12b, *Eruvin* 53b), or I can bless you with immense wealth, for both you and your children, and you will never lack for anything material."

The Chassid thought for a moment and said, "I'll take the second gift."

When telling the story to Rav Yisrael, the Chassid concluded, "And from that day, I was blessed with great riches and saw the Rebbe's berachah come to full fruition."

When Rav Grossman related this story, he remarked that he never understood the intent of the Chassid; instead of choosing to be with his righteous Rebbe for eternity, he selected the blessing of material wealth in this world. It just didn't seem to add up.

Rav Grossman shared his bewilderment with his mechutan, Rav Knobloch, a respected Belzer Chassid, who offered an enlightening thought.

"It's quite simple. The Chassid was most virtuous in choosing the gift of wealth," he explained. "What does 'imi b'mechitzasi' mean? It means that I am focused on myself: I am benefiting. I am in a good place. I am enjoying the spiritual holiness and nourishment of being with the Rebbe. It is 'tov li v'tov l'nafshi — good for me and good for my soul.' Although this is an outstanding blessing of supreme spiritual delights, it is all about myself.

"On the other hand, with a little money, and certainly with a lot of money, a person can acquire a phenomenal amount of ruchniyus. He can engage in tzedakah and chesed. He can assist almanos and yesomim. He can support hachnasas kallah endeavors. He can use his wealth for pidyon shevuyim and for the establishment and maintenance of mosdos haTorah. He can support lomdei Torah generously. Think about all that can be done for others!

"This pious Chassid wasn't going to trade all of this for something that would benefit only himself."

A Taste of Leadership

Hiddur Mitzvah

What started as a disappointment over an inheritance morphed into a full-fledged internecine conflagration. It would have raged on indefinitely but for the wisdom of an *adam gadol*.

The issue was a *yerushah* passed down to five brothers. The rosh yeshivah of Yeshivas Mir Yerushalayim, Rav Eliezer Yehudah Finkel, tried desperately to extinguish the flames of this family feud, but his efforts were futile. This matter so pained him that before he was *niftar*, he requested of his son and eventual successor, Rav Beinish Finkel, that he do everything possible to bring peace to this family.

By the time Rav Beinish got involved, the situation had given rise to a lot of tension and none of the brothers were on speaking terms. No matter how hard he tried to mediate between them, he met with failure, as each one of the heirs was convinced that he was right, that his unscrupulous siblings were wrong, and that they were attempting to usurp what was rightfully his. The more Rav Beinish spoke to each party, the more each one hardened his stance. It appeared that the dilemma was unsolvable.

Then one evening, Rav Beinish knocked on the door of one of the brothers. "Reb Reuven, I have a private matter to speak to you about," he said with emotion. "May I come in?"

The two made small talk for a few minutes and then Rav Beinish got to the point.

"I want you to know that I really put a lot of thought into this argument, and I am fully convinced that you are 100 percent right," he said. Rav Beinish proceeded to prove with sound logic why Reb Reuven's cause was a just one and that there was no room for argument.

Reb Reuven's satisfaction was evident on his face.

"*Baruch Hashem*," Reb Reuven exclaimed, "the truth finally emerged like oil that rises to the top of water. I always knew that I was right and that my brothers were thinking irrationally. But that's what a *nogei'a b'davar* is. When there is self-interest involved, one is blinded from seeing the truth. The rosh yeshivah is the only one who was able to discern between truth and falsehood, between integrity and dishonesty."

"Thank you for your complimentary words," said Rav Beinish, "but now I have something else on my mind. I would like to solicit funds from you for a most worthy cause, a great *dvar mitzvah*."

"Why, of course," said Reb Reuven excitedly. "I am ready and willing to donate generously to any *tzedakah* that the rosh yeshivah is collecting for."

"You are well aware," said Rav Beinish, "that for a *hiddur mitzvah*, to beautify a mitzvah, one should spend up to a third of the mitzvah's original cost. For example, if one can acquire an *esrog* for $60 and a more beautiful one for another $20, he should buy the more beautiful one, if possible."

"Yes, yes, I am well aware of that," said Reb Reuven.

"Similarly, and perhaps even more so," said Rav Beinish, "to beautify the mitzvah of *shalom*, which is the foundation of the entire creation, it is surely worthwhile to spend at least an extra third to keep the words of David, '*Seek peace and pursue it*' (*Tehillim* 34:15). If so, I ask that you donate one-third of your inheritance for the mitzvah of peace with your brothers."

Without any hesitation, Reb Reuven replied, "I agree wholeheartedly. All of my life I have made an effort to be *mehader* in mitzvos. I never scrimped when it came to spending money on mitzvos and *tzedakah*. The main thing is now clear: The money is mine, and it does not belong to my brothers, who wanted to extract funds that weren't really theirs."

Once he was successful with the first brother, Rav Beinish proceeded to visit the other brothers. By week's end, the heated dispute was finally settled, to the satisfaction of all the parties.

Interestingly enough, after many years, one of the brothers commented to a friend, "Rav Beinish was the only one who understood me and was totally on my side throughout the dispute with my brothers."

The Tchebiner's Heart Attack

Rav Dov Berish Weidenfeld, the Tchebiner Rav and author of Shailos U'Teshuvos Doveiv Meisharim, was one of the leaders of Torah Jewry in Eretz Yisrael during the past century.

The rav shared a close bond with Rav Aharon Kotler, rosh yeshivah of Beth Medrash Govoha. The rav considered Rav Aharon a world-class *gaon* and recommended that his most qualified *talmidim* learn Rav Aharon's *sefer*. Rav Aharon, in turn, used to speak about the rav in glowing terms. He would often point to the Tchebiner as an example of *gadlus* in Torah. He once told his *talmidim* in Lakewood, "You need to know the entire Torah the way the Tchebiner Rav knows it."

Rav Avrohom Kabalkin is one of the directors of Machon Yerushalayim, whose mission is to disseminate works of Torah scholarship. Rav Avrohom visited the Tchebiner Rav immediately after Rav Aharon's *petirah* and asked him to submit a *teshuvah* for a *sefer* that was to be published in Rav Aharon's memory.

A short time after their conversation, the Tchebiner Rav suffered a heart attack and was rushed to the hospital. Soon after the rav was discharged, a messenger from Rav Kabalkin went to remind him about the piece he was asked to submit for the memorial *sefer*.

"You should know," the rav explained, "that it was this *sefer* that caused my heart attack. When Rav Kabalkin came to tell me that he was putting out a memorial *sefer*, I remembered that Rav Aharon is no longer with us and I began to feel ill!"

His Profit Is Yours

Rav Yosef Goldberg, son-in-law of Rav Hershele of Liska, once approached his father-in-law and said, "The *shver* gives *berachos* to all those who seek him out, and yet I, your son-in-law, am not *zocheh*?"

Rav Hershele replied, "Do you approach me like everyone else?"

Rav Yosef immediately went home to make preparations, as if he were traveling to visit his Rebbe. His rebbetzin asked him, "Where are you traveling?"

"To Liska, to spend Shabbos in the presence of the *tzaddik*, Rav Tzvi Hirsch!"

His rebbetzin was perplexed, but bid him farewell as he packed a small suitcase and went to the local *hachnasas orchim* house, where guests used to stay when spending Shabbos or Yom Tov in Liska. It seemed a bit strange to the other guests when Rav Yosef settled into the *hachnasas orchim* house as a simple Chassid spending Shabbos in the presence of his Rebbe. But no one asked any questions throughout Shabbos.

On Motza'ei Shabbos, the Chassidim bid farewell to the Rebbe, and before long it was Rav Yosef's turn to enter the inner sanctum of Rav Hershele. After the customary questions, Rav Hershele asked his son-in-law, "Do you have a specific request?"

"Yes, I do," he said. "I would like a *berachah* for *parnassah*!"

"What is your *parnassah*?" asked Rav Hershele.

"I am a timber merchant. I travel periodically to the city and negotiate the acquisition of timber to resell in local markets."

"Please tell me the process," urged Rav Hershele.

"I bargain with the non-Jewish sellers until I get the price down."

"Ah— I have heard enough!" Rav Hershele said. "When you begin your discussions and the price is fair, do not attempt to push the price down further in order to spread out your profits. When you allow someone else to profit, you will always have *hatzlachah* in your business ventures!"

> *It is said that from then on, Rav Yosef amassed much wealth.*
> — *heard from Pinchos Ben Tzvi*

"An Oil Merchant I Am Not"

A Yid once visited Liska to ask Rav Hershele for a *berachah* for *parnassah* and other worldly matters. Rav Hershele asked him, "How do you conduct yourself in regard to *shemiras Shabbos* and other *yesodos* of *Yiddishkeit*?"

The man replied, "I came to the Rebbe to ask for a *berachah* for *parnassah*. I didn't come to discuss my *Yiddishkeit*."

"Let me tell you a story," Rav Hershele replied.

> *A Yid traveled to the big city to purchase goods to sell back home; most of his business was conducted with one wholesaler, who sold him all types of items for his store. One year, as he was returning from his trip to the city in the middle of the night, this Yid's wagon got stuck in the mud. He got out of the wagon to check what was wrong and saw that one of the wheels of the wagon was broken, and he would need a certain oil to fix it. He didn't know what to do, until he thought of an idea: to return on foot to the wholesaler and ask him if he had oil. He knocked on the man's door and asked for his help. The wholesaler handed him the oil and wished him a safe journey home.*
>
> *As he continued on his way, he noticed another wagon stuck in the mud, with the same problem. He told the owner of the other wagon that if he needed oil to fix the wheel, he should go to the wholesaler in the city and he would surely be helpful. The man followed the merchant's advice and went to the wholesaler's house.*

The wholesaler, who was being roused from his sleep for the second time that night, came to the door and asked grumpily, "Who is bothering me in the middle of the night?"

The man replied that he needed oil to fix his wagon.

The wholesaler responded, "I am not an oil merchant. Let me go back to sleep."

"But I was told that you possess this oil," replied the hapless traveler. "I met a man who said that you gave him the oil graciously."

The wholesaler responded, "Why don't you understand what happened here? A man comes to me and spends a whole week purchasing merchandise for his business. He encounters a problem on his way to home, so of course I help him out by giving him oil that I have in my possession. But you just come here for my oil!"

Rav Hershele explained, "When a man comes to me for a *derech* in *avodas Hashem*, wishing to improve his state of *Yiddishkeit* and be close to Hashem — and he also wants a *berachah* to be *matzliach* — it is my duty to give him the *berachah*. But an oil merchant I am not!"

— heard from Pinchos Ben Tzvi

A Gadol's Pain

Rav Yechezkel Sarna, rosh yeshivah of Yeshivas Slabodka in Chevron and Yerushalayim, would recount the following story.

It was the height of the Russo-Turkish War and Jewish men were being drafted to fight against the army of the Ottoman Empire. Naturally, the women whose husbands had been called to serve were worried sick that their husbands would be missing in action, leaving them *agunos* who could not remarry without verification that their husbands had died.

They decided to go to Rav Yitzchak Elchanan Spector, the rav of Kovno, for a *berachah*. When Rav Yitzchak Elchanan heard about the group of women who had come for a *berachah*, he went out to meet them. He so empathized with their pain that he cried together with them for quite a while. Suddenly, as the tears continued to fall from his eyes, he proclaimed, "I am certain that all of your husbands will return."

And that is exactly what happened. Although there were many casualties, these women's husbands all returned home.

> When Rav Sarna would relate this story, he would add, "This story should not be misinterpreted. The crux is that Rav Yitzchak Elchanan empathized so much with these women. When such a tzaddik really takes to heart the troubles of his fellow Jews, it is no wonder that he is able to decree that the husbands return home safely."

True Mesirus Nefesh

Rav Shaul Brus, rosh yeshivah of Beth Hatalmud in Bensonhurst, Brooklyn, would often state, "I am not a rosh yeshivah; I am a *melamed*. But Rav Baruch Ber Leibowitz was also just a *melamed*."

Rav Brus would then add, "Rav Baruch Ber could have taught many pages of Gemara a day, but his primary concern was teaching his *talmidim* how to learn, and establishing within them the foundations upon which their future learning would be built. To that end, he made sure to understand every detail of the *sugya* with utmost clarity, and was therefore not able to teach his *talmidim* as much as he would have liked.

"To give up one's heartfelt wish to learn more for the sake of one's *talmidim* is true *mesirus nefesh!*"

— *heard from Rabbi Aryeh Dovid Spiegel*

The Consummate Partner

Rebbetzin Sarah Pam, wife of Rav Avrohom Pam, rosh yeshivah of Yeshiva Torah Vodaath, was the quintessential *eizer k'negdo*. She was always ready to help further her husband's spiritual growth, to preserve his health, and to ensure that his time was utilized for *avodas Hashem*.

In his introduction to his sefer Atarah LaMelech, Rav Pam writes:

"Hashem did further wondrous kindness for me in sending me an eishes chayil, the mainstay of my home, through whom all our household needs are cared for. She has withheld from me all domestic duties so that I can devote myself to learn and to teach. Also, in the raising of our children, her spirit has been faithful to my own, so that with a united approach and goal we merited, with Hashem's help, that they all go in their forebears' ways and Torah is their lifelong occupation. May Hashem grant her a long and pleasant life, and may the words 'A glad mother of children' (Tehillim 113:9) be fulfilled through her, forever and ever."

A person acquainted with Rav Pam ran into financial difficulty and desperately needed to borrow $60,000. The individual found someone who was willing to lend him the money on one condition: that Rav Pam serve as an *areiv*, a co-signer, on the loan. When the time came to repay the loan, the individual was still having difficulties and most of the loan remained outstanding. The lender was left with no choice but to ask Rav Pam, the *areiv*, to repay the loan. Rav Pam went to discuss the matter with the rebbetzin, and they decided to withdraw the money that the rebbetzin had earned as a pension for her decades of teaching in the New York City public school system. Together, they went to the bank to take care of the matter — in order to repay someone else's loan.

A *talmid* of Rav Pam, who experienced much travail in his life, would constantly consult with him for his sage advice regarding how to address many of the challenges he faced. Toward the end of Rav Pam's life, when Rav Pam was ill and in much pain, he stopped coming; he felt that he could not impose on his beloved rebbi when his rebbi was in such a state.

A short while after his decision, he met Rebbetzin Pam on the street and she asked him, "How come you haven't been calling?"

The *talmid* replied, "Rebbi is not feeling well. I don't feel that I should bother him."

The rebbetzin answered, "It is your job to call and my job to decide whether or not he can speak on the phone. You keep on calling."

More Than Anyone Else

Several *gedolim* were once discussing which prominent figure had done more than anyone else for the Torah of previous generations.

One of them said that it was Rav Chaim Soloveitchik of Brisk, who introduced his innovative *derech* in learning.

Another one said that it was the Chofetz Chaim, with his *tzidkus* and revolutionary *sefarim*.

Rav Yechezkel Sarna, however, said that he felt it was Sarah Schenirer.

Everyone looked at Rav Sarna in surprise and asked, "She did more for *Yiddishkeit* than anyone else? More than Rav Chaim Brisker and more than the Chofetz Chaim? How can that be?"

Rav Sarna explained, "Before Sarah Schenirer opened Bais Yaakov, Rav Meir Shapiro of Lublin once visited the Mirrer Yeshivah, which had 400 *talmidim* at the time, and spoke with the *bachurim* in learning. He was sincerely impressed with their level of learning. As he was preparing to leave, the rosh yeshivah went over to him and said, 'Well, what do you think of my *talmidim*?' Rav Meir replied, 'When I reach their age, I hope that I know as much as they do.' In other words, the *bachurim*, the unmarried *talmidim*, in the yeshivah were quite advanced in age.

"They had never married because there was no one for them to marry."

Rav Sarna continued, "Thanks to Sarah Schenirer, the Torah revolution reached the girls, and then there were girls for the *yeshivah bachurim* to marry. That is why I feel that she contributed more than anyone else to the Torah of this generation."

— heard from Rav Yitzchak Scheiner

Mistreated for the Sake of Torah

*D*uring the winter of 1939, the economic situation of Yeshivas Rabbeinu Yisrael Meir HaKohen/Chofetz Chaim in Williamsburg, Brooklyn, was critical. America was still trying to emerge from the Great Depression, and with the financial flourish that would accompany World War II still years away, Yeshivas Chofetz Chaim, like other yeshivos in America, found itself struggling for survival.

The yeshivah couldn't pay its coal bill, and the *bachurim* learning in the yeshivah's building on South Ninth Street were so cold that they sat in the *beis midrash* with their coats on. To keep warm, they would take turns learning in the dining area adjacent to the kitchen, so they could absorb some of the steam emanating from the large pot of soup on the stove.

To alleviate some of the yeshivah's financial problems, Rav Dovid Leibowitz, the rosh yeshivah and founder, undertook a trip to Miami, where he made appointments to meet with some wealthy people he thought would be able to help the yeshivah.

Accompanying him was one of his beloved *talmidim*, Abba Zalka Gewirtz, who later became the vice president of Telshe Yeshivah in Cleveland. The train ride, which took from Wednesday night until Friday morning, was not all that comfortable, for they could not even afford accommodations in a Pullman car, which provided sleeping berths. They had to get whatever rest they could while sitting erect.

Finally, they arrived in Miami. They entered the town with great anticipation, hoping to get the yeshivah on a solid financial footing. They made their way to the home of a prominent person in the community, expecting a generous donation. They arrived just at the appointed time, knocked on the door, and were greeted by their host with something less than enthusiasm. Rav Dovid tried to explain that they had just come from New York on an important mission to save the yeshivah from going under, but the man had no time or patience for them. He told them to leave at once, as he had no desire to hear their story.

Rav Dovid, in his ever-gracious manner, thanked the man for his time, but as they left, his young *talmid*, Abba Zalka, was incensed. "That was an awful way to treat you," he told the rosh yeshivah. "Where was the *k'vod haTorah*?"

Rav Dovid sighed and smiled. "You are mistaken," he said lovingly to his *talmid*. "The man gave us great honor."

"Honor?" the surprised *talmid* asked. "He hardly gave us the time of day, and he certainly didn't act with respect."

Said Rav Dovid, "Regarding the *navi* Yechezkel ben Buzi, Chazal say (*Vayikra Rabbah* 2:8) that Buzi was actually a title for the family of Yechezkel. Buzi comes from the word *boz*, meaning shame, signifying that this family was willing to suffer shame and embarrassment as long as their actions would bring honor or glory to Hashem and His Torah. But why would the verse ascribe to a noble family a title that connotes disgrace and contempt?

"Chazal are telling us that it is an honor to be abused or mistreated for the sake of Torah. It is proper and fitting for people to be remembered this way, for it depicts the exalted life they lived.

"Thus, this man's action makes us part of an exclusive group, one that we should be proud to be a part of. We are from Yechezkel ben Buzi's people! And all because we came here for *k'vod Shamayim*."

— *heard from Malkeal Yusupov*

"You've Been Accepted"

The following story was related by Rebbetzin Sarah Finkel about her son, Rav Nosson Tzvi Finkel:

Rav Nosson Tzvi once saw a *bachur* at Yeshivas Mir Yerushalayim who looked downcast. When he asked the *bachur* what was bothering him, the *bachur* answered that he had tried to get accepted into a different yeshivah in Yerushalayim, but unlike his friends, he was turned down. He was deeply disappointed and very upset.

Upon hearing this, Rav Nosson Tzvi called his driver to take him to the house of the rosh yeshivah of the other yeshivah. Rav Nosson Tzvi climbed up the steps to the rosh yeshivah's house and asked the rosh yeshivah to please accept this *bachur* into his yeshivah.

"How can I turn you down?" the rosh yeshivah said to Rav Nosson Tzvi, and he immediately agreed to accept the *bachur*.

Rav Nosson Tzvi returned to the Mir, found the *bachur*, and told him to pack his bags. "You have been accepted to the yeshivah of your choice."

The *bachur* was stunned, but overjoyed.

Emunas Chachamim

In Kislev 5775, Rav Chaim Kanievsky was visited by four brothers whose sister was in desperate need of a kidney transplant. She had experienced kidney failure and was receiving painful and difficult dialysis. The brothers had gone for testing to determine who is a match for their sister. The tests had revealed that the four brothers were equally eligible.

The brothers then agreed to visit Rav Chaim and have him draw lots to determine who would be the benefactor. The youngest brother was hesitant about undergoing the process of kidney donation, but he agreed, for the benefit of his dear sister, to go with his brothers to Rav Chaim.

As fate would have it, Rav Chaim's lottery determined that the youngest brother should donate his kidney.

The brother became emotional. As tears filled his eyes, he shared that he has a family of young children and is afraid to undergo the surgery. He added that at no point had he been ready to donate his kidney and had only agreed to visit Rav Chaim's home after being persuaded to come.

Everyone present was sure that Rav Chaim would say to hold the lottery again and leave this brother out.

To their surprise, Rav Chaim was firm. "Since you were selected via the *goral*, you should be the one to donate the kidney. You won't lose or suffer because of it," added Rav Chaim. "This will be to your benefit." The brother reiterated his fear of the procedure, but Rav Chaim persisted, saying, "You need to have the surgery and it will be good for your health."

On Sunday, 22 Kislev 5775, the brother lay in one room of Beilinson Hospital, while his sister lay in an adjacent one. He was going to be saving her life.

After removing his kidney, the doctors were shocked to find a malignant growth underneath, with metastasis to the pancreas. The doctors said that they would not have been able to identify the growth without removing the kidney. If some more time had passed, the growth would have expanded and posed a serious threat to the young man's life.

The brother had undergone the procedure to save his sister's life, but had, instead, saved his own.

Because of the growth, the kidney of the younger brother could not be used for the sister. Thus, a lottery of the remaining brothers was once again drawn by Rav Chaim and one of them was chosen.

As an addendum to this story, it is interesting to note the following regarding *emunas chachamim*.

Rav Yitzchak Zilberstein, Rav Chaim's brother-in-law, related that he was once learning with Rav Chaim, when there was a knock on the door. Rebbetzin Batsheva Kanievsky opened the door to find a harried *yungerman*, who muttered something about having an urgent *shailah* for the rav. The rebbetzin ushered in the *yungerman*. The man told Rav Chaim that his wife was in critical condition. A particular treatment had been recommended by her doctors, who claimed that the treatment must be done; otherwise, her life would be in serious danger. The woman had told the doctors that she would not consent to the treatment until she received the approval of Rav Chaim.

After hearing the details, Rav Chaim dismissed the doctors' claims. "She does not need the treatment," he said simply. "Everything will be O.K., *b'ezras Hashem.*"

One of the people in the room mustered the courage to ask Rav Chaim what everyone else was wondering: "We're not dealing here with doctors who don't know what they are talking about," he said. "If a doctor says that there is an urgent need to perform a certain treatment, how can the rav rule for the woman not to listen to their recommendation?"

Rav Chaim waved his hand once more and repeated, "Everything will be all right, *b'ezras Hashem.*"

The *yungerman* left the house satisfied, fully accepting the advice he had been given by Rav Chaim. Those who remained behind were still looking for answers. One of them again articulated the question: How come Rav Chaim felt comfortable dismissing what seemed to be the expert advice of experienced physicians?

Rav Chaim turned to the questioners and said, "Of course, the doctors know what they are talking about. They don't recommend such things without reason. In general, they direct a patient to a course of treatment that is appropriate and necessary. However, in this case, by sending her husband to ask a *shailah*, this woman demonstrated that, in her mind, there is something more significant than the views of the doctors. It is this very act — her submission to *emunas chachamim* — that is the deciding factor.

"By demonstrating this belief, she is no longer under the control of conventional medicine and the knowledge of the doctors; she has entrusted her well-being elsewhere. Accordingly, she has the power to nullify the natural medical channels followed by other people and adhere to a completely different approach."

Majority Rules

A childless couple was at their wits' end in their mission to have children of their own. It seemed like there was no natural way that was going to work. They certainly had tried everything known to medicine.

Finally, they approached the Klausenberger Rebbe for a *berachah*. The Rebbe said, "The halachah is that we follow the majority. Our Sages say in *Yevamos* 119a that most women give birth. *Shoin!* If that's the case, then, please, Hashem, let it be so."

And so it was.

Hashem Will Care for the Children

The Chasam Sofer used to learn the sefer Chovos HaLevavos of Rabbeinu Bachya with his talmidim. Some people felt that it was beneath the Chasam Sofer's dignity to be teaching such a text — which speaks about recognizing the Omnipotence of G-d and discusses topics that were seemingly obvious to someone of the Chasam Sofer's stature — but others recognized that this was actually a sign of his greatness.

> *Some say that he was zocheh to have many generations of descendants who carried on his legacy because he gave of himself so completely for the sake of his generation. He worked to see to it that every community had a rav, and wherever there was no yeshivah, he founded one. He fought against every breach in observance and dispatched messengers on his behalf to intervene on every issue of concern.*

The *gaavad* of Pressburg, Rav Simchah Bunim Schreiber Sofer, a direct descendant of the Chasam Sofer, related the following. One time, the Chasam Sofer seemed despondent, and one of his *talmidim* asked him what was wrong. He answered that he was so busy dealing with communal matters that he had no time for his own children. In response, his *talmid* shared with him a *vort* on the *pasuk* (*Tehillim* 37:26) that states, "All day long he is gracious and lends, and his offspring will be blessed." This *pasuk* can mean that if a person is gracious and gives up his own day for others, then Hashem promises him that his children will be blessed. The Chasam Sofer was pleased by the *vort*, and that Shabbos he repeated it publicly, quoting his *talmid*.

The Chasam Sofer then added a thought of his own: The Torah (*Devarim* 7:14) says, "There will be no barren male or barren female among you." The Gemara (*Bechoros* 44b) explains that this is a promise that a teacher of Torah who teaches for the sake of Heaven will not be "barren" of *talmidim*. This can also be applied to the *pasuk* in *Shemos* (23:26), which states, "There will be no woman who loses her children or is barren in your land; I will fill the number of your days."

However, when a person has many *talmidim*, he will not have time to pay attention to his own children, since he will be forced to spend his days tending to others. The Chasam Sofer explained that the end of the *pasuk* from *Shemos*, "I will fill the number of your days," addresses this concern: Hashem promises, as it were, that He will "fill in" for the days when one must give to others. In other words, Hashem Himself will care for the children of the man who spends his days serving others, seeing to it that his children will be a source of blessing.

A lesson, and a source of chizuk, in caring and devoting time for others.

Late Arrival

It was a half-hour after midnight and the waiters and workers of Lake Terrace Hall in Lakewood were almost finished cleaning up from the Goldstein-Munk wedding. It had been a truly uplifting *simchah*, celebrating a *shidduch* of "*invei hagefen b'invei hagefen* — grapes of the vine with grapes of the vine," i.e., a combination of two like-minded individuals from wonderful stock (*Pesachim* 49a). The *mechutanim* were gathering their belongings in the lobby when someone mentioned that a car was pulling up outside.

"That's strange," one person commented. The wedding was long over. There are always latecomers, but this late?

The onlookers figured that it must be some workers arriving for the final cleanup of the hall. But then they saw a black-hatted individual emerge from the vehicle. The person appeared to be a rabbinic figure.

As the guest made his way up the wedding-hall steps, the *mechutanim* took note that it was none other than Rav Dovid Schustal, rosh yeshivah of Beth Medrash Govoha. It was 12:30 a.m., but he had made it to the wedding.

Upon entering the hall, Rav Schustal, with his characteristic warmth and ebullience, wished the *baalei simchah* mazel tov. Noting their wonderment regarding his early-morning arrival, Rav Schustal explained that the wedding had been marked on his calendar, but numerous pressing issues had arisen throughout the course of the night. First one person needed the rosh yeshivah's assistance. Then a *bachur* had come to him for help. Then a third issue of urgency had been brought to his attention. And so it went, hour after hour, until before he knew it, the night had passed.

We would say that the rosh yeshivah had every "excuse" to call it a night and chalk up his absence to a hectic schedule that he could not have foreseen. But Rav Schustal wasn't looking for excuses. He genuinely wanted to participate in the *simchah*. So, despite the late hour, he had headed for Oak Street to participate in the wedding.

With his eyes shining and with the exuberance of a *bachur*, Rav Schustal took the hands of the *mechutanim*, Reb Daniel Goldstein and Reb Ezriel Munk, and began a spontaneous dance in the lobby of Lake Terrace Hall. A person looking at a snapshot of the spirited *rekidah* would never have known the time of day or the fact that there weren't hundreds of other celebrants dancing around this intimate circle led by the rosh yeshivah.

Upon concluding the dance, Rav Schustal wished the *baalei sim-*

chah a heartfelt mazel tov and, still radiating joy and happiness, headed back out into the winter cold, leaving behind the warmth of his gesture for a stunned *chassan* and *kallah* to cherish.

The Loan

During the period in which Rav Naftuli Tzvi (Naftulche) Halberstam served as *s'gan nasi* of the Bobover institutions led by his father, the Bobover Rebbe, Rav Shlomo, the Bobover *mosdos* faced a serious deficit. Since the burden of coming up with the funds fell squarely on the shoulders of Rav Naftulche, he was constantly seeking ways to procure the money.

As he went over his options in the Bobover offices one day, someone suggested that he ask Mrs. Bochner of Bochner's Grocery in Boro Park for a loan. Mrs. Bochner was known as an outstanding *baalas chesed* who would help anyone she could. Rav Naftulche explained that he had just recently taken a large loan from Mrs. Bochner and did not feel comfortable approaching her again so soon.

Rav Naftulche was still analyzing the possibilities when a man walked into the office looking distressed. Rav Naftulche went over to him and the man whispered something into Rav Naftulche's ear.

"How much?" asked Rav Naftulche.

"$4,000," the man told him.

"Wait here, please," said Rav Naftulche, as he headed for the door. "I'll be right back."

Without hesitation, Rav Naftulche headed straight to Bochner's Grocery to ask Mrs. Bochner for a loan to help this Yid. She happily gave Rav Naftulche the money for the loan, which he handed to the very relieved man as soon as he returned to the office.

Rav Naftulche wouldn't trouble a previous donor for his own mosdos, but to help another Yid he had no qualms.

Rav Naftulche possessed the rare trait of a genuine leader: putting the welfare of others before one's own well-being and even the interests of the public institutions under one's auspices.

For Another's Benefit

A *talmid* once approached Rav Tuvia Goldstein, rosh yeshivah of Yeshiva Emek Halachah, for advice. The man had been told that his newborn son was blind, and the doctors wished to perform a procedure in an attempt to enable him to see. Rav Tuvia told his *talmid* to wait a few months and that no medical intervention should be pursued in the interim.

After the passage of a short amount of time, the baby's parents noticed signs indicating that their child was able to see. During an examination about a month later, the doctors confirmed that the child's vision was within normal range.

The father returned to Rav Tuvia to inform him of the good news.

"I have been davening for your son every day in the *berachah* of *Refa'einu*," said Rav Tuvia humbly. He then added, "I am personally of the opinion that one should not add a *tefillah* to the *berachah* of *Refa'einu*. However, after hearing of your predicament and seeing your pain, I decided to rely on those who permit doing so."

Rav Tuvia was the consummate posek, whose every move, down to the smallest detail, was governed by halachah. On his exalted level, relying on a divergent opinion to insert a tefillah in a berachah in Shemoneh Esrei was perhaps a sacrifice, but if it was for the benefit of another, he allowed the divergent opinion to prevail.

A Taste of Hadrachah

Indispensable Images

Rav Chaim Leib Epstein, rosh yeshivah of Yeshivah Zichron Meilech in Brooklyn, kept several items on the desk in his home, including small placards with *maamarei Chazal* and two pictures. Each summer, as he headed to Camp Toras Chesed in the Catskills, Rav Chaim would ask his son to take along the two photos from his desk.

Why did the great rosh yeshivah need these two photos as he continued learning and teaching in the mountains? What was so important about them?

When asked about it, Rav Chaim explained: "One photo is of my rebbi, Rav Aharon Kotler, speaking to his rebbi, Rav Baruch Ber Leibowitz." This famous photo shows Rav Aharon with Rav Baruch Ber on dacha (vacation) in a forest environment. The reverence with which Rav Aharon is speaking to his rebbi is almost tangible in the still photo.

"At all times, I wish to have in front of me the image of the way my rebbi spoke to his rebbi, so that as a *talmid*, I will know how I am to revere my rebbi, Rav Aharon, even though he is no longer with us," explained Rav Chaim.

"The second photo," the rosh yeshivah continued, "shows young children in the Warsaw Ghetto learning Torah. This picture is a reminder that no matter where one is, and no matter what the circumstances, there is never a legitimate reason not to be engrossed in *limud haTorah*."

*Rav Chaim, as was his wont, saw depth, insight, and profundity
where they are so easily missed or ignored by others. Furthermore, we
see that despite having already reached heights in Torah and gadlus, Rav
Chaim was constantly working toward further perfection and aliyah.*

You Don't Remove the Wheels

Rav Binyamin Kamenetsky, rosh yeshivah of Yeshivas Toras
Chaim of South Shore and eldest son of Rav Yaakov Kamenetsky (rosh yeshivah of Yeshiva Torah Vodaath), shared a story
that took place in the United States not long after his marriage.

"We lived in Brooklyn, and there was a grocery store near our
home owned by a Mr. Epstein, a *shomer Shabbos Yid*," Rav Binyamin
related. "One day, my rebbetzin was doing some grocery shopping
when she heard an elderly woman in the store talking Yiddish with
the identifiable accent of a Tzitavianer."

Tzitavian was a small Lithuanian town where Rav Yaakov had
served as rav.

Rebbetzin Tzirel Kamenetsky approached the woman, who told
her that she was the mother-in-law of the storeowner.

"My rebbetzin," continued Rav Binyamin, "asked her from where
she hailed. Sure enough, she answered, 'Tzitavian.' When my wife
informed her that I, too, was from Tzitavian and that I was the rav's
son, she exclaimed, '*Voz redt ihr*?! What are you saying?!' She was
so excited that she came by later with an entire stack of letters and
notes that she had received from my father."

As he looked through the letters, Rav Binyamin noticed that they
were thank-you notes written by his father, Rav Yaakov, in appreciation for small donations Mrs. Epstein had made to various communal institutions, such as the mikveh, the shul, and the upkeep of
the rav's home.

There was one particularly fascinating letter. Apparently, the
woman had informed Rav Yaakov that her parnassah was not what
it used to be, and she was unable to donate her regular sums of

money. Rav Yaakov replied in the letter with a *mashal* from the Dubno Maggid:

> *There was once a wagon driver who lived in a small town. He would frequently travel to the big city to purchase food supplies, such as flour and sugar. Once, before Pesach, he was transporting a large shipment and the wagon got stuck. All efforts to extricate the wagon from the mud were fruitless. It simply would not budge. There was no other way but to lighten the load. The simple wagon driver, however, did not want to sacrifice the precious food cargo. Instead, he decided to remove the heavy iron wheels from the carriage. Incredulous passersby came over and asked, "How can you be so foolish? The first things you remove are the wheels?! How silly! The wagon cannot move without the wheels!"*

Rav Yaakov concluded the letter by stating, "When times are difficult, the first budget cuts that people feel compelled to make is to their *tzedakah* giving. Do they not realize that it is the *tzedakah* that is the most integral component of their success?"

> *The Gemara in Maseches Gittin (7a) teaches: "If a person sees that his provisions are dwindling, he should take from them to give to charity." By acting mercifully toward others, one may bring upon himself the necessary merit for Hashem to act mercifully toward him.*

One More Stroke

An older *bachur* once approached Rav Mendel Kaplan, *maggid shiur* in Chicago and later at Talmudical Yeshiva of Philadelphia, and related that he was having immense difficulties in *shidduchim*. He had been dating for years, with no end in sight. He was ready to give up on ever finding his mate, and was in dire need of emotional support.

Rav Kaplan, who always seemed to have the right response to every question and request, shared a memory.

> *When I was a student at the Grodno Yeshivah, I came down with a painful stomach malady. I consulted with a local physi-*

cian, who was unable to pinpoint the cause of my pain, but he said that perhaps my diet, which consisted of little more than bread and tea, could be causing the pains I was experiencing.

The doctor suggested that I undertake an exercise regimen to help alleviate the discomfort. And so, I began swimming on a regular basis in a local lake.

While swimming one day, I got caught in a current, which began to sweep me away from the shore. I tried desperately to swim toward land, but my efforts were no match to the strong current. The harder I tried to swim, the farther I was drawn in. I did my best to remain calm, knowing that if I flailed or panicked, I would be in even more danger. But it was so difficult. Before long, I felt I couldn't hold out anymore.

I was about to give up when I heard someone yelling, "Keep going! Just one more stroke! You're going to make it! You're almost there! Keep it up!"

"With the encouragement of the onlooker standing on the shore," Rav Kaplan told the *bachur*, "I found the strength needed for one more stroke, and then another, until, slowly but surely, I was out of the current. Before I knew it, I reached dry land."

So often, people need to push just a little further to reach their goal. But in order to find the strength for that next step, they require outside support. An encouraging remark can have powerful results, even saving lives as it helps others arrive at their destination.

Falling From Above

T his parable was first related by Rav Zev Rosenthal to his family just days before his passing, which followed intense suffering. It was retold by Rav Yaakov Feitman.

A man who worked on the 50th floor of a skyscraper was working after hours, and unknowingly became locked inside his office.

When he realized his predicament, he tried to figure out how to get out of there before morning. This was before the cell phone era, and the phones in the office had already been turned off for the day. In addition, the custodial staff and all the others had long gone home. His screaming out the window to pedestrians below went unheeded, so he returned to his desk with an idea.

An executive with a sweet tooth, he had a drawer full of sugary little treats. He tossed his goodies to the street below, thinking that surely someone fortunate enough to find one would look up to discover its source. However, to his chagrin, everyone happily picked up the candies and hurried off. Even dollars thrown to the wind failed to elicit any meaningful attention. Various stationery and desk items did not work either, and desperation was slowly setting in.

Finally, the man took a large, expensive paperweight from his desk and threw it out the window. It narrowly grazed the neck of a passerby, who called the police in his outrage. When the policemen looked up, they immediately understood why the tiny figure was flailing his arms so wildly.

> *Rav Rosenthal taught his family a practical lesson: Our merciful, loving Father does so much for us. He hopes that we will recognize His beneficence and act in accordance with His will. When we don't, he gently nudges us, reminding us with increasingly louder messages. Sometimes, though, only when we are in pain do we look up to the One Above and make the changes needed.*

Learning to Be Givers

F or years, several weeks after Succos, many of us were reminded that Chanukah was coming when we received a box of Chanukah candles in the mail, compliments of the Telshe Yeshiva of Cleveland. This half-century-old project involved much time and effort, and helped the yeshivah raise badly needed funds. Rabbi Yitzchok Tzvi

Schwarz shared the following anecdote related to the Telshe Chanukah candles.

In those days, *bachurim* at Telshe in need of pocket money would spend their lunch break packing candles into boxes. The one or two pennies earned per box would accumulate, supplying them with a humble allowance.

One day, the yeshivah's office director, Rav Meyer Zelig Mann, walked into the room where the boys were working and announced that from now on, the yeshivah would not pay for this service. Instead, it would ask for volunteers to do it for free.

One boy, Shmuel, was upset at this loss of income and politely asked for the reason for this new development. Rav Mann said that it was not his decision and suggested that he take the matter up with the rosh yeshivah.

Not being the bashful type, Shmuel approached the rosh yeshivah, Rav Elya Meir Bloch. "I don't understand," he protested. "*Bachurim* have a chance to earn some much-needed money in the candle room, and the rosh yeshivah wants to deprive us of this?"

Rav Elya Meir listened patiently as the *bachur* voiced his gripe. With a feeling of empathy, he answered, "Shmuel, do you really believe that I would begrudge my beloved *talmidim* some extra money?"

The *talmid* was beginning to feel a bit uneasy and was having second thoughts about questioning the rosh yeshivah. But now he was even more curious to know what prompted the change in policy.

"Of late, the yeshivah has not been doing well financially. There are bills to be paid and we are behind in paying the rebbeim's salaries. That is why I traveled to the East Coast to collect the necessary funds. I was hopeful that our old *talmidim* would come through in our time of need and fill the void in our bank account. What can I tell you? I was very disappointed. I returned with much less than expected.

"During the long trip home, I was thinking about how this was possible. Here were *talmidim* whose souls we nurtured with Torah while providing all of their physical needs. How could it be that in our time of need, this kindness was not reciprocated? I came to the conclusion that we taught our *talmidim* how to learn in a yeshivah, how to eat in a yeshivah, and how to board in a yeshivah, but we were lax in teaching them how to give to a yeshivah. We have to teach them how to be givers, not just takers! This is a lesson I want to inculcate in my *talmidim*. Hence, the *bachurim* will voluntarily donate their services to the yeshivah from now on by packing candles — to give to the yeshivah."

The message did not miss its mark. The recipient of the lesson would become Rav Shmuel Kaufman, a dynamo of harbatzas Torah and kiruv rechokim, one of the great pillars of the Detroit Jewish community, and an inspiration to thousands of talmidim and acquaintances.

Breaking the Engagement

R*av Yosef Shalom Elyashiv's chizuk and advice were always penetratingly on the mark, delivered with precision.*

A boy and girl were engaged to be married, but during the engagement, the girl's parents realized that the *chassan* was not the lifelong learner or *masmid* they had hoped for, and they wished to break off the *shidduch*. They presented their dilemma to Rav Elyashiv, who seemed confounded by their question.

"Did you make a *tenai kodem le'maaseh*, a condition prior to their engagement, that the boy has to be of such and such standard?" asked Rav Elyashiv.

The girl's father answered in the negative.

"So then how can you even contemplate breaking off the *shidduch* and embarrassing someone?"

Thus, the masmid of the generation taught a lesson to a father seeking a masmid for his daughter: Basic kavod for another person comes first, no matter what.

Proper Appellation

*R*av Chaim Epstein often commented that he considered it a unique privilege that his yeshivah was located in close proximity to the home of Rav Yosef Rosenblum, rosh yeshivah of Shaarei Yosher in Boro Park.

Rav Chaim once related the following to his *talmidim* in a *shmuess* given during *seudah shelishis*. "I met the rosh yeshivah of Shaarei Yosher on Succos and observed that he was carrying his *esrog* box in a paper bag. I asked Rav Yosef, 'Why are you carrying it in a bag? Why not carry it in your hand?'

"He responded that there are those in the streets who are not from the Jewish community. He was concerned about *hisgarus ba'umos*, antagonizing the nations, and he didn't want to publicly display a religious article while walking in the street, lest it be viewed with disdain by non-Jewish passersby who would feel provoked by it." Rav Chaim went on to share a *mussar* thought based on this story and proceeded with the rest of his thoughts.

About five minutes after concluding his *shmuess*, Rav Chaim began speaking again and the room grew quiet once more. He then referenced the story he had mentioned.

"Just to clarify, when I addressed Rav Rosenblum, I didn't call him by his first name, as it may have sounded from the story. I actually said, 'Rosh yeshivah.' "

Rav Chaim, a senior rosh yeshivah and aged gadol baTorah, felt that it would have shown a lack of respect had he addressed Rav Rosenblum by his first name, rather than as "rosh yeshivah." Thus, although he had already concluded his shmuess minutes earlier, this seemingly minor detail was on his mind, and he stopped to make sure that this point was crystal clear.

Deference to Daas Torah

The following is a story that Rav Chaim Epstein would relate in the name of his rebbi, Rav Aharon Kotler.

There was a charismatic *maggid* whose oratorical skills and deep discourses captivated his audiences and moved his listeners. One of those who were inspired by his *derashos* was Rav Hillel of Grodno, a son-in-law of Rav Chaim Volozhiner and a towering *talmid chacham* in his own right.

Rav Chaim Volozhiner himself was strongly opposed to the *maggid* and his teachings, and he made his feelings known publicly. He had substantial reason to feel that the *maggid* was not the virtuous individual others thought he was. Upon learning that his son-in-law, Rav Hillel, had become a follower of the *maggid*, Rav Chaim dispatched a messenger to Grodno with a paper containing a personal message for him.

Arriving in Grodno, the messenger found Rav Hillel sitting on the floor of the local shul listening to none other than the *maggid* in question. The *maggid* was speaking with great effectiveness, and Rav Hillel was completely involved, tears streaming down his face as he hung onto the powerful words of the master rhetorician.

Rav Hillel's spiritual uplift was interrupted by the messenger, who handed him the note from his father-in-law. Rav Hillel stopped to read the communiqué, in which Rav Chaim Volozhiner made clear that the *maggid* was not a person from whom Rav Hillel should be seeking spiritual direction, and that Rav Chaim had already spoken out against him.

Immediately upon concluding the note, Rav Hillel wiped the tears from his face, composed himself, and stood erect. He turned to the *maggid* and said pointedly, "*Der shver zugt nit tzu redden un ihr redt*? My father-in-law says that you shouldn't speak and yet you still speak?" With that, Rav Hillel walked out of the shul.

That was it. He never sought spiritual enrichment from the maggid again.

His father-in-law had given him a directive and there were no questions asked. The fact that he was benefiting from the maggid was irrelevant in the face of the trenchant words of his father-in-law. Tears wiped away, he moved on. (It was later revealed that the maggid was indeed a charlatan.)

This, Rav Chaim Epstein would explain, was the deference to daas Torah seen in the days of yore. Rav Hillel was from the geonim of Lithuania and could have averred that he had his own view on the matter. But he had no such thought. His emunas chachamim guided him fully.

Time Release

One day, a young Avigdor Miller, who was learning in the Slabodka Yeshivah in Lithuania, came across a young man he had known when they had both studied at Yeshivas Rabbeinu Yitzchak Elchanan several years back. This young man had been a light-headed fellow and a joker, yet here he was, in the Slabodka Yeshivah, a yeshivah reserved for elite students.

When Avigdor went over to the young man and gave him *shalom aleichem,* the *bachur* told him, "Do you remember that day we met in the corridor of the yeshivah in New York? You looked at me and said, 'When will you make something of yourself and take life seriously?' Your words penetrated deeply and shook me up. That was my turning point."

Rav Miller, who later became a rav, mashgiach, and well-known disseminator of Torah, would tell this story to his students and add that if they had an opportunity to influence another person to be better, or even a chance to just say something thought provoking, they should take advantage of the opportunity, even if they're not sure the other person will accept it. "Once it goes down the hatch, it's there," Rav Miller would say. "It may take a week, a month, or even years, but it never leaves the person's brain. One never knows when it will bear fruit."

Taking Vacation

*R*av Yisrael Zev Gustman possessed one of the great Torah minds of his generation. He was just 11 years old when he joined Rav Shimon Shkop's yeshivah in Grodno. His diligence in learning was reflected by the fact that he slept minimally, and during the month of Elul, he would leave the beis midrash only on Fridays.

In his younger years, he would take a Gemara that he had never learned and a blank piece of paper. After learning the Mishnah thoroughly, he would create his own version of the Gemara, Rashi, and Tosafos on the Mishnah. Before comparing it to the actual text in the Gemara, he had already independently devised the means to discern the true objectives of the sugya, thereby growing in his analytical approach to learning. By age 16, he was fluent in Shas Bavli and Yerushalmi.

Over the years, Rav Gustman learned b'chavrusa with some of the greatest gedolim of his time, including Rav Chaim Ozer Grodzensky, who appointed him to the Vilna beis din, as well as the Chazon Ish, Rav Chaim Shmulevitz, Rav Shmuel Rozovsky, Rav Shlomo Heiman, and later Rav Moshe Feinstein and Rav Yitzchak Hutner. The author of the Marcheshes, Rav Chanoch Henoch Eiges, despite his seniority on the Vilna beis din, would stand up for Rav Gustman when he entered the beis din chambers.

From 1979 until 1985, Rabbi Yerucham Silber learned under Rav Gustman at Yeshiva Netzach Yisrael in Yerushalayim. That period changed his life, and to this day, Rabbi Silber remains inspired by the sensitivity and depth of compassion of his rosh yeshivah. The Silbers' youngest son, Yisrael Zev, proudly bears Rav Gustman's name, and Rabbi Silber says Kaddish every year on 28 Sivan, Rav Gustman's yahrtzeit.

When Rabbi Silber got married in 1982, he and his wife settled in Eretz Yisrael. Mrs. Silber had never been to the Holy Land, but she bravely followed her husband as they began their married life there. They arrived during the summer of 1982 and found an apartment in Rechavia, near the yeshivah. Mrs. Silber set out to find work almost immediately in order to support her husband in kollel.

The Silbers' oldest son was born during the summer of 1983. During that *bein hazmanim*, with a newborn in the house, it was not an appropriate time to vacation, so the Silbers stayed put. Throughout the next year, they eagerly anticipated the *bein hazmanim* in the summer of 1984, when Mrs. Silber would take off from work and the Silbers would be able to spend quality time with their young son while touring the country.

Much to their chagrin, Mrs. Silber's boss announced to his entire staff that they would need to take their vacations in July, as he was sponsoring an important international conference during August. Mrs. Silber worked at Hadassah University Medical Center under Professor Rami Rahamimoff, who was co-sponsoring the prestigious conference with Sir Bernard Katz, Nobel Prize-winning biophysicist. Rahamimoff made it clear that he needed all his employees on hand for the event.

That year, *bein hazmanim* fell fully in August, which meant that the Silbers' long-anticipated plans were in jeopardy. The news was upsetting to the Silbers. Mrs. Silber suggested to her husband that he ask his rosh yeshivah, Rav Gustman, for permission to take a week off from yeshivah.

"I don't have the nerve to make such a request from him," Rabbi Silber replied.

Undeterred, Mrs. Silber went to speak to Rav Gustman herself. When she entered his office, she introduced herself as Mrs. Silber.

"No," replied Rav Gustman with a twinkle in his eye. "You are Rabbanit Silber," he said, indicating his immense respect for the fact that she was working to support her husband, who spent his days learning Torah.

She explained the situation to Rav Gustman, relating that though she had never been in Eretz Yisrael before, she came because she knew that her husband could *shteig* there. She shared that she went to work immediately to enable her husband to learn. But now, at their first opportunity after two years to take a vacation, her work schedule precluded them from their long-anticipated tour of the country during *bein hazmanim.*

After listening to her carefully, Rav Gustman called in Rabbi Silber and said to him, "*Yerucham, nem dein veib oif vacation.* Take your wife on vacation. She is entitled."

Rav Gustman asked that Rabbi Silber come back on Thursday for his *shiur* before leaving for the trip.

"Do you need extra money for your trip?" Rav Gustman then asked.

Rabbi Silber replied that he had what he needed.

"O.K.," said the rosh yeshivah. "By the way, there's a very good restaurant in Tzfas where you can go for supper." Rav Gustman provided the details and then wished Rabbi Silber an enjoyable trip.

Rabbi Silber departed from the rosh yeshivah amazed by his thoughtfulness and compassion. Here was Rav Gustman, a phenomenal Torah giant, who understood the mesirus nefesh of the wife of a kollel yungerman and realized that she deserved time away to rejuvenate along with her husband, the ongoing zman notwithstanding.

And the great gaon also knew of a restaurant where he thought the young couple would enjoy a meal!

A Taste of Fortitude

Today's Pain...

A woman from the family of Rav Isaac Sher, the Slabodka rosh yeshivah, once approached him, asking for words of chizuk. She had broken her leg in a fall and the pain was unbearable, affecting her spirit as well.

"Remember the discomfort you experienced," said Rav Isaac, "when you were expecting a child. And remember the excruciating pain during birth. When you remind yourself of that experience, you have happy thoughts, because the child you bore turned out to be a great talmid chacham and a tremendous nachas to you. In comparison to the results, the pain does not even register today."

Continued Rav Isaac, "The agony that you are experiencing right now will also result in happiness. For with every hardship that a person experiences, great spiritual edifices are created. We just don't see them. But we must believe they exist. And if you believe, you will be able to withstand the hardship of these days."

Such appropriate words for these most troubling times. Today's pain will bring tomorrow's prize.

How to Achieve Success

A bachur once approached Rav Moshe Yehudah Schneider to ask for a *berachah* before his wedding. Rav Schneider asked him what *berachah* he wanted. The boy responded that he would like a blessing that everything should go smoothly in his life and that he should have no difficulties. Rav Schneider said that that is not a *berachah*.

Instead, he blessed the *chassan* that when faced with challenging situations, he should have the ability to overcome them successfully. He explained that living a tranquil existence is not an ideal; something attained effortlessly has little value. It is only by surmounting difficulties that we achieve success.

Grabbing the Opportunity

When Mattis was 9 years old, he was not exceptionally smart, to put it mildly. It took him such a long time to catch onto things that his family members and peers would become upset and frustrated with him, sometimes making sharp comments. "You're a fool," they would tell him. "You have no *seichel*."

Despite his other shortcomings, Mattis had exceptional *middos*, so he didn't respond to their comments. He just remained quiet. However, at one point, something seemed to have changed. When the boy was insulted by others, he would mumble under his breath.

His father was concerned. After he saw this happening a few times, he asked Mattis what was going on. Mattis replied that the insults of others at home and in school had always bothered him. Then, one day in shul, he opened the *sefer Aleinu LeShabei'ach* by Rav Yitzchak Zilberstein. There he read the following story:

> *A couple was married for 24 years, but did not have any children. After trying whatever they could from a medical standpoint, the woman went to Rav Chaim Kanievsky and told him of her challenging circumstances. Rav Chaim told her that she should seek out someone who fulfills the qualifications of "hane'elavin v'einan olvin — those who are insulted and do not insult back" (Yoma 23a); such a person, he explained, has incredible powers, and she should get a blessing from that person.*

The woman went on a long search. When she witnessed an exchange in which a person was shamed but did not respond, she knew she finally had found the one she was looking for. She immediately approached the person who had been humiliated and asked her for a berachah.

A short while later, the woman was blessed with a child.

Mattis said that reading this story transformed him. Instead of feeling bad when he was insulted, he suddenly became filled with happiness. *I'm insulted constantly*, Mattis said to himself. *This means that I'm constantly being filled with holiness and being given the opportunity to have my blessings fulfilled!*

Suddenly, Mattis viewed every insult as a huge opportunity. He had a problem, though: No one was coming to him for blessings. "These opportunities are getting lost," he said.

He decided to take action. He searched in shul for notices containing names of sick people. He also looked through the newspaper for similar announcements. He studied all the names until he knew them by heart — no easy task for a boy who was not blessed with a strong intellect.

He then waited until someone insulted him, whereupon he would pray for all those whose names he had memorized.

Who knows how many yeshuos this young boy has brought about?

— heard from Rabbi Dov Brezak

Cellular Humiliation

On 25 Teves, 5773/2013, Rav Asher Zelig Rubenstein, rosh yeshivah of Yeshivas Toras Simchah in Yerushalayim and talmid muvhak of Rav Chatzkel Levenstein, was niftar at the age of 71. Rav Rubenstein knew how to mold bnei Torah and how to influence others with sensitivity. He left a legacy of gadlus in Torah and middos.

During the week of *shivah*, a man entered the Rubenstein home, and from his expression it was clear that he had something to share. This is the story he related to the family:

> A well-known rosh kollel in Yerushalayim was going to be delivering a shiur at his own kollel, and your father, Rav Asher, had received permission to attend as a guest. One of the ordinances of this kollel was that no cell phones were allowed, and the rule was strictly enforced.
>
> During the shiur that Rav Asher attended, a cell phone began ringing. The rosh kollel was visibly disturbed, and he paused for a moment before resuming the shiur. A short while later, the cell phone began ringing again. Apparently, the owner of the phone was too embarrassed to reach into his pocket and turn it off, so it rang a few times and then stopped. This time, the rosh kollel not only paused, but also expressed his displeasure regarding the lack of k'vod haTorah. After a few moments, he resumed the shiur. A short while later, the phone rang again. This time, the rosh kollel closed his sefer and declared, "If the avreichim in the kollel cannot follow rules, I will close the kollel!" Clearly frustrated, the rosh kollel began to walk out.
>
> Immediately, Rav Asher stood up. "I apologize," he told the rosh kollel, and said something about needing to be contacted by someone. "It was my fault. It will not happen again. Please do not close the kollel." With that, Rav Asher, enduring great embarrassment for the invidious disturbance, headed for the exit. With the source of trouble removed, the rosh kollel, somewhat mollified, returned to his shtender and continued with his shiur.

The visitor concluded, "Look how great your father was! He subjected himself to public shame for the sake of Torah. He could not bear to see the rosh kollel halt the *shiur* or for the kollel's future to be threatened."

The visitor departed.

Two hours later, a *yungerman* arrived at the Rubenstein home to be *menachem avel*. He, too, related this story, but he added: "The cell phone was not your father's. It was mine! I was the owner of the ringing cell phone. I was too ashamed to stand up and take responsibility. Your father, in his greatness, was willing to take on the *bizyonos*. He did not feel it beneath himself to publicly accept the blame for something he did not do, as long as the *shiur* — and the kollel — would continue."

Rav Asher emulated Shmuel HaKatan, as recounted in the Gemara in *Maseches Sanhedrin* (11a).

> *Rabban Gamliel would convene a court to proclaim a leap year and the court would meet in a specific attic. Rabban Gamliel gave instructions that seven judges should awaken early in the morning and come to the attic. In the morning, when Rabban Gamliel arrived, he found eight judges instead of seven. He proclaimed, "Whoever came here without permission should exit."*
>
> *Shmuel HaKatan stood up and said, "I am the one who ascended without permission, but I did not come to add a month to the year as the others did. I wish to learn the halachos of how to extend the year, so I came to observe the proceedings." Rabban Gamliel told Shmuel HaKatan, "Sit, my son, sit. It would be worthy for each leap year to be extended by you, but the Chachamim said that we add a month to the year only with judges specifically designated for that purpose." Since Shmuel HaKatan said that he hadn't been explicitly designated, he could not participate.*
>
> *The Gemara then relates that it was not really Shmuel HaKatan who went to that attic without permission, but a different person. It was only because of the humiliation that the undesignated person would have suffered that Shmuel HaKatan falsely admitted to arriving without authorization.*

Many centuries after this incident recorded in the Gemara, Rav Rubenstein demonstrated the same strength of character, taking the blame and earning disgrace, when he had, in fact, done nothing objectionable.

> *Upon pondering this story, I had two observations. First, at the time of the incident, Rav Rubenstein had no way of knowing that the truth would ever emerge. For all he knew, it would forever be thought by those who heard of the incident that Rav Rubenstein had allowed his cell phone to disturb the shiur not*

once, but three times, leading to the rosh kollel's stinging response.

Furthermore, even after the truth emerged, there was no way of knowing whether all the people present at that shiur were aware of what truly occurred. It is possible that every single one of them, to this day, maintains the image of Rav Rubenstein walking out, cowering in shame for allowing "his" cell phone to create such a scene.

But to Rav Rubenstein, that mattered little. What mattered was saving someone else from shame and ensuring that a shiur would resume.

Never Too Late

Rav Avigdor Miller was the rav of Bais Yisroel Torah Center, mashgiach in Yeshivas Rabbeinu Chaim Berlin, and a popular author, lecturer, and disseminator of Torah. Unquestionably, his accomplishments were remarkable.

I was fortunate to grow up just blocks from his shul and to pass him on his regular walks down Kings Highway in Flatbush, Brooklyn, and I found the following tidbits about Rav Miller's life to be even more inspiring than what he actually accomplished:

Rav Miller was 57 years old when he wrote his first book.

He was almost 60 years old when he began teaching his congregants Gemara. He was 65 when his first tapes began to spread throughout the Jewish world.

His greatest accomplishments took place when he was in his 60's, 70's, and 80's, and he continued to influence the world until his passing at the age of 93. Perhaps one can say that he spent his first 50-plus years preparing for his last 40.

Rav Miller reached his 93rd birthday brimming with plans to publish more *sefarim*. Just a month or so before his *petirah*, he published the final *sefer* of his commentary on *Chumash*. At the time, he was preparing three volumes on the Aggados of *Shas*. He was working on three volumes on the Holocaust. He had prepared outlines to finish his history series. He had taped *shiurim* on *Shaarei Teshuvah, Mesillas Yesharim, Chovos HaLevavos,* and *Pirkei Avos,* which he was considering putting into written form, including 83 90-minute tapes of *shiurim* he had given on *Mesillas Yesharim.* He had 49 tapes on *Perek Cheilek* of *Maseches Sanhedrin.* When he davened, he always asked Hashem to give him more years so that he could continue to disseminate Torah and inspiration for Torah living to the public.

People often remark that they are "over the hill." Some look at the ages of 50, 60, and 70 as benchmarks, dividing the young and the old. Rav Miller showed us that one is never too old to make a colossal impact on others, one at a time and on a community as a whole.

Forgiven

Rav Avrohom Pam often spoke about "simple" greatness, stating that one must be vigilant never to speak negatively about *any person or act disrespectfully to anyone, because one never knows a person's true value and accomplishments. He illustrated this by relating the following incident.*

When Rav Pam was a young boy in Brownsville, a poor widow performed household chores for his mother in their home. This widow worked for other families of rabbanim in the neighborhood, as well, and over a lengthy period, she saved up $100, a small fortune at that time.

One day, a friend of hers, who was also a widow, asked her for a loan. The housekeeper took the money she had saved up over years of penny-pinching and lent it to this woman. A short time later, the borrower died, leaving no children or assets.

The money that had been lent was gone.

Upon arriving at the woman's funeral, Rav Pam's mother saw her housekeeper trailing the casket, softly mouthing words as she followed the procession. When she moved closer, she heard the housekeeper uttering, "*Ich bin dir mochel! Ich bin dir mochel!* [I forgive you! I forgive you!]"

Realizing that the debt would never be paid, the housekeeper did not want her departed friend to suffer in the next world on her account.

When Rav Pam's mother observed this outstanding act of nobility, conduct befitting a tzaddik or a tzaddeikes, she realized that this housekeeper was not a simple woman at all. To completely forgive such a large sum of money, which had been collected over years of self-deprivation, displayed genuine greatness.

— heard from Rabbi Sholom Smith

A Taste *of* Ethics

Better Not to Run

Rav Naftali Friedler, rosh yeshivah of Yeshivas Ner Yisroel in Toronto, was once walking with his rebbi, Rav Eliyahu Eliezer Dessler. They were at the 184th Street train station in Washington Heights, New York, heading for the A train going downtown. When they were at the top of the steps just above the subway platform, they noticed the train pulling into the station at the bottom of the steps. Rav Friedler started to rush down, expecting Rav Dessler to follow him.

Rav Dessler stopped Rav Friedler and explained that this is not the proper way, as one has to be in constant control of oneself.

"If one rushes, one can lose control," said Rav Dessler. "It is better to go at a regular pace than to run, even if it means missing the train."

They walked down and missed the train — but they were in complete control.

A Visit of Gratitude

The son of Rav Shalom Eisen, a *dayan* in Yerushalayim, was going to be celebrating his bar mitzvah, so Rav Shalom brought the boy to his rebbi, Rav Isser Zalman Meltzer, rosh yeshivah of Yeshivas Eitz Chaim, for a *berachah*. During the visit, Rav Eisen also intended to stress that Rav Isser Zalman should not burden himself to make the trek to the Eisen home that Shabbos for the Kiddush in honor of the *simchah*.

Rav Isser Zalman greeted the bar mitzvah *bachur* warmly and gave him a heartfelt *berachah* in honor of the upcoming milestone. He also thanked Rav Eisen for his sensitivity and understanding in not wanting to trouble him to come to the Kiddush.

That Shabbos, many well-wishers made their way up several flights to the Eisen home to wish mazel tov to the bar mitzvah *bachur* and his illustrious family. Then, in the middle of the celebration, the crowd grew quiet; a special guest had arrived, none other than Rav Isser Zalman.

Rav Eisen welcomed his rebbi and arranged a seat for him. He was honored that Rav Isser Zalman had decided to personally partake in the Kiddush, but he felt bad that the great *gaon* had strained himself, walking all the way from his home and then up the many steps to the Eisen home, to do so.

"Let me explain why I decided to come," Rav Isser Zalman said. "After you visited my home the other day with the bar mitzvah *bachur*, I thought to myself that it seems like just yesterday that I served as *sandak* at your son's *bris*. I began to think about how time flies! I pondered my own life and how soon my years will be up, and it will be time for me to face the Heavenly Court. I realized that I must perform an accounting of my life and make improvements where necessary.

"Since your visit triggered these thoughts of *teshuvah*, I owe you immense gratitude. It is out of this sense of *hakaras hatov* that I came to participate in your *simchah* in person."

Valuing Life — and Money

Rav Yitzchak Zilberstein, in his *sefer U'Firyo Matok*, relates a story about a religious Jewish man who was waiting for a subway train in New York City when he suddenly felt unwell, lost his balance, and fell onto the tracks. He was not able to get up and pull himself off the tracks, and although a train was due in the station very soon, not one person in that entire station offered to help this unfortunate Jew.

Soon, however, a man who was waiting on another train in the station heard all the noise and realized that something was going on. "What's the ruckus about?" he asked. People told him that someone had fallen onto the tracks. Without a moment's hesitation, the fellow jumped up from his seat, got off the train, ran over to the tracks, jumped down, pulled the man up, jumped back onto the platform, and ran back to his seat, where he continued waiting for his train to depart.

Onlookers were stunned by this man's behavior. In an instant, he had become the new American hero by risking his life and jumping onto the train tracks to save a fellow human being. But the strangest part of his behavior was that after his heroic rescue operation, he simply returned to his seat on the train and sat down nonchalantly, as if nothing had happened, as if he hadn't done anything noteworthy.

People asked him why he wasn't excited or at all emotional about what he had done.

"Listen here," he replied. "I work in a restaurant washing dishes and I earn $10 an hour. I'm on my way to work now. When I heard that the trains were stopped because someone fell onto the tracks, I realized that if this fellow were to get run over and killed, they would close down this whole station for at least five hours and there would be no trains running at all. That means that I would lose five hours of work. Five times 10 is 50. I'd have lost $50!

"Are you going to pay me the $50 I'd be losing? I doubt it! I knew I had to get up and save that fellow so I could get to work on time and I wouldn't lose any money."

> When relating this story, Rabbi Dov Brezak observed that when we hear the savior's motive and see how little he — along with all the others in the subway station — valued human life, we can appreciate the meaning of the words we say in davening (U'Va LeTzion), "Baruch Hu Elokeinu shebera'anu lichvodo v'hivdilanu min hato'im — Blessed is He, our G-d, Who created us for His glory, and separated us from those who stray."

Punctiliousness Personified

*R*av Yehuda Schwab of Monsey was similar to his illustrious father, Rav Mordechai Menachem Schwab, mashgiach in Mesivta Beth Shraga, in many ways. However, chief among the similarities were their attributes of humility and self-effacement.

Rav Yehuda taught many lessons in middos tovos and general hanhagas hachaim just by the way he carried himself and communicated with others. I recall one incident in which I personally witnessed his greatness. My wife gave birth to our second child, a boy, a week before Pesach, leaving us scrambling to figure out how and where we would hold a bris on Chol HaMoed Pesach, with a "diverse" menu of matzah, cream cheese, yogurt, and seltzer. It was Rav Yehuda and his devoted rebbetzin who offered to host the bris in their basement.

I don't think I will ever forget the image of Rav Yehuda, who was very sick and weak at the time, smiling as he schlepped tables to help us set up the room, and telling us not to worry about the inevitable mess and inconvenience.

The following story was related by Reb Aron Aderet, who grew up on Locust Hollow Drive, around the corner from Rav Yehuda.

At Aron's bar mitzvah, Rav Yehuda approached the head table holding a small wrapped box. With a big smile, he asked the bar mitzvah *bachur* if he could guess what it contained.

"An *esrog* box," replied Aron.

"No," said Rav Yehuda. "It's a set of HaMaor *Chumashim*."

"So small?" replied the bar mitzvah *bachur* innocently.

Rav Yehuda grinned. "You know what? I'll get you a big one for your *chasunah*."

A decade passed and the exchange was all but forgotten by the *bachur*. Then, on the Erev Shabbos of Aron's *aufruf*, Rav Yehuda pulled up in his car in front of the Aderet home. Since he was already ill, he asked the *chassan* to come out to his car, where he presented a stunned Aron with a large box.

He hadn't forgotten.

"I promised it to you at your bar mitzvah," said Rav Yehuda, pointing to the large set of *Chumashim*, "so here it is."

Rav Yehuda then showed Aron a letter he had written to his son, Yitzie, while in Atlanta, Georgia, where Rav Yehuda had undergone surgery several years prior. The letter read:

> *Dear Yitzie,*
>
> *I don't know if I'm going to live much longer and I wanted to ask you for a favor. I have no debts in this world except for one, and that is to Aron Aderet. At his bar mitzvah, I promised him a set of Chumashim for his chasunah. The set has been up in your closet ever since. I don't want to come up to Shamayim with any chovos, so please deliver the Chumashim to him immediately upon my petirah.*

Rav Yehuda gave Aron a hug and said into his ear, "How good is the Ribono Shel Olam that He gave me more years to live."

Aron asked Rav Yehuda if he could keep the precious letter.

Rav Yehuda demurred. "I'm going to take it with me to the *Olam HaEmes*," he answered with a smile.

Signed With Tears

*I*n 1951, the Israeli government passed legislation to draft women into its army, causing much apprehension within the frum community. The rabbanim in Yerushalayim and Bnei Brak issued a ruling stating that under no circumstances should any frum girl join the army.

A committee of Torah leaders, among them Rav Zelig Reuven Bengis, then the rav of the Eidah HaChareidis of Yerushalayim, immediately penned a letter to the government to protest the proposed draft. The letter was sent to various leading rabbanim for their signatures. Afterward, it was returned to Rav Bengis, who had not yet signed it.

As he was getting ready to sign the letter, Rav Bengis reviewed the page. All of a sudden, he put down his pen, closed his eyes, and sat silently in concentration. Several minutes later, he heaved a sigh and his eyes filled with tears. Then he lifted his pen and signed the letter carefully.

"Why did the rav have to re-evaluate whether to sign the letter?" someone standing nearby asked him. "Wasn't he involved in formulating the letter in the first place?"

"Yes, I was," responded Rav Bengis, "but I just reread the letter and noticed that someone had added the phrase 'hachosmim b'dimah — those who sign with tears.' Until now, I had not shed tears over this state of affairs. I could not sign the letter under false pretenses, so I sat down to ponder the dreadful reality of girls being forced to serve in the army. When tears came to my eyes, I was able to sign."

Rav Bengis was known for his tremendous diligence in Torah learning and his incredible brilliance. But his Torah learning was not just in the intellectual realm. He had integrated it into his very personality to the point that he could not possibly attach his name to a document unless he fully meant every word.

Greater Pleasure Above

Rav Gamliel Rabinovich, rosh yeshivah of the yeshivah in Kishinev, authored a comprehensive *sefer* on the entire commentary of the *Pri Megadim*. The reason no one reading this story has ever seen that *sefer* is because it was never published. Rav Rabinovich's manuscript was destroyed in a large conflagration that consumed his home.

His son, Rav Levi Rabinovich, related that his father was initially tormented by this personal loss. He had spent an untold number of hours authoring his work, and apparently it had all been for naught. But then Rav Rabinovich regained his composure and remarked, "If this is Hashem's will, then I accept it with a full heart and with love, because, in truth, the entire purpose of writing the *sefer* was only to create a *nachas ruach* for the Ribono Shel Olam."

From that moment on, Rav Rabinovich never uttered another word about his frustration in losing the manuscript.

> *His grandson who carries his name, Rav Gamliel Rabinovich, remarked that perhaps his grandfather's humble and quiet acceptance of this Heavenly decree actually created greater pleasure for the Ribono Shel Olam than the entire sefer he had written.*
>
> *Rav Levi Rabinovich, whose sefer Maadanei HaShulchan has seen widespread acceptance and immense popularity across the Torah world, attributed the success of his own sefer to the merit of his father's reaction to his personal nisayon with equanimity.*
>
> *Thus, while the senior Rav Gamliel Rabinovich never saw the publication of his own chiddushei Torah, he merited witnessing, from Above, his son's sefer gracing the shelves of batei midrash and homes across the globe.*

Life Lessons

Rav Zelik Epstein, rosh yeshivah of Yeshivah Shaar Hatorah in Kew Gardens, New York, was an individual whose immersion in Torah was unrelenting and uncompromised. When spending the summers in Camp Ohr Shraga, Rav Zelik would become so engrossed in his learning that he'd be shocked to find a large crowd standing around him ready to begin davening at his private *minyan*.

On one occasion in camp, he planned to end his *shiur* as soon as a scheduled fire drill had begun, yet he continued delivering the *shiur* right through the fire alarm, completely oblivious to the sound. He later remarked to his rebbetzin that the drill must have been postponed. "Not only didn't I hear the alarm, but the *bachurim* didn't hear it either," he said.

Rav Zelik offered a parable to demonstrate the role that To-rah should play in our lives. There were two apartment buildings: one run by the owner of the building and one run by a hired superintendent. The owner and superintendent were both very knowledgeable in the makeup and maintenance of their respective buildings. From the backgrounds of their tenants to the electric wiring, plumbing, and rental payments, the owner and hired superintendent knew it all.

The difference between the two was discerned when each of the buildings required maintenance. The superintendent tended to the repairs as he did his other responsibilities, while the owner displayed a sense of urgency and was bothered that his very own building needed fixing.

"*Es iz nit genug tzu zein nahr shomrim oif der Torah,*" Rav Zelik would say by way of a *nimshal*. "*Mir darf zein baalei batim oif der Torah.* It is not sufficient to be superintendents over the Torah. We need to be owners of the Torah." Knowledge of Torah is not enough. We need to have a sense of urgency and genuine concern for the Torah. Torah is, and must remain, the core of our lives.

Before leaving to yeshivah in Eretz Yisrael, Dovid Steinberg, Rav Zelik's *talmid*, asked Rav Zelik if he could recommend a particular *gadol baTorah* to visit. Rav Zelik responded that he should focus on what he is learning in yeshivah.

"But this is a once-in-a-lifetime opportunity, a chance for me to visit these *gedolim*, and certainly the rosh yeshivah could send me to one of them," the *talmid* persisted.

Rav Zelik responded with a smile, but with his typical sharpness. "If you will be busy with 'once-in-a-lifetime' opportunities, *vuss vet zein mit der leben*? What will be with the main point of life?"

At Rav Zelik's levayah, his son, Rav Kalman, related that his father would tell him that at the end of one's life, one will not be certain if all the Torah he learned found favor before Hashem or if the talmidim he raised were taught correctly. The only merit a person can be sure he will retain is the merit he acquired when a Yid came to him feeling depressed, fearful, or sad and left that person's presence with a smile.

Who better than Rav Zelik, to whom life was Torah and Torah was life, to share this penetrating lesson?

Being Mechazeik Even One Person

Rav Chaim Ozer Grodzensky, rav in Vilna and leader of all prewar Jewry, once asked the Chofetz Chaim to travel to Vilna in order to be *mechazeik* the people there in the mitzvah of *taharas hamishpachah*. "If Rav Chaim Ozer asks, then I must go," said the Chofetz Chaim.

The Chofetz Chaim was already quite elderly and his family was hesitant to let him travel. Much of the trip would have to be taken by horse and wagon, which, in the best of circumstances, was very uncomfortable. However, the Chofetz Chaim was not going to be dissuaded and was ready to push himself beyond his natural *kochos*. Left with no choice, his family made the arrangements for his travel.

A young *talmid chacham* who looked after the Chofetz Chaim went along on the trip. Thousands of men and women heard the Chofetz Chaim speak on separate occasions over Shabbos. On Shabbos afternoon, a large group of people assembled in front of the home where the Chofetz Chaim was staying, hoping to receive *berachos* and advice from him.

One such person told the Chofetz Chaim that he needed strengthening in his *emunah*. The Chofetz Chaim spent a considerable amount of time with this person, who went away with much *chizuk*, feeling very encouraged.

It was after this that the Chofetz Chaim's assistant heard the Chofetz Chaim repeating something over and over. When he listened closely, he heard him say, "Whether or not I accomplished something for *taharas hamishpachah* is hard to say, but that I helped one Yid with his *emunah* is certain. And that made the trip worth it."

A Taste of Sensitivity

In the Face of Tears

*R*av Dovid HaLevi Segal, known as the Taz (ז"ט), which stands *for* טורי זהב, the name of his commentary on the Shulchan Aruch, was one of the Torah giants of his day. The Taz served as chief rabbi of the Polish cities of Potylicz and later Ostrog, where he established a yeshivah and became known as one of the prominent halachic authorities of his time. He spent the latter part of his life in Lemberg.

During his younger years, the Taz concealed his greatness in Torah and Talmudic acumen. He traveled to a distant city, accompanied by a close *talmid*, where he occupied himself in learning. His *talmid* faithfully protected his rebbi's secret, not revealing his name or the fact that he was a spiritual giant with a grasp of all segments of Torah.

The rav of this city was extremely strict in his rulings, and just about every time a question was presented to him, he ultimately found a stringency and *paskened* accordingly. One time, the Taz became aware of a *shailah* regarding a chicken that had been presented to the rav, who had, as usual, ruled stringently. The Taz disagreed with the ruling, believing that the chicken was kosher, and he shared his feelings with the owner of the fowl.

The chicken owner ran to the rav and told him that an unknown visitor claimed that the chicken was kosher. The rav asked that the visitor be summoned. When the Taz arrived at the rav's home, the rav rebuked him sternly, "How dare you argue with the local rabbinic authority?"

At that time, rabbanim wielded tremendous power and were

able to impose penalties and punishments when necessary. In this case, the rav ordered that the man who had the audacity to disagree with his ruling be forced to sit at the entrance of the shul, while the congregants walked by and shamed and disgraced him. The Taz accepted the punishment, happy to maintain his anonymity.

A period of time passed. One day, as he was walking in the street, the Taz came upon a young girl who was holding a chicken and crying. The Taz asked the child what was troubling her. She explained, "I come from a poor home, where every *zloty* is precious. My mother saved up *zloty* after *zloty* for weeks, finally collecting enough money to purchase a chicken. My siblings and I were so happy and we looked forward to this treat, which we hadn't tasted in months.

"I am now returning from the home of the rav," the girl continued. "There was a halachic question about the *shechitah* of the chicken, and I was sent to inquire of the rav whether it is kosher. The rav said that the chicken is *treif* and cannot be eaten! Here is the chicken," she said, indicating the fowl, "which I am bringing home, where my mother will dispose of it."

The girl, who had stopped crying in order to relate her story, now burst into a fresh bout of tears. After comforting the child and assuring her that he will help, the Taz asked if he could take a look at the chicken.

He examined it carefully and then said, "Go back to the rav, and ask him to please look in the *sefer Turei Zahav*" — and he specified which chapter and which subsection — "where he will find a clear *heter* for this chicken."

The girl did as she was told. The rav, stunned by the girl's instructions, headed to the shul's library to look up the source he was given. Indeed, he found the *heter* in the *Turei Zahav*. The rav returned home and instructed one of his household members to track down the man who had advised the girl, and discovered that he was the very individual whom he had reprimanded for disagreeing with his ruling. Recognizing that he was not dealing with a simpleton, but an outstanding Torah scholar, the rav pleaded with the Taz for forgiveness for disgracing him. The rav then asked the Taz for *mechilah* in front of the entire *kehillah*.

The Taz's identity, however, was still unknown, and the rav commanded that he reveal who he is and where he had come from. Reluctantly, the Taz told the rav his name and that he was the author of *Turei Zahav,* the very *sefer* that had been referenced in resolving the chicken *shailah.*

The Taz's talmid asked him why, after trying to conceal his identity, he got involved in the question regarding the chicken, which ultimately led to his divulging his identity. Earlier, the talmid pointed out, the Taz had chosen to endure embarrassment rather than disclose his identity. What changed?

The Taz replied, "I would have liked to remain hidden from the public eye, so that I could learn Torah and serve Hashem without being disturbed," answered the Taz. "But that was only until I came across a Jew in pain! Here was a girl, forlorn and dejected, whose mother was surely going to be devastated when her hard-earned chicken would have to be thrown out.

"I couldn't stand by while tears were being shed; I had to step in and do what I could! In the face of the pain and tears of my brethren, my personal concerns and preferences completely fell away."

Out of the Conversation

There was great excitement at Yeshivas Ohel Torah in Baranovich, as Rav Dovid Rappaport had just been appointed to the faculty of the yeshivah. Rav Rappaport, while still a young man, wrote a sefer, Tzemach Dovid, on the chiddushim of his grandfather, Rav Akiva Eiger. His second major work, Mikdash Dovid, covered the masechtos of Kodshim, Taharos, Bechoros, and Sanhedrin. The talmidim in Baranovich were thrilled to imbibe Torah wisdom from such a brilliant mind.

At the time of Rav Dovid's appointment, the rosh yeshivah, Rav Elchanan Wasserman, was out of town collecting funds to sustain the yeshivah. Upon Rav Elchanan's return, a *bachur* from the yeshivah went to the train station to greet the rosh yeshivah and tell him about the impact of the new *maggid shiur* upon the students.

A wagon driver was hired to take Rav Elchanan and the *bachur* from the train station to Baranovich. Joining them in the wagon was another Jew, who happened to be heading in the same direction. The *bachur* was eager to tell the rosh yeshivah all about Rav Dovid's *shiurim*. Strangely, though, Rav Elchanan didn't seem interested. Instead, he conversed with their fellow passenger, asking the simple Jew what he did for a living, among other mundane questions. Rav Elchanan even asked the man about his gastronomic preferences. The *bachur* was surprised to hear the rosh yeshivah engage in idle chatter, but he sat silently out of respect as Rav Elchanan and the Jew spoke.

After the Jew disembarked, Rav Elchanan turned to his *talmid*. "I must apologize to you," he said. "I know that you wanted to talk to me about Rav Dovid's *shiurim* and tell me about the yeshivah, but that would have left our fellow passenger out of the conversation. He would not have been able to join in our Torah discussion, which would have been insensitive. That is why I spoke to him about matters with which he was familiar and which interested him.

"Now that he has left, please tell me about Rav Dovid's *chiddushim*."

Don't Hold Up the Bus!

*E*very morning, Rav Yosef Leizerson, a talmid chacham who lived in Bnei Brak, would take the number 318 bus to Rechovot, where he headed a kollel. The bus driver was familiar with his distinguished passenger, who waited patiently at the bus stop every day.

One morning, Rav Leizerson was running late and the bus pulled up at the stop before he arrived. The rav hurried to the bus but the driver signaled to him to take his time. Rav Leizerson, for his part, continued moving at a rapid clip. When he boarded the bus, slightly out of breath, the driver exclaimed, "*K'vod harav*, why did you run? I would have waited for you!"

"I appreciate that you were willing to wait for me," Rav Leizerson replied, "but what about all the other people on this bus? None of them gave their consent and I have no right to make them late."

The bus driver was so impressed by the rav's sensitivity to others that he began to take an interest in Yiddishkeit and eventually became a baal teshuvah.

— heard from Rabbi Shraga Freedman

Tzaros and Reconciliation

*R*av Yisrael Yaakov Fisher, rav of the Zichron Moshe neighborhood in Yerushalayim, would often speak about the need to be scrupulous in matters of bein adam la'chaveiro. His derashos made frequent mention of the fact that many of the troubles experienced by Yidden are due to transgressions between man and his fellow man.

Rav Gamliel Rabinovich, the noted *mekubal* and rosh yeshivah of Yeshivah Shaar HaShamayim in Yerushalayim, was once approached by a *yungerman* who was suffering terribly in the rearing of his children. His tribulations in this regard were so dire that he asked Rav Gamliel if his wife should change her name, since she was named after a relative who had suffered all her life. Perhaps a name change would bring about a positive transformation in their *chinuch* fortunes.

Rav Gamliel replied that he does not deal with such matters, but he offered to accompany the *yungerman* to Rav Yisrael Yaakov Fisher, whose expertise in these matters, big and small, was well known. When Rav Yisrael Yaakov heard the man's question, he stated that changing a name is not the solution, because the intention when giving one's child the name of a relative is to perform a *tovah*, a favor, for that person's *neshamah*, and nothing negative can result from that good deed.

"However," advised Rav Yisrael Yaakov, "what you should do is perform a *cheshbon hanefesh* to determine if you possibly harmed another person who has not forgiven you."

The man left with Rav Gamliel and began to think deeply. Had he ever slighted someone and not sought forgiveness? After a period of time, he remembered that years prior, at a small yeshivah where he had studied, he had had a serious spat with another *bachur*, whom he had humiliated in public. The *bachur* had been severely hurt and the two had not spoken to each other from then until they both left the yeshivah.

The *yungerman* began searching for his former acquaintance and learned that he resided with his family in a different city. He called him and asked if they could meet.

At the meeting, the man confirmed that he had indeed harbored resentment all the years toward this former yeshivah-mate for embarrassing him. He added that he was unable to be *mochel* him because of how much that incident still tormented him.

The *yungerman* pleaded with the man, relating that Rav Fisher felt that this was the source of the *tzaros* he was experiencing. But the man was unyielding.

"I understand your grief," he said, "and I understand what Rav Fisher said, but what can I do? I am still angry. Even if I say that I forgive you, it will be mere lip service; in the depths of my heart, I am in pain. I can't just wipe it away."

The crestfallen *yungerman* returned to Rav Gamliel and shared his predicament. Rav Gamliel advised him to offer the man a sum of money as compensation for granting forgiveness.

The next day, the *yungerman* returned to his former yeshivah-mate's city and handed him an envelope containing a significant amount of money. The man was very touched by the gesture, explaining that he was in dire financial straits and this monetary gift would help extricate him from his fiscal quagmire.

The two reconciled, with the man stating that he now realized that the quarrel had taken place during their younger, immature years, and there was no justification in maintaining the grudge forever. He repeated this several times, forgiving the *yungerman* wholeheartedly.

Amazingly, before long, the *nisyonos* that the *yungerman* had been experiencing either disappeared or were resolved.

Rav Gamliel said that this approach — of giving money to a friend to encourage him to grant forgiveness — is one that he learned from the Steipler Gaon, Rav Yaakov Yisrael Kanievsky.

Humble Greatness

*T*hey say that great men are not born great, but grow great. Others say that greatness lies in the small things one does.

And most would agree that greatness is manifest in the way one responds when one is caught off guard and unprepared.

One of our senior *gedolei Torah* demonstrated that sort of greatness. A student of Talmudical Yeshivah of Philadelphia was asked to leave the yeshivah for a given reason. Years later, when he spotted the rosh yeshivah, Rav Shmuel Kamenetsky, he still harbored resentment over his forced departure from the yeshivah. The man approached Rav Kamenetsky and let loose.

"I know you!" he said to the rosh yeshivah with a huff. "You're Shmuel Kamenetsky! And I am not going to say 'Rabbi'!"

Without missing a beat, and with the genuineness that characterizes his every word, Rav Kamenetsky softly responded, "*Farshteit zach nit!* Of course not! *Mir zenen yedidim!* We're friends. And among friends there are no titles."

With that, Rav Kamenetsky deflected the barb and proceeded to ask the fellow how he was doing.

Greatness with simplicity and compassion.

Precise Dialing

During the last period of Rav Chaim Greineman's life, an urgent medical matter arose late one night. Rav Chaim wished to contact a doctor and ask him to come to his home immediately.

Rav Chaim asked his grandson to bring him a telephone book so that he could look up the exact phone number of the physician. "But Zeide," the grandson said, "you called this doctor many times; surely you remember his number by heart. Why must you look it up in the phonebook?"

Rav Chaim replied, "Yes, it is true. I usually rely on my memory when calling the doctor, but right now it is the middle of the night. If I make a mistake while dialing the number and call someone else, I am going to wake up a different family. That would be a transgression of *gezel sheinah* [stealing another's sleep]. How can I do that? I must therefore look up the number, so that I get every digit correct."

Thousands have benefitted from Rav Greineman's Torah insights, recorded in his many volumes of Chiddushim U'Biurim. In this instance, he imparted a priceless insight of sensitivity and understanding.

Never Without a Goodbye

When Rav Michel Yehudah Lefkowitz was a *yungerman* in kollel, he and his fellow *avreichim* received their kollel stipend each Erev Shabbos. One Friday, Rav Michel Yehudah was not in kollel, so the rosh kollel brought the check to his home. Upon arriving, he found Rav Michel Yehudah learning in the front room of his humble house. He knocked on the window and passed the check through.

Rav Michel Yehudah invited the rosh kollel to come inside, but the rosh kollel explained his hesitation. "I am sure that you had a good reason for not coming to the kollel today, but I thought that perhaps your rebbetzin doesn't know. I figured that I'll just hand you the check and leave, so as not to bring any attention to it."

Rav Michel Yehudah was confused by the rosh kollel's suggestion that his rebbetzin would not be aware of whether he had left the house or not. "What do you mean?" he asked the rosh kollel. "I have never left my house without saying goodbye to my wife."

Decades later, when he was over 90 years old, Rav Michel Yehudah was scheduled to address a major *atzeres*. For whatever reason, he was running late and it was unclear whether he would make it to the event in time. He was already on his way to the gathering, about 10 blocks out of Bnei Brak, when he turned to his driver and asked him to turn around and return home. The driver was taken aback, since it was already late, but he figured that Rav Michel Yehudah had forgotten something important at home.

When they arrived at his house, the driver offered to run inside and get whatever it was that the rosh yeshivah needed. Rav Michel Yehudah waved him off. With great difficulty, he got out of the car and made his way to his home. Upon entering and seeing his wife, he said, "Rebbetzin, I am so sorry! This is the first time in all our years that I left the house without saying goodbye and wishing you *kol tuv*." He then asked his rebbetzin *mechilah* and wished her well before heading back to the car.

Call Your Wife

Rav Shea Ozer Halpern once went with Rav Nosson Tzvi Finkel to the home of a wealthy Yid, to collect money for Yeshivas Mir. The philanthropist asked Rav Nosson Tzvi to tell him about the well-known visit of Rav Chaim Shmulevitz, a previous rosh yeshivah of Yeshivas Mir Yerushalayim, to Kever Rachel. Rav

Nosson Tzvi turned to Rav Halpern and said, "You took Rav Chaim on the trip. You tell him."

Rav Halpern proceeded to relate the story:

I had the zechus to take Rav Chaim Shmulevitz on a walk every morning at 6 a.m. One day, I asked him if he wants to go to Kever Rachel. He asked if there was a public phone nearby, because he wanted to let his wife know that he would be home 45 minutes later than usual. I found a phone and called the rebbetzin and then told Rav Chaim that the rebbetzin had been notified.

From that moment on, he began sobbing and crying as if the biggest calamity and tragedy had occurred. When we arrived at Kever Rachel, even the soldiers asked us what happened.

Rav Chaim entered Kever Rachel and said, "Mamme, your son Chaimke is here." He then began davening for all the ill people he knew and everyone who needed salvation.

He said, "Hashem tells you to stop crying, but your son Chaimke says that you should carry on crying for your children!"

Rav Nosson Tzvi asked the wealthy Yid, "What do you see in this story?"

The Yid responded, "I see the feeling and heart that Rav Chaim had for Klal Yisrael."

Rav Nosson Tzvi smiled. "While that is certainly true," he responded, "I see the *middos tovos* in how he was concerned about his wife. If you are going to be home late, call your wife and let her know."

Good Morning

Young Moshe Sherer often assisted Rav Elchanan Wasserman during Rav Elchanan's visit to America in 1938. This took place while Moshe — who later became president of Agudath Israel of America — was still a talmid in Mesivta Torah Vodaath, and his first encounter with the great sage left an indelible imprint on the impressionable teenager.

Moshe Sherer arrived at the Broadway Central Hotel one morning and made his way to the room of the visiting rosh yeshivah. The two left the hotel room together and walked toward the elevator.

Before it arrived, Rav Elchanan turned to Moshe and asked, "*Vi azoi zugt men 'Gut morgen' oif English*? How does one say 'Good morning' in English?" Moshe told him, and Rav Elchanan began to pace back and forth in the hallway, repeating over and over, "Good morning. Good morning. Good morning."

When the elevator arrived, Rav Elchanan turned to the non-Jewish attendant and said, "Good morning."

Then he asked Moshe, "*Hub ich gut gezugt*? Did I say it right?"

— *heard from Rabbi Shraga Freedman*

Rav Aryeh's Secret

Rav Aryeh Finkel, rosh yeshivah of Yeshivas Mir Brachfeld, used to spend every Pesach in Givat Shaul at the home of his son-in-law and daughter, Rav and Rebbetzin Saar Maizel. While he was there, his son, Rav Binyamin Finkel, arranged a *minyan* for him at the Maizel home.

Once, the morning after the Pesach Seder, Rav Aryeh decided to join his son-in-law at the *vasikin minyan* where he usually davened as a show of respect for his gracious host. When he returned from the lengthy davening, Rav Aryeh knew that his son would soon appear along with several of his own sons and a group of other men who had been invited to the *minyan*. Thus, instead of taking a rest, the rosh yeshivah waited in the living room for the *minyan* to arrive. Not wanting to cause them distress by revealing that he had already davened, Rav Aryeh moved his lips and pretended to daven along with them.

When the rest of the *minyan* finally reached *Shemoneh Esrei*, they were surprised to discover that Rav Aryeh's *siddur* was still open to *Pesukei DeZimrah*. Rav Binyamin signaled to the other men to wait, not only out of respect for his father, but also because the *minyan* had been arranged solely for his sake; it would not be proper to begin *Shemoneh Esrei* without him. There was also another very simple reason that they could not begin *Shemoneh Esrei*: Since there were only nine other men aside from Rav Aryeh, they would not have a *minyan* until he began *Shemoneh Esrei*. The men sat and waited, each of them immersed in his own thoughts or *sefarim*. From time to time, they glanced at Rav Aryeh's *siddur*, failing to understand why he was davening at such a slow pace.

Rav Aryeh, meanwhile, scanned the room and saw that there were only nine other men present. Since he had already davened, he didn't want to be counted as part of the *minyan* for *Shemoneh Esrei*, and he decided to draw out his davening until a 10th man arrived. And so they waited: Rav Binyamin for his father to finish *Pesukei DeZimrah* and to reach *Shemoneh Esrei*, and Rav Aryeh for a real 10th man. Even as the minutes ticked by, Rav Binyamin remained firm in his insistence on waiting for his father, to enable him to be part of the *minyan* that had gathered for his benefit.

Finally, two latecomers arrived, and when the two of them reached *Shemoneh Esrei*, Rav Aryeh "somehow" managed to catch up with them and was ready to begin, as well.

One of the few people who were aware of Rav Aryeh's secret was his granddaughter, Digla Maizel (who is known today as Rebbetzin Rauchberger). "Zeide," she whispered to her grandfather later, "why didn't you motion to them that you had already davened?"

Rav Aryeh looked at his granddaughter and smiled his famous smile. Lowering his own voice to a whisper, he said, "How could I have done that? How could I offend all those people who made the effort to come here for my sake, especially my righteous son?"

The young lady kept her grandfather's secret to herself, but the next day her uncle had a surprise for her. "Do you really think I didn't know that your zeide had davened *vasikin*?" Rav Binyamin asked her with a smile.

"But then why did you make everyone wait and cause Zeide to have to draw out his davening?" she asked.

Rav Binyamin replied, "I had to do that. How could I cause him distress, when he worked so hard to keep it a secret so that we wouldn't be offended?"

— heard from Rabbi Tzvi Yaakovson

Marlboro Versus Time

*N*othing escaped the eye of Rav Nosson Tzvi Finkel. He noticed everything.

A *yungerman* once asked the rosh yeshivah if he could join Yeshivas Mir Yerushalayim. He added that he was financially comfortable, so he would not need to accept any money from the yeshivah.

"Yes, you may join," Rav Nosson Tzvi said, "and when you have a *shtickel Torah*, come and tell it to me."

A few months later, the *yungerman* went to the rosh yeshivah and shared a *chiddush* with him. When he finished, Rav Nosson Tzvi asked him, "How is *parnassah*?"

The *yungerman* replied, "*Baruch Hashem*, fine."

Rav Nosson Tzvi asked him again, "How is *parnassah*? Do you have what you need?"

Once again, the *yungerman* replied that all was well, but then he asked, "Why is the rosh yeshivah questioning so much?"

Rav Nosson Tzvi said, "Because I noticed that when you first came to the yeshivah, you had a packet of Marlboro cigarettes in your pocket. But now you have Time cigarettes, which are much cheaper. I'm just wondering if you can still afford the Marlboro or if you need assistance."

He Truly Cared

*T*hrough their example, our gedolim have always taught us that maintaining *k'vod habriyos*, respect for all people, is of fundamental importance.

A group of workers was once hired by the Talmudical Yeshivah of Philadelphia to complete an urgent job with only a few days' notice, so it would be ready in time for the new *zman*. Since the workers did not live near the yeshivah and it was necessary for them to work long hours to complete the job in time, the administration offered them sleeping accommodations in one of the yeshivah buildings. Mattresses were provided, but the workers found these accommodations uncomfortable and were unable to fall asleep.

One night, at 1 a.m., the rosh yeshivah, Rav Shmuel Kamenetsky, entered the room where they were bedded down. "Do you mind if I stay here with you?" he asked.

"You should go to sleep. There's no reason for you to stay here with us," the supervisor protested.

Rav Shmuel shook his head. "I noticed that you are having trouble sleeping," he explained. "I feel very bad that you are losing sleep because you are working for me, so I can't sleep either."

The rosh yeshivah remained with the workers throughout the night, alternating between conversing with them and learning from his *sefarim*.

When the workers later shared this story with others, they commented that the rosh yeshivah had made them feel very important and they could tell that he truly cared.

— heard from Rabbi Shraga Freedman

All for Show

During his younger years, Rav Sroya Devlitzky, noted mekubal, posek, and prolific mechaber sefarim, merited a close relationship with the Chazon Ish. Rav Devlitzky once needed to annul a vow and went to the home of the Chazon Ish to take care of it. At that time, another Jew was at the home of the Chazon Ish, asking him various questions. When the Chazon Ish heard what Rav Devlitzky needed, he told him, "This Yid and I are two people, so go out to the street and bring in a third person. Then we'll have a beis din of three and we'll be able to be matir your neder."

Rav Devlitzky went outside and returned a short while later with another fellow, a clearly unlearned Jew, who was, perhaps, ignorant in even the basics of Yiddishkeit.

The Chazon Ish immediately began addressing the three men in front of him, explaining the details of hataras nedarim, including the pesach — literally, an opening, or a reason — for annulling the vow, how they were to proceed, and what they should say. Led by the Chazon Ish, the process of hataras nedarim was carried out with precision, and the three dayanim declared, "Mutar lach. Mutar lach. Mutar lach."

Rav Devlitzky thanked the fellow he had brought in from the street and wished him well.

Once the man had departed, the Chazon Ish turned to Rav Devlitzky. "I regret to tell you this," he said, "but that fellow, unfortunately, had no understanding of what was taking place. As such, the hataras nedarim was invalid. Please go back out and call in another Yid who is more familiar with the procedure, so that we can do it again and really be matir your neder."

Rav Devlitzky was inspired by the righteousness of the Chazon Ish, who had apparently picked up on the man's ignorance from the moment he began speaking to him. Yet, to protect the man's dignity and avoid causing any embarrassment to him, the Chazon Ish went through every component of hataras nedarim and carried out the process without letting on that it was all for show.

What a lesson in sensitivity!

My Pain...and Theirs

When Rav Moshe Dovid Lefkowitz — rosh yeshivah of Yeshiva Bais Dovid of Bnei Brak, mashgiach of Yeshiva Be'er Yaakov, and rav of Chanichei HaYeshivos in Bnei Brak — lost a son in a drowning accident, the *niftar's* grandfather, Rav Michel Yehudah Lefkowitz, was one of the *maspidim* at the *levayah*. On the first day of *shivah*, Rav Michel Yehudah went to be *menachem avel* his son, his daughter-in-law, and the rest of the family.

On the third day of the *shivah*, Rav Michel Yehudah asked a grandson, Rav Yitzchak Karlansky, to accompany him to the *beis avel*. When they got there, the *aveilim* were sitting at one end of the room. Rav Michel Yehudah asked his *einikel* to place a chair at the other end, where he sat down. People came and went, asking him to move closer to the crowd, but he declined. After over an hour, Rav Michel Yehudah stood up, said, "*HaMakom yenacheim eschem…*— May the Omnipresent console you…" to the *aveilim* and left.

Perplexed, Rav Karlansky asked his zeide about the seemingly strange visit. He had already been *menachem avel*. Why the additional visit?

"At the *levayah* and on the first day of *shivah*, I was present for my pain. But how was I being *mishtateif* with the pain of my son and daughter-in-law and the rest of the family? How did I share in their pain? That's why I went back — just to be *mishtateif* in their *tzaar*."

Price of Comfort

One summer, a *talmid* of Yeshivas Torah Vodaath who came from a non-*frum* home did not have a place to stay and asked the rosh yeshivah, Rav Avrohom Pam, and his wife if he could stay in their house. They gladly agreed.

Rebbetzin Pam made an accounting of exactly how much the stay would cost her, down to the last penny. She told the *talmid* that at the end of his stay, that is the amount she wanted in order to cover the costs.

When the month ended and the *bachur* approached her with the money, the rebbetzin refused to take it.

"I won't take your money," she insisted. "I just wanted you to be completely comfortable taking everything that was given to you during your stay at our home."

Also a Person

Rav Michel Yehudah Lefkowitz once received a ride from a *yungerman* whose 6-year-old son was sitting in the back seat of the car. Upon arriving at his destination, Rav Michel Yehudah thanked the driver and exited.

After a few moments, however, the driver was surprised to see Rav Michel Yehudah returning to the vehicle. Rav Michel Yehudah approached the back door of the car, opened it, and smiled at the young boy sitting there. "*Kol tuv!*" said the rosh yeshivah. "I forgot to say goodbye to you."

Turning to the stunned father, Rav Michel Yehudah remarked, "*Ehr iz oich ah mentch* — He is also a person."

Not That Gan Eden

Rav Meir Tzvi Bergman, rosh yeshivah of Yeshivas Rashbi in Bnei Brak, was once at the home of his father-in-law, Rav Elazar Menachem Man Shach, rosh yeshivah of Yeshivas Ponovezh, when a group of distinguished *talmidei chachamim* came to tell him about a new initiative: a Friday-afternoon kollel. They explained that Fridays, especially the short winter Fridays, are a time when people tend to be lax about their learning, and they felt it would be a good innovation.

They waited expectantly for Rav Shach to bless them warmly for their initiative, but he sat in silence.

After a few minutes, he looked them in the eye and demanded, "And who will help the wife? On such a short Friday, when she is busy cooking and cleaning and there are small children at home, if her husband is learning all day, who will help her?"

The men stood there quietly, not knowing what to say.

Then Rav Shach added, "I am not belittling it, *chas v'shalom*, and a person who learns on Fridays will certainly have a portion in Gan Eden. But I do not want to be in that Gan Eden."

Ensuring Their Honor

Late one night in the Ohel Moshe neighborhood of Yerusha-layim, Rav Isser Zalman Meltzer sat with one of the city's accomplished *talmidei chachamim,* Rav Matisyahu Davis. They were involved with the final editing of one of the volumes of Rav Isser Zalman's magnum opus, *sefer Even HaAzel* on the Rambam, which was going to the publisher the next day. While examining the final manuscript, Rav Isser Zalman exclaimed, "*Oy vey!* In the *sefer* I quoted a conversation I had with two roshei yeshivah of a certain yeshivah. But I did not mention any *chiddushim* from its third rosh yeshivah. I'm afraid that his feelings will be hurt."

Immediately, he asked Rav Matisyahu to escort him to the home of the rosh yeshivah who wasn't mentioned in the *sefer.* They both proceeded to make the long trek to his house, and when they arrived at their destination, Rav Isser Zalman knocked gently on the door. The rosh yeshivah came to the door and was startled to see the two distinguished visitors. He was even more astounded when he found out the purpose of the visit: Rav Isser Zalman, many years his senior, had come to ask him *pshat* in a Rambam.

It is well known that Rav Chaim Brisker said about him, "When I speak to Rav Zunya Mirrer [Rav Isser Zalman's nickname] in learn-ing, all of the windows of my brain open up." Yet now this tow-ering giant of Torah had come to this rosh yeshivah for his help in clarifying a Rambam. The rosh yeshivah was astounded by Rav Isser Zalman's humility and related this in a *hesped* on Rav Isser Zalman after his passing. Little did he know the real reason for the visit: to hear a *chiddush* from him in order to record it in the *sefer Even HaAzel* so that his honor wouldn't be slighted.

When Rav Isser Zalman returned home with his mission accom-plished, his rebbetzin was concerned. She was always worried for his welfare, working hard to maintain the health of his fragile body, and eating and sleeping properly were crucial. "Was it so necessary to leave the house at such a late hour?" she asked now.

"Yes, yes," answered the *tzaddik.* "It was of upmost importance. How can I have my *sefer* published knowing that in the process I may have hurt someone's feelings?"

— heard from Rabbi Yitzchok Tzvi Schwarz

True Refinement

*R*av Moshe Feinstein's brilliance is well known. Just as amazing were his sensitivity and tzidkus, as demonstrated in this story related by Rav Tzvi Hirsch Meir Ginsberg, menahel of Yeshivas Rabbi Jacob Joseph:

A young rabbinic leader was getting divorced. Rav Moshe Feinstein was on the *beis din* presiding over the divorce and was taking care of sending the *get* with a messenger to the person's wife, who lived elsewhere.

Before Rav Moshe signed the papers, he walked over to the man giving the *get* and apologized. "Please forgive me. The halachah requires that I refer to you as 'you,' using the informal Yiddish term '*du*,' as opposed to the third person honorary term of '*ihr*.' "

Avoiding Distress

*T*he Shinova Rav, Rav Yechezkel Shraga Halberstam, was also known as the Divrei Yechezkel, after the *sefer* he authored. He was careful to always read the letters presented by individuals collecting *tzedakah.* This seemed odd to some, since he had set amounts that he gave for various requests and never increased the sum based on the letters he read.

When he was asked why he bothered reading the letters, he replied, "I read each letter to avoid causing pain to the poor person. If I don't read the letter, the person may think I would have given more if I had."

The Robe Maneuver

W hile still in his 20's, Rav Avraham Genechovsky received semichah from Rav Yosef Shalom Elyashiv, who, it is said, only farhered three yungeleit for semichah in his entire lifetime. Of Rav Avraham, he marveled, "I didn't know who was farhering whom."

In addition to serving as rosh yeshivah at Yeshivas Kochav M'Yaakov-Tchebin in Yerushalayim for 45 years, Rav Avraham was renowned for his popular shiurim. But Rav Avraham was also a giant in bein adam la'chaveiro. "A person should be like this planet," he once said. "Just as the outside of the world is primarily water, so should a person not be harsh with people, but he should be flexible, like water. However, in terms of his core, a person should be like a rock and encompass within himself the fire of Torah."

That is exactly how Rav Avraham was. Though he encompassed the fire of Torah, when simple people came to speak to him, he treated them with immense respect and humility, and he was always sensitive to their feelings.

One Shabbos, a visitor mistakenly rang Rav Avraham's doorbell. Rav Avraham realized that the person would be embarrassed if the door were opened right away. He quickly instructed his family members to hide at the back of his apartment.

He then proceeded to put on a robe so that the person would think he was relaxing in a bedroom and had not heard the doorbell. After waiting a short while, during which the person had time to gather his wits and knock on the door, Rav Avraham opened the door with a pleasant greeting to his guest.

Through this complicated maneuvering, the person thought that no one had taken note of his breach of Shabbos.

The Three-Dollar Sweater

*A*t the end of World War II, broken in body and shattered in soul, the weary survivors of the Holocaust made their way to safer shores. Thanks to the efforts of the Vaad Hatzalah, a large group of Mirrer talmidim traveled across the Pacific to California, and from there to New York, where the Mirrer Yeshivah was reborn under the leadership of Rav Avraham Kalmanowitz, Rav Chaim Shmulevitz, and Rav Yechezkel Levenstein.

Rav Shmuel Brudny was one of those talmidim. Shortly after he arrived in New York, Rav Brudny became engaged to Rochel Leshinsky, daughter of Rav Dovid and Batsheva Leshinsky. While yet a chassan, Rav Shmuel was invited by the roshei yeshivah, Rav Avraham Kalmanowitz and Rav Chaim Shmulevitz, to become a maggid shiur at the Mir, a position he would hold for the next four decades. Rav Shmuel delivered his shiur with such a sense of commitment and responsibility that he showed up on the day of his wedding and delivered a shiur.

As he ended the shiur 10 minutes early, he apologized. "I am sorry," he said. "I am a bit busy today."

A "bit" busy!

Rav Brudny was a marbitz Torah in every sense of the term. Talmidim vied to be accepted into his shiur. The kesher between rebbi and talmid was forged with bonds of love. The talmidim revered Rav Shmuel and appreciated what he represented.

A *talmid* recalled: "During one of the first *shiurim* I attended, we were discussing the concept of thirds. Rav Shmuel wanted me, the new *talmid*, to understand the concept. I was wearing a sweater,

274 ❖ FOOD FOR THOUGHT

and Rav Shmuel said to me, 'Imagine if your sweater cost $3. A third of your sweater would be a dollar.' The discussion ended and the *shiur* was over. Rav Shmuel, who was by then ailing and weak, went home.

"A half hour later, Rav Shmuel returned to the yeshivah. 'I am looking for the new *bachur*,' he announced. It took only a few minutes to track me down.

"Rav Shmuel smiled at me and said, 'I have to ask you *mechilah*. Earlier, when I said that your sweater is worth $3, I may have offended you. Actually, it could be worth much more than that.'

"I assured Rav Shmuel that I was not in the least bit slighted, and he turned once more to go home."

Three days later, Rav Shmuel passed away.

A Taste of Humility

The "Worker"

In the 40 years of his tenure, Rav Shmuel Brudny never once sat on the *mizrach* wall of the Mirrer Yeshivah *beis midrash*. In addition, Rav Shmuel never accepted visitors without first donning a hat and jacket. Even if a young *talmid* would come over to his home to speak words of Torah, he would excuse himself and put on a hat and jacket.

Once, a *talmid* was ill for several days and the phone rang in his home. His mother picked up the phone.

"Hello, this is Shmuel Brudny. Can I speak to Yankel?"

"Shmuel who?" asked the mother.

"Shmuel Brudny. *Der vuss arbet in Mirrer Yeshivah.* [The one who works in Mirrer Yeshivah.]"

Nothing more. A worker in the Mirrer Yeshivah!

Giving Honor, Not Taking

The Unsdorf-Frankfurter Rav, Rav Yosef Yonah Tzvi HaLevi Horovitz, once attended a wedding at which the host forgot to honor him with *siddur kiddushin* or with a *berachah* under the *chuppah*, even though the renowned rav was generally a recipient of such honors.

"Rav Horovitz, Rav Horovitz!" the host cried, when he realized what happened. "I'm so sorry to have overlooked the rav. Please forgive me. There were many obligations and my mind was in a haze on this momentous occasion." The man, who was beside himself with guilt and shame, kept excusing himself, over and over again.

"My dear friend," the Unsdorfer Rav consoled him when he was able to get a word in edgewise. "Please do not aggravate yourself over an issue of such insignificance. *Mir zenen gekumen geben kavod, nisht nemen kavod!* I have come to your *simchah* to give you honor, not that you should honor me."

Thus, the discussion was finally closed, with heartfelt wishes from both ends. And the celebration continued in an atmosphere of warmth and friendship.

— heard from S. Horowitz

"This Call Was for You"

Rabbi Moshe Sherer, president of Agudath Israel of America, was particularly devoted to the Daf Yomi and its cause. At the Tenth Siyum HaShas, Rabbi Sherer, with eloquence and emotion, pointed out how the Nazis had recognized that the "Talmud-lehrers," the teachers of Talmud, were the greatest threat to their diabolical plans to obliterate the Jewish people, and how a celebration of this magnitude a half-century later was the most powerful testimonial to the eternity of the am Hashem.

For many years, Rabbi Sherer attended the Daf Yomi *shiur* at the Agudah of 14th Avenue in Boro Park, which was delivered by Rav Moshe Meir Weiss, rav of Agudas Yisrael of Staten Island.

One Erev Yom Kippur, Rabbi Sherer called the Weiss home, and one of Rav Weiss's daughters answered the phone. When Rabbi Sherer asked to speak to her mother, the girl thought she hadn't heard him correctly.

"Do you want to speak to Tatty?" she asked.

"No, to Mommy," clarified Rabbi Sherer.

Rebbetzin Miriam Libby Weiss got on the phone and Rabbi Sherer explained why he had called.

"Your husband gives the Daf Yomi *shiur* at the Agudah of Boro Park and the Agudah of Staten Island," said Rabbi Sherer. "He is out every night from 8 p.m. until midnight. So I called to thank you and wish you a good year."

Rebbetzin Weiss thanked the venerable Agudah leader for the call and asked him if he was sure he didn't want to speak to Rav Weiss.

"Wish your husband a good year," he said, "but this call was for you."

Toting Tefillin

*I*n his younger years, my rosh yeshivah, Rav Nechemya Kaplan, rosh yeshivah of Yeshivas Shaar HaTalmud in Yerushalayim, learned at Yeshivas Toras Emes Kaminetz in Woodridge, New York, where Rav Levi Krupenia served as rosh yeshivah. Like the others who learned in that oasis of Torah decades ago, Rav Nechemya's memories are vivid and warm.

Nechemya had been away from the yeshivah one night and returned early the next morning, in time for Shacharis. When he arrived at the building that housed the *beis midrash*, he realized that his *tefillin* were in the dormitory building, which was located across the campus. He figured that since the *bachurim* would be walking to the *beis midrash* building for davening, it would not be a big deal for one of them to bring him his *tefillin* bag. He called the public phone in the dormitory building and explained to the person who answered where he had left his *tefillin* bag, requesting that it be brought to the *beis midrash*.

A short while later, Nechemya noticed someone approaching the building, and he was gratified to see that the person was carrying what appeared to be his *tefillin* bag. But when he looked more closely, he saw that the one carrying his *tefillin* was none other than the rosh yeshivah, Rav Levi Krupenia, himself!

A Clever Response

Once, during Rav Shlomo Zalman Auerbach's *shiur* at Yeshivas Kol Torah, a *talmid* raised a difficulty regarding the Rashash's commentary. Rav Shlomo Zalman spent several minutes struggling to resolve the question, and his distress at his inability to come up with an answer was evident on his face. Another *talmid* wondered aloud, "Why is the rosh yeshivah so troubled? I heard that the Rashash [Rav Shmuel Shtrashun of Vilna, who was also a businessman] was wealthy and his family paid to have his commentary included in the Vilna *Shas*."

> *Try to envision the dilemma that confronted Rav Shlomo Zalman at that moment. What would any of us have done in such a situation? Would we have rebuked the talmid for his insolence? What if he had made the comment in complete innocence? Even if he hadn't, was his rebbi justified to embarrass him in front of his peers? At the same time, how could anyone disregard such a comment? Silence would have been interpreted as tacit agreement, which would have been an affront to the honor of the Rashash.*
>
> *Using ingenuity coupled with humility, Rav Shlomo Zalman responded in a way that accomplished his goal, without hurting anyone in the process.*

"My dear *talmid*, that story is incorrect," Rav Shlomo Zalman said. "But I agree with you in principle. I, too, would have been prepared to pay a fortune for the Rashash's commentary to be included in the Gemara."

Camera Consideration

Rav Yosef Shalom Elyashiv once attended the wedding of the son of a *yungerman*. Arriving at the wedding during the meal, Rav Elyashiv approached the dais, gave the father of the *chassan* a hearty mazel tov accompanied by a heartfelt *berachah,* and sat down.

A short while later, Rav Elyashiv suddenly stood up, stuck out his hand toward the father of the *chassan*, and again wished a warm mazel tov. The father of the *chassan* assumed that Rav Elyashiv was getting ready to leave the *simchah.* But Rav Elyashiv sat right back down. The father of the *chassan* was mystified. What was that all about?

A fellow *yungerman*, who paid close attention to Rav Elyashiv's conduct, later explained to the father of the *chassan* what had transpired. When Rav Elyashiv arrived at the wedding, the photographer was taking pictures in the women's section. After Rav Elyashiv had sat down, the photographer came over to the men's section. Seeing this, and feeling that the *baal simchah* would feel important and honored to have a picture of Rav Elyashiv wishing him mazel tov, the *gadol hador* stood up and gave him his wishes once again so that the photographer could capture the moment.

"His Fame Harmed Him!"

*R*av Mordechai Altusky, rosh yeshivah at Yeshivas Torah Ore *in Yerushalayim, shared the following story about his father-in-law, Rav Abba Berman, rosh yeshivah of Yeshivas Iyun HaTalmud.*

> *In 5684/ 1924, when Abba Berman was 5 years old, the Chofetz Chaim visited the city of Lodz, where the Berman family lived. The government had issued an edict requiring yeshivah students to learn secular studies, and the Chofetz Chaim, though already over 90, went to fight the decree.*

When the Chofetz Chaim arrived, the area was so packed with people that it looked like the streets had turned black. Tens of thousands of people gathered around the house where he was staying, as everyone wanted to see the Chofetz Chaim. Of course, they wanted a *berachah,* as well, but with thousands of people crowding around the house, most of those gathered there knew that they had no chance. Only important *askanim* and close *talmidim* of the Chofetz Chaim were allowed into the house.

Rav Berman's father, Rav Shaul Yosef, was a *talmid* of the Chofetz Chaim, so he was permitted to enter. He went inside with his young son and said to the Chofetz Chaim, "My son has learned the Gemara, Rashi, and Tosafos of *Perek HaMafkid*, and the rav can test him."

The Chofetz Chaim asked 5-year-old Abba several questions, mainly on Tosafos, and he answered them well. Then the Chofetz Chaim said to Rav Shaul Yosef, "I have some advice for you: Do not let it become public knowledge that your son is an *iluy*, because publicity is always damaging."

He added a frightening statement: "Even the Vilna Gaon could have been greater, but once he became famous, the fame harmed him!"

Letting Go

*R*av Chaim Kreiswirth's genius in Torah was well known, but he was no less a gaon in middos. When his father-in-law, Rav Avraham Grodzensky, was inquiring about the young Rav Chaim as a match for his daughter, he wanted to find out about "how he speaks in learning." Rav Grodzensky maintained that from the way a bachur speaks, one can tell whether he is of good character. Rav Chaim visited Slabodka at the time; the shidduch that resulted was evidence of the positive outcome of the examination.

Once, while conversing with a group of people, Rav Chaim advanced an explanation of his own. One member of the group, a respected individual, denounced Rav Chaim as being "*megaleh panim baTorah she'lo k'halachah* — one who perverts the Torah contrary to the halachah" (*Pirkei Avos* 3:15). A number of *talmidim* were present, and although they were pained upon hearing this severe censure, they knew that Rav Chaim was not fond of people defending his honor.

Nevertheless, one of them opened a Gemara and discovered that Rashi stated exactly what Rav Chaim had just said. He rushed over to Rav Chaim's critic and asked him, "Would you say the same thing about Rashi?"

By this time, Rav Chaim had left the group. When he later heard what had happened, he summoned the *talmid* and protested, "One must learn to let things go — not only in worldly matters, but in learning, too!"

Emended Envelope

Rav Nesanel Elbaz, a rav in the Givat Shaul neighborhood of Yerushalayim, once sent a letter containing a halachic *shailah* to Rav Shlomo Zalman Auerbach. Along with his own missive, he enclosed a stamped envelope bearing his address: "Nesanel Elbaz, Rechov Kotler 7, Yerushalayim."

When the self-addressed stamped envelope arrived in the mail, Rav Elbaz observed that, along with his response to the question, Rav Shlomo Zalman had included two corrections: The title "Rav" had been added to Rav Elbaz's name, and the name of the street had been altered to "Rechov Harav Kotler."

"What's His Number?"

Rav Elyashiv was once approached regarding a halachic dispute between a rav and another individual. Rav Elyashiv indicated that the halachah was in accordance with the rav, who had posed the question to him.

The rav called the other party and conveyed Rav Elyashiv's *psak*, adding that Rav Elyashiv said that he should feel free to call him for clarification.

With great audacity, the other person responded, "If Rav Elyashiv would like, he can call me."

The rav followed up with Rav Elyashiv and, despite the chutzpah inherent in the response, relayed the reaction of the other party. Without hesitating, Rav Elyashiv said, "What's his phone number?"

The Driver

A close friend of Rav Shimshon Pincus, rav of the Negev city of Ofakim and prolific author, was Rabbi Avraham Deutsch, a member of the Ofakim city council. When Rabbi Deutsch's wife was ill and required treatment abroad, Rav Pincus traveled with Mrs. Deutsch and her sister overseas several times, so Rabbi Deutsch could stay behind in Ofakim and care for his children. Rav Pincus was a respected and busy rav and *mashpia*, yet he thought nothing of picking himself up and traveling thousands of miles to ensure that his friend's wife receives the best medical care possible. When Rav Pincus first brought up the suggestion and Rabbi Deutsch objected, Rav Pincus waved away Rabbi Deutsch's protestations. Since Rav Pincus was American-born, he felt that his involvement would ensure that Mrs. Deutsch would be tended to properly.

At one point, Rav Pincus accompanied Mrs. Deutsch to Santiago, a municipality in Mexico. "They were there, in some place off the beaten track, for seven weeks," Rabbi Deutsch later recalled. During this entire period, Rav Pincus, the venerated rav and *tzaddik*, served as personal chauffeur and attendant to Mrs. Deutsch and her sister. For two months, he drove them around, purchased the food they needed, and took care of other mundane tasks. Whenever they weren't seeking medical assistance or guidance, and he wasn't otherwise needed, Rav Pincus sat by himself in a room and learned Torah, while Mrs. Deutsch's sister kept her company.

Professor Schreiber of Bar Ilan University was in Santiago at the same time. Impressed by the diligence, professionalism, sensitivity, and care of Mrs. Deutsch's driver, he utilized the man's services himself; in his humility, Rav Pincus did not say a word. Eventually, Professor Schreiber discovered the identity of the respected personage he had hired. "What did I do?" he later told Rabbi Deutsch. "Whom was I using as my driver?"

He was using a malach Elokim, an individual who had so perfected himself that his humility was a part of his very essence.

One of Mrs. Deutsch's operations took place in Manhattan. That morning, Rav Pincus drove to the Shomrei Shabbos shul in Boro Park to daven. Someone in the Deutsch family received a call from a friend, who wanted to know what tragedy had taken place in the Pincus family. A person had seen Rav Pincus davening *Shemoneh Esrei* for 45 minutes and crying profusely, so the woman on the phone was convinced that something awful must have happened within his own family. When she was told that Mrs. Deutsch had undergone an operation that day and that Rav Pincus was davening for her, the woman said, "It can't be. He was crying as if the most personal tragedy had occurred."

But that was Rav Shimshon Pincus.

A Taste *of* Chinuch

The Future Gedolim in Our Hands

*I*n Tehillim (34:12), David HaMelech says, "Lechu vanim shimu li yiras Hashem alamedchem — Go, O sons, heed me, I will teach you the fear of Hashem." The question arises: Why did David say, "Go, O sons," and not, "Come, O sons"?

Perhaps one can interpret David's words to mean that good chinuch should become an intrinsic part of a child's being, so that long after a child has left the parental abode and goes on in life, the teachings remain with him.

At an annual gathering of the heads of *mesivtas* in Eretz Yisrael, Rav Aharon Leib Shteinman, rosh yeshivah of Orchos HaTorah in Bnei Brak, said: "Some individuals think that one may act toward *talmidim* as one desires, shouting at them and getting angry at them. At times, the *talmidim* suffer major damage later in life from having been shamed in this manner. One must know that he is dealing with *neshamos*, and every one of them has the ability to become a great *talmid chacham* who can be *mashpia* on the entire world with his Torah, *yiras Shamayim*, and *middos tovos* — and, *chas v'shalom*, to the contrary, as well.

Rav Shteinman related that the Gemara (*Bava Basra* 134a) says that Hillel HaZakein had 80 *talmidim*. The Gemara tells us that 30 of them were fitting to have the *Shechinah* rest upon them like Moshe Rabbeinu, 30 of them were fitting to have the sun stop for them as it did for Yehoshua bin Nun, and 20 of them were "*beinonim*," mediocre. The greatest of his *talmidim* was Yonasan ben Uziel and the smallest was Rabban Yochanan ben Zakkai. The Gemara then details the wide-ranging Torah knowledge of Rabban Yochanan ben Zakkai — the smallest among Hillel's *talmidim*.

"We don't know who the *talmidim* of Yonasan ben Uziel were," said Rav Shteinman. "Rabbi Akiva and all the great Tannaim were *talmidim* of Rabban Yochanan ben Zakkai, who perpetuated the Torah among Klal Yisrael. Yet he was the smallest of Hillel's *talmidim*.

"Everyone working with youngsters must know that he is involved in *avodas hakodesh*, with holy *neshamos*. You are not performing a regular job like one who fashions tables or chairs, which do not have a soul. These are the holy *neshamos* of Klal Yisrael, and we do not know what will become of each of our students…

"There are well-known stories in recent times involving *talmidim* who were disobedient and mischievous, who then went on to become *gedolei Yisrael*. If a *bachur* commits mischief, one should definitely respond appropriately, but one must respond carefully — and not excessively, *chas v'shalom*, in a way that the child will be ashamed, disenfranchising him and pushing him away."

Loving Rebuke

*A*s an illustration of the benefits of effective reproof carried out in a pleasant, private manner, Rav Avrohom Pam often recalled an incident about his mother, Rebbetzin Rochel Leah.

When she was 9 years old, she wanted to fast the whole day on the *taanis* of Asarah B'Teves. Knowing that her father, the Shedlitzer Rav, would not approve, she spent the day at the home of friends, so that her parents wouldn't realize she was fasting until the day was over.

At nightfall, she returned home and explained where she had been all day. At that moment, the *dayan* of Shedlitz was in the house of the rav, and hearing what had occurred, he became incensed.

"You should give that girl a *potch*!" he exclaimed. "I would teach that little *fasterke* [fasting one] a lesson she will never forget! I would not tolerate such behavior!"

Rochel Leah's father ignored the suggestion of the *dayan*. Instead, he gave her supper and sent her to sleep. Once she was in bed, he went into her room and sat down next to her.

"My dear daughter," he said, "you wanted to perform the mitzvah of fasting like an adult. However, you should know that if someone is not required to fast, it is a sin to do so. In fact, it is a mitzvah for a growing girl to watch her health by eating properly. When you will be a bas mitzvah, you will then be obligated to fast.

"Now, you must be exhausted. Go to sleep and have a sweet rest! Good night."

The loving words of the Shedlitzer Rav pierced the heart of his 9-year-old daughter. Eight decades later, when the rebbetzin would relate the story, those words were still fresh and warm in her mind.

— *heard from Rabbi Sholom Smith*

Still Speaking This Way

Jewish secular author Shalom Yehuda was once taking a stroll with the well-known Zionist leader, Dr. Max Nordau. Mr. Yehuda had a question for Dr. Nordau: Dr. Nordau was known for his antagonism toward religious Judaism, yet at the First Zionist Congress, which was held in Basil, Switzerland in August 1897, he had spoken favorably about the Jewish religion, quoting the Rashi about Rachel Imeinu crying for the welfare of her children. Now Mr. Yehuda complimented Nordau for his oratory skills, but expressed wonder that Nordau would quote a Rashi. And besides, he queried, how did Nordau know this Rashi? Did he ever learn in *cheder*?

The doctor answered with a story:

Not long ago, a poor woman came to my medical practice in Paris with her young son. They were obviously from the Jewish quarter of the city. The boy's face was pale and drawn. He didn't speak French, only Yiddish. I asked him where he learns, and he answered, "In the cheder."

The woman started complaining that her fanatical husband did not allow the boy to attend a modern school, where the child could gain the skills to earn a living, and I said to myself, "How pitiful are these people who discard the modern culture for their old-fashioned teachings."

I asked the boy cynically, "Nu, so tell me what you learned in your cheder."

Suddenly, the boy perked up and some color returned to his face. He recited the passage (Bereishis 48:7) that speaks of Yaakov's words to Yosef, explaining why Rachel was not buried in Me'aras HaMachpeilah along with the rest of the Patriarchs and Matriarchs: "When I came from Padan, Rachel died on me in the land of Canaan on the road, while there was still a stretch of land to go before coming to Efras. I buried her there on the road to Efras, which is Beis Lechem."

Then the child quoted the Rashi, in which Yaakov said to Yosef: "I am burdening you to bury me in the land of Canaan even though I did not do the same for your mother, for she died near Beis Lechem. And don't think the rains prevented me, for it was the dry season, and I didn't even carry her to Beis Lechem to bring her to a settled land. I know that you have resentment toward me, but know that it was by the word of G-d that I buried her there."

Now the boy perked up as he continued quoting the words of the Rashi, which give Yaakov's explanation to his son: "So that she will help her descendants when Nevuzaradun will send them into exile. And when they pass by her grave, she will emerge from her grave and cry and beseech mercy for them."

I looked at the boy who, just moments ago, had seemed lethargic and weak. Now he had come alive and there was fire in his eyes, as he concluded with the words from Yirmiyahu (31:14-15), "A voice is heard from Ramah, Rachel is weeping for her children. She refuses to be consoled for her children who are not here." And, as is cited in Rashi and quoted by this child, Hashem answers her: "There is reward for your toil for your children will return to their border."

"This left an indelible impression on me," explained Dr. Nordau, "and it made me think that if Jews still speak this way and remember such a story after so many years of exile, then we can be confident that our nation will survive. This boy changed my views on the future of Israel."

This is the result of a strong chinuch.

— *heard from Rabbi Yitzchok Tzvi Schwarz*

Only Kosher

The *menahel* of a *cheder* in an American town tried his best to get the local residents to enroll their children in his school. During one of his rounds to homes in the city, he stopped at the residence of a Jew, who, unfortunately, was far removed from religion. Not having received a Jewish education himself, the man's knowledge of *Yiddishkeit* was virtually non-existent.

Still, despite his lack of connection to Judaism, the man graciously welcomed the *menahel* into his home. However, when he heard that the *menahel* had come to persuade him to send his children to the local *cheder*, he immediately rejected his visitor's overtures. "There's no reason my children should receive an education that is any different from the one I received," he said tersely. "What was good for me is good for them."

Despite his insistence on not enrolling his children in the Jewish school, the man assured the *menahel* that he respects, and maintains a relationship with, the *frum* institutions in the town, and proceeded to write out a generous check for the *cheder*.

During the course of the visit, in his desire to demonstrate warmth and hospitality, the host brought the *menahel* a cup of tea. The *menahel* politely declined. The host sensed that the *menahel's* refusal was based on his concern regarding the kashrus of the home.

"If you are concerned about it being kosher," the man said, "I can assure you that you have nothing to worry about. Everything in this house is 100 percent kosher, according to the strictest letter of the law. We only purchase foodstuffs bearing the most respected certifications and keep separate utensils for milk and meat. And every year, before Pesach, a rabbi comes to our home to make it kosher for the holiday. Believe me, you can trust our kashrus!"

The *menahel* looked at the man in surprise. This was the strangest thing. Why did this non-religious Jewish man keep kosher, and with such fastidiousness to boot?

"Let me explain," the man said, responding to the *menahel's* unarticulated question. He then told his story:

> In my younger years, I served in the American Army. During World War II, I was sent to Occupied Poland to fight the Nazis. I was completely ignorant about Judaism, but I had a Jewish heart and wished to do whatever I could to assist my Jewish brethren. Thus, after the war, I joined a group of soldiers who went from concentration camp to concentration camp. I brought along bars of chocolate, which I gave to the very grateful survivors, whose gaunt faces made it clear just how malnourished they were.
>
> Arriving in one of the camps, I encountered a Jew who was completely emaciated. He was lying on the ground, on the verge of death. I hurried to place some chocolate in his mouth, but the man refused. He closed his mouth and muttered feebly, "Nahr kosher! [Only kosher!]"
>
> Due to my ignorance, I had no idea what "kosher" was, so I tried again to push some food into the mouth of the dying man, but once again he refused. And again he began muttering. I put my ear to his mouth and I heard him repeat those two words: "Nahr kosher!"
>
> I tried to absorb and understand what the man was saying, but I was at a loss. Before I knew it, this man, lying right in front of me, had departed to a better world. I was gripped by the horror of what had just taken place. This man had survived the concentration camps only to die in my presence due to a lack of understanding between us.
>
> I decided right then that when I returned to America, I would find out the meaning of this strange word "kosher." After all,

if a Jew's last words on this world were related to this term, it must be something significant.

When I arrived in America after the war, I learned from a local rabbi the meaning of kosher. I finally understood what that dying Holocaust survivor on the other side of the world had been trying to convey to me, and I accepted upon myself never to put into my mouth food that is not kosher.

"It is for this reason that in our home we are scrupulous about the laws of kashrus, to the nth degree," concluded the man.

Hearing the moving tale, the *menahel* smiled. "If this is the case," he said, "you surely want your children to also follow the strict dietary laws of kosher. Like all fathers, you wish for your children to continue in your path of tradition. However, they didn't witness the enormous sacrifice for kashrus that you saw firsthand in Europe. They have only observed it as the custom of their father's home. This will not in any way ensure that they keep this tradition in the coming years.

"The only way to ensure that your tradition is followed by your children and future generations is by providing your children with an authentic Jewish education. In a Jewish day school, they will receive a pure Torah education, training them to live like Jews and, of course, to meticulously follow the laws of kashrus."

The man knew that the *menahel* was speaking words of truth. The plea penetrated the man's heart and he agreed to enroll his children in the local *cheder*.

His children ultimately became upstanding bnei Torah, carrying on the mesorah of their forebears.

That unnamed Polish Jew, through his resoluteness during the final moments of his life, brought about the return of an entire family to the ways of Torah.

The Truth Above All

A soon-to-be bar mitzvah *bachur* had the opportunity to receive a *berachah* from Rav Aharon Leib Shteinman. In preparation for his big day, when he would become a *bar chiyuva*, he asked the *gadol* what *kabbalah* he should accept upon himself.

As the young *bachur* posed his question, myriad possibilities ran through his mind, from extra learning and *kavanah* in *tefillah* to other areas of mitzvah observance to which he could pay extra heed.

Rav Shteinman looked at the sweet *bachur* with a smile and answered him. *"Tzu zuggen der emes*, to say the truth," said Rav Shteinman, who is known for his precision, exactitude, and meticulousness in all discussions, *"viel dos iz der ershte zach*, because that is number one."

The *bachur*, a bit surprised by the answer, pressed on, asking Rav Shteinman if by accepting upon himself to always say the truth, he will merit becoming an *adam gadol*.

"Yes," Rav Shteinman said and then repeated, *"vayl dos iz der ershte zach."*

Shabbos in Middle of the Week

R av Gamliel Rabinovich *was acquainted with the well-known Kopschitz family who resided in Yerushalayim, and was most impressed by the wonderful children they raised.*

Rav Gamliel related that when he got married, he approached the Kopschitzes to find out the secret to their success.

"Whenever one of our children brought home a good report card," they told Rav Gamliel, "we would serve a Shabbos meal in the middle of the week — all because 'Yankele brought home a *tzetel.'* In contrast, if a child brought home a bad report, we didn't say a word to him, but both of us would fast."

Rav Gamliel later said that this original form of chinuch shaped his outlook on educating Yiddishe kinder.

"Ah Gefunene"

As a yungerman living and learning in Lakewood, life was idyllic for Rabbi Mordechai Levin. He lived in a beautiful fifth-floor apartment overlooking Lake Carasaljo, and he and his wife enjoyed each day, along with their two adorable children. One fateful day, shortly before Rosh Hashanah, his innocent life was forever changed.

Reb Mordechai had just put his two children in for a nap and was sitting down for lunch. Suddenly, he heard his daughter scream, "Chesky fell out the window!" He rushed to the children's room, where he saw an open window next to the bed. The screen was missing. He rushed to the window, looked down, and saw something that no parent should ever have to see. Five stories below, he saw the tiny figure of his almost 3-year-old son, apparently lifeless.

He ran out of his apartment and flew down the five flights of steps. While it likely took no more than 10 seconds for Reb Mordechai to make it to the ground floor, it felt like forever. With a prayer on his lips, Reb Mordechai rushed out the side door to find his son lying on a grass strip, which was about three feet wide and surrounded by cement steps and an asphalt driveway.

Reb Mordechai leaned over his son, who lay there motionless. His eyes were closed, his angelic face framed by blond curls. As Reb Mordechai bent closer to see if his son was breathing, Chesky's eyes fluttered open. The boy at first looked confused, but then broke into a beautiful smile, as if he had just woken up from a light nap and his father had come to greet him.

A Hatzolah call went out for a toddler who had fallen out of a fifth-story window at 426 North Lake Drive. Two Hatzolah members responded within minutes and the child was rushed to the hospital. Amazingly, he suffered only two minor hairline fractures. The Levins were told to keep Chesky off his feet for two weeks, but the rambunctious child had other plans and was up and running in two days. Soon enough, the story of the "miracle boy" was written up in the local paper, with the headline: Boy Falls from Fifth Story Window, Survives.

"How did he survive?" people still ask when they recall the story. "Is it true that the screen fell with him and acted as a type of parachute? Is it true that he bounced off a small bush, which helped cushion his fall? Isn't it amazing that he landed on a small patch of grass versus the wide area of cement all around?"

Reb Mordechai smiles, gives a slight nod, and responds, "All true, but not the whole truth."

The day after the incident, Reb Mordechai received a phone call from his grandmother, Rebbetzin Zlata Ginsburg. Rebbetzin Ginsburg was the wife of Rav Efraim Mordechai Ginsburg, rosh yeshivah of the Mirrer Yeshivah in Brooklyn, and also the daughter of the famed mashgiach, Rav Chatzkel Levenstein, after whom Chesky is named. The rebbetzin immediately put the incident into perspective.

"Your son is a 'gefunene,' a 'found' person," she said. "In Europe, if one went through a traumatic experience, such as a fire or an accident, and miraculously survived, he was then referred to as a 'gefunene,' for in truth, he should no longer have been alive and yet was given newfound life by HaKadosh Baruch Hu."

The rebbetzin said that raising a "gefunene" comes with achrayus. "Now you must be certain to make something special of your son's life," she concluded.

Nowadays, Reb Chesky and his wife, Leah, are also living an idyllic life in the very same Lakewood where the incident took place so many years ago. Reb Mordechai, for his part, is never more than a few thoughts away from the "gefunene" mindset. He knows that he must cherish every moment in which he has this matanah from the Aibeshter.

As we look at our own lives, can we identify the "gefunenes" we've been blessed with? Do we cherish and guard each one as we should?

"I Never Thought About Myself"

Stories of the Torah greatness and sterling character traits of Rav Michel Yehudah Lefkowitz continue to inspire Jews around the globe. In addition, Rav Michel Yehudah was the *address for many rebbeim and mechanchim*, who turned to him with their *chinuch shailos*.

One veteran *mechanech* in Eretz Yisrael posed all his *chinuch* questions to Rav Michel Yehudah. One day, he presented a very personal question to the rosh yeshivah.

"I feel like I am not *shteiging* as an individual," the *mechanech* related. "I am considering taking two years off to recharge. I will go back to kollel and rejuvenate myself. I have been promised that I won't lose my *shteller*. I just feel that I need some time off to get to where I want to be in terms of *aliyah*."

The *mechanech* had little doubt that Rav Michel Yehudah would support his plan. He was thus stunned when the rosh yeshivah advised him to present the *shailah* to someone else for a decision.

"But rosh yeshivah," asked the *mechanech*, "in all the years, you have answered every question of mine. Never have you referred me to someone else. Why now?"

Rav Michel Yehudah explained, "I have been in *chinuch* for 65 years. *Ich hub kein mol nit getracht vegen zich alein.* I never thought about myself. *Ich hub nahr getracht vegen der shteigen fun meine talmidim.* I focused only on the growth of my *talmidim*. If you are thinking about yourself, you have to ask your *shailah* of someone who understands someone who thinks about himself."

The mechanech got his answer.

A Mother's Prayers

Rav Eliyahu Cheshin was a talmid of the famed Talmud Torah Eitz Chaim and Yeshiva L'Metzuyanim of Rav Chaim Aharon Turchin, and was among the first talmidim of Rav Avraham Ye-

hoshua Soloveitchik in Yeshivas Brisk. He now serves as a melamed at a cheder in the Ramot section of Yerushalayim. Rav Cheshin, a star mechanech for over three decades, is wholly devoted to chinuch habanim.

Rav Cheshin spends some time in the United States before Pesach each year, providing consultation to mosdos hachinuch on American shores. It is always a treat for me to see him during these visits.

During one such visit, Rav Cheshin shared that when he has a *talmid* who is struggling in his learning and requires tutoring help outside of school time, he advises the *talmid*'s father to learn with his son.

"I understand that sometimes it is more difficult for the father to do so and some people prefer to hire a tutor, but I feel strongly that it should be the father," Rav Cheshin stated. "In fact, in cases where the father does not know the *limud* well enough to review it with his son, I encourage him to hire a *talmid chacham* to learn with him *be'chavrusa*, so that he will understand the material we are learning, and will be able to learn successfully with his son."

Rav Cheshin surprised me as he shared the reasoning for his stance on this particular topic.

"I feel that the father, rather than a tutor, should be learning with his son because the father will truly comprehend, firsthand, the struggles his child is having in grasping what the class is learning. The father will ultimately share this fact with his wife, the child's mother. Sensing the genuine need for help from Heaven, she will engage in intense *tefillah* for the success of her son.

"It is because I want the mother's heartfelt prayers and pure tears on behalf of her son that I encourage the father to learn with his struggling son. That is the most potent recipe for the success of a *Yiddishe kind*."

In his youth, Rav Moshe Shternbuch of the Eidah HaChareidis was a member of the *shiur* of the Tchebiner Rav, Rav Dov Berish Weidenfeld. One day, the rav challenged his students with a difficult question, and Rav Shternbuch offered a dazzling answer, which resolved the query.

The rav smiled, appreciating his *talmid*'s profound response. He then said, "In truth, this answer is not your own."

Observing the quizzical looks on the faces of his students and young Moshe, Rav Weidenfeld clarified, "In truth, this answer is your mother's. It is due to her tears and prayers when you were young that you merited such brilliance in Torah, enabling you to offer such a deep and insightful reply."

Wait for Bein Hazmanim

Rav Michel Yehudah Lefkowitz suffered from poor eyesight for many years and underwent several operations. Despite his thick eyeglasses, as he aged he struggled to see. When he was given expensive new glasses that allowed him to read the Gemara with ease, his excitement was obvious. It was the first time in years that he could see clearly.

His *talmidim* were surprised when, the very next day, Rav Michel Yehudah was seen in yeshivah wearing his old glasses. He later explained, "I will have to wait until *bein hazmanim* to make the change. If I enter yeshivah with the new glasses, it will create a distraction among the *talmidim*, and that will cause *bitul Torah*."

After wearing the glasses during *bein hazmanim*, he said, the issue wouldn't cause such a tumult when the next *zman* commenced.

Chocolate Pudding Chinuch

Years ago, a *cheder* in Eretz Yisrael gave out chocolate pudding to its students each month, in honor of Rosh Chodesh. The boys stood in line, their mouths salivating as they waited to receive this delectable treat.

One Rosh Chodesh, a youngster sneaked back into line after polishing off his pudding, looking for doubles. When the boy reached the front of the line, the yeshivah cook realized that he had already had one portion and loudly chastised him for his transgression: "How dare you try to take a second portion?" Then the cook ordered the child to leave the room.

Thoroughly embarrassed, and seething at the cook for berating him in front of the other students, the boy took the pot of pudding from which the cook had been dishing out the portions and dumped it on the floor.

The cook was furious. He grabbed the boy and schlepped him to the *menahel*. The *menahel* spoke to the lad briefly and told him that he was at serious risk of expulsion from the yeshivah. But first, he was to meet with Rav Aryeh Levin, the *tzaddik* of Yerushalayim, with whom the yeshivah's *hanhalah* consulted regarding important decisions.

The next day, the boy arrived at the home of Rav Levin. As he sat in front of the *tzaddik*, his fingers were cold and numb, and he shook with fright. *What*, he wondered, *was going to happen*?

Turning to the boy, Rav Levin asked him, "Do you regret what you did?"

"Yes."

"Would you ever do such a thing again?"

"No, definitely not."

"O.K., then," said Rav Levin, stroking the boy's cheek. "I see that you like chocolate pudding. And you know what? So do I!"

With a smile, Rav Levin promptly took out two servings of chocolate pudding for him and the boy to enjoy.

The Challenges of the Street

W hy do children go off the derech? Says Rabbi Dov Brezak: Because of the enormous forces pulling children away from anything that has to do with kedushah. This pull is stronger today than ever before. Unless someone — especially a child — is anchored strongly to Yiddishkeit, he is in danger of being pulled away. Some are more strongly anchored and others are less so. Yet even those who are not going off face a constant struggle to fight the temptations and trials the yetzer hara places before them. Today, one need not do anything to be pulled away from Yiddishkeit. One needs to take positive action so that he not be pulled away.

To back up his point, Rabbi Brezak related the following story:

A yeshivah *bachur* was offered a *shidduch* with a young woman who was purported to have special *middos* and pure *hashkafos*. She was also the daughter of a well-known rosh yeshivah. The boy was very interested.

Still, there was a problem: The girl's brother had gone off the *derech*. The *bachur* was troubled by the dictum of Chazal (*Bava Basra* 110a) that one should check out a woman's brothers before considering her as a possible candidate for marriage, since most children are similar to their mother's brothers.

The *bachur*, who very much wanted to move forward with the *shidduch* but was steadfast in his loyalty to the teachings of Chazal, went to Rav Elazar Menachem Man Shach, hoping that the *gadol* could help. Rav Shach responded that there was no problem with his accepting the *shidduch*. He added that according to the Chazon Ish, these words of Chazal apply only to character traits — which can be hereditary and dependent on familial associations — but not to matters of one's *hashkafos* or worldview, which depend on *bechirah*, free will, and are not hereditary.

The young man was relieved and told his mother about Rav Shach's response. His mother countered that this case certainly involved *middos*. The pain the girl's brother caused his parents by going off the *derech* is immeasurable, yet this did not prevent him from leaving his parents' ways, nor, as of that point, had it caused him to return. Anyone so oblivious to the pain he is causing his parents is a paradigm of bad *middos*, said the mother. The young man returned to Rav Shach and relayed his mother's take on the matter.

"Tell your mother," said Rav Shach, "that the challenges of the street today are so great, and the pull is so strong, that one cannot judge a person's *middos* by his lack of ability to stand up to these trials. The wayward child's reluctance to come back does not stem from bad *middos*, but from the difficulties involved and from his own inability to withstand the attraction of the street.

"Proceed with the *shidduch*, and I give you my blessing," Rav Shach concluded.

The necessary introductions were made, and eventually the couple married and successfully raised a Torah family.

> *After sharing this story, Rabbi Brezak quoted the following prescient words written in the Chovas HaTalmidim (Chapter 6) by the Piaseczna Rebbe, Rav Klonimus Kalman Shapira, some 75 years ago:*
>
> *First, we must explain the difference between one generation and another. Why, in previous generations, did every style of chinuch succeed and almost every person was an oveid Hashem? The simple and principal reason is that today young people consider themselves mature adults well before their time. The entire world is complaining about this. We are not here to explain why it is so, but this is the fact.*
>
> *Our Sages informed us long ago that in the times of Mashiach, there will be abundant chutzpah in the world. One way that this chutzpah presents itself is that a child thinks he is mature enough to rely on himself. This spirit has become so prevalent that we are sometimes shocked to see even in very small children how this spirit of independence and boldness is already becoming apparent, such that they think themselves to be adults.*
>
> *Rav Shlomo Wolbe would comment that we can observe this phenomenon in a 3-year-old child. When he is given a potch, he will often raise his hand to hit his father or mother back; the only thing that prevents him from following through is the fact that the parent is bigger than he is.*

But the spirit of rebelliousness is there even from a young age, as the Chovas HaTalmidim continues to explain:

Because of this, every child views his parents and educators as cruel tyrants who are trying to rule over him by force and rob him of his independence. A type of resistance — even a hatred — is aroused in the youth toward his parents and educators, to the point that he pays no attention to what they have to say, but cares only about how to free himself of their authority and be liberated from their rule.

It is not sufficient to tell the child that he has to listen, because this will not work. The main thing is to teach the child that he is his own mechanech (i.e., that he is in charge of himself). He has to view himself as a vine planted in the vineyard of the House of Yisrael, and to realize that Hashem has entrusted him with the obligation to grow this small vine into a big tree, a tree of life.

His educators and parents are here only to instruct him how to be mechanech himself. This can be compared to someone who goes to a rav to ask a shailah. All the rav will do is tell him what is kosher or nonkosher, but the responsibility to throw away the part that is treif lies entirely with the one who asked the shailah, not with the rav.

Rebbi and Student

Rav Yechiel Mendelson — who heads the Mendelson's Girls High School in Yerushalayim, serves as the rosh yeshivah of Yeshivas Birchas Aryeh, and founded Yeshivas Ohr Elchanan L'Tzeirim in Givat Shaul — related the following:

Rav Simcha Wasserman was once going to Radin to see the Chofetz Chaim. On the way, he paid a visit to Rav Yerucham Levovitz in Mir. After greeting him, Rav Yerucham asked him for his name, and Rav Simcha replied that he was a son of Rav Elchanan Wasserman and that he was on his way to the Chofetz Chaim.

There was no point in Rav Yerucham asking Rav Simcha to stay and learn in the Mir, as he was on his way to Radin. Instead, Rav Yerucham shared brief but forceful words of wisdom with the young *talmid chacham*.

"I want to tell you something that I generally tell only to my *talmidim*," said Rav Yerucham. "Even though you are not my *talmid*, I will tell you because you are Rav Elchanan's son. There is a saying (*Pesachim* 112a) that more than the calf wants to suckle, the cow wishes to nurse. The common explanation for this is that a cow feels pain if its milk is not expressed. Clearly, then, the mother wishes to nurse more than her offspring wants to drink, because otherwise she will be in pain.

"But this is not the way I understand it," Rav Yerucham said. "The calf doesn't yet understand the benefit of what it receives along with its milk. The mother cow knows very well what her calf needs, and how much the milk nourishes it and causes it to grow, and that is why she wishes to nurse her young — not because she feels the need to rid herself of her milk."

Rav Yerucham then went on: "This is often compared to the relationship between a rebbi and a student. It is said that more than a student wishes to learn, the rebbi wishes to teach. Here, too, it must be made clear that if the rebbi's desire to teach is due to the fact that he has a good *vort* to say and he feels intense pressure to tell it to someone — and his *talmid* is merely his medium — then that is just plain awful. Rather, a rebbi must carefully ascertain what is good for his student, what *vort* will help him understand a *sugya*. That is how a rebbi must teach."

Rav Simcha would often share these words with *talmidim* and others with great enthusiasm.

> *Rav Simcha added a postscript to the story: Rav Yerucham concluded by telling him, "You may not understand what I am telling you now, but the day will yet come when you will." And yes, that day did arrive. In fact, this actually encapsulates the essence of Rav Simcha himself. It is exactly what Rav Simcha, a loving rosh yeshivah and rebbi, was all about.*
>
> *Rav Dovid Feldman, the head of Yeshivas Ohr Elchanan L'Tzeirim in Kiryat Sefer, compiled the sefer B'Hikavetz, which*

contains an index of all of Rav Elchanan Wasserman's sefarim and a brief synopsis of each of his chiddushim, and was published under Rav Simcha Wasserman's auspices.

Rav Feldman remarked: "I consulted with Rav Simcha on every detail, including what to write in the introduction. He instructed me to mention the incident with Rav Yerucham. He then told me that he felt that his father's Torah became so famous and is commonly learned throughout the yeshivah world because his father always taught his students in accordance with what they needed to hear, not what he felt he needed to share."

The Responsibility of a Rebbi

Rav Achikam Shevach, rosh yeshivah of Yeshivas Ohr El-chanan in Teveriah, related the following in the name of Rav Moshe Mordechai Chodosh:

Rav Simcha Wasserman once entered a class in an elementary school in Los Angeles and told the rebbi, "You must understand the enormous responsibility you have. In a *talmud Torah* in Yerushalayim called Bnei Tzion, 80 years ago, there were boys named Bentzion, Yehudah, and Ovadiah. Their rebbi took his responsibility toward them very seriously.

"If he had been negligent in his task, *chas v'shalom*, and if he hadn't given them everything they needed to grow, then the world would have lost Rav Bentzion Abba-Shaul, Rav Yehudah Tzadkah, and Rav Ovadiah Yosef."

An All-Encompassing Love

Rav Achikam Shevach also related the following vignettes, which show Rav Simcha Wasserman's love for all yeshivah students:

After traveling on a public bus that was packed with young yeshivah students, Rav Simcha declared, "I should have hugged them and kissed them!"

A different time, on Rosh Hashanah, Rav Simcha was with the *talmidim* of Yeshivas Ohr Elchanan in the yeshivah's dining room. He remarked, "I don't need an apple or honey. All I have to do is place my hand on a student's head and say the *Y'hi Ratzon* for a sweet new year."

A Taste *of* Teaching

A Mashgiach's Job

Rav Shlomo Wolbe once interviewed a candidate for the position of mashgiach at the *yeshivah ketanah* in Be'er Yaakov. Everything, in Rav Wolbe's words, was "beautiful," a term that he often employed.

But the "beauty" of the interview ended when the candidate inquired about the extent of his authority.

"Regarding what?" Rav Wolbe asked.

"Who has the authority to expel a *bachur*? Would it be me or the *hanhalah*?" the would-be mashgiach asked.

Rav Wolbe was silent for a moment. Then he said, "You can't be a mashgiach here. The job of a mashgiach here is not to expel anyone. It is only to help."

Playing Pretend

Rav Moshe Mordechai Chodosh defined the educational approach of his revered father, Rav Meir Chodosh, mashgiach in Yeshivas Chevron:

"In his *shmuessen* in the yeshivah, and certainly in his private conversations with *bachurim*, my father was always very careful not to offend a *talmid*. When Rav Aharon, my brother, became the mashgiach at Yeshivas Mir Yerushalayim, my father said to him,

'Some people think that a mashgiach is considered successful when he catches a *bachur* acting improperly, but I feel that a mashgiach is successful when he knows how to practice self-restraint.'

"In other words," said Rav Moshe Mordechai, "a mashgiach should learn to pretend that he doesn't see certain things. A mashgiach needs to know what is happening, but he also needs to make sure that the *talmid* doesn't know that he knows."

Raising Masmidim

Dayan Aharon Dovid Dunner of London related the following eye-opener: A newly appointed mashgiach of a yeshivah visited Rav Yosef Shalom Elyashiv and asked him how to approach his new position.

Rav Elyashiv answered, "*B'derech hateva*, a *masmid* usually becomes a *talmid chacham*. A *baal kishron*, one with a good head, does not necessarily become a *talmid chacham*. Your job is to see to it that a *bachur* becomes a *masmid*.

"But one doesn't make *masmidim*," Rav Elyashiv went on. "*Hasmadah* comes from inside the person. Often, though, there are worries within the *talmid*'s heart that prevent him from totally dedicating himself to learning. These worries vary from family issues and relationships with friends to doubting one's own abilities. Your job as a mashgiach is to clear these worries from the *talmid*'s heart so that it is free to imbibe the wonderful words of Torah."

Who Succeeds?

Eliezer came from a somewhat traditional family. He possessed exemplary *middos* and *yiras Shamayim*, but he was academically weak and found it difficult to learn.

A *yungerman* who learned with Eliezer took him to visit Rav

Michel Yehudah Lefkowitz, hoping that the rosh yeshivah would be able to offer encouragement and guidance to the boy.

Eliezer told Rav Michel Yehudah about the difficulty he experienced in his learning.

"I try my hardest," he said. "I really do. But I can't seem to grasp the Gemara."

"What does your father do?" Rav Michel Yehudah asked.

"He is a carpenter," said the boy.

"Is he *shomer Torah u'mitzvos*?"

"Not really," said the boy, a bit embarrassed.

"Do you have any brothers in yeshivah?" asked Rav Michel Yehudah.

"No."

"Are your sisters in *frum* schools?"

"No."

Rav Michel Yehudah stroked the boy's face. "Do you know what kind of responsibility rests on your shoulders? You are the only one in your family learning Torah! You must carry your entire *mishpachah*!"

Eliezer was still heartbroken. "But I just can't learn!" he said, sobbing. "I try and I try, but it is impossible!"

Rav Michel Yehudah's eyes also filled with tears. He said to the boy, "I have been the rosh yeshivah of the Yeshivas Ponovezh L'Tzeirim for many decades. Experience has shown me that it is not the brilliant boys who succeed, but the *masmidim* who keep at it.

"But how can you become a *masmid*? I will tell you how to go about it: Learn during your yeshivah's *sedarim*; don't learn late at night and don't skip meals. Sleep during the time designated for sleeping, eat during the times designated for eating, and learn during the times designated for learning. Just keep at it and you will see the gates of learning suddenly open for you. You will begin to understand the Torah you are learning, and you will see great success."

As the boy hung onto every word, his face slowly began to brighten.

"And one more thing," concluded Rav Michel Yehudah. "Any time you are having a hard time or are feeling discouraged, please come back to me and we will talk. I am always here, available to speak to you."

Proper Sleep

One of the *talmidim* of Rav Chaim Elazar Spira, the Minchas Elazar of Munkatch, was an incredibly diligent *bachur* who only slept two hours each night. The Rebbe called him in to discuss his daily schedule.

"I hear that you sleep for two hours every day," the Rebbe said. "Why so many? Do you know how much you can accomplish in two hours of learning? You are wasting two full hours to sleep."

The boy didn't understand what the Rebbe wanted from him. Most people sleep three or four times that amount.

The Rebbe explained: "When a Yid sleeps the amount he is supposed to, in accordance with Chazal and the *gedolim*, he is sleeping in order to clear his head to learn and perform his *avodas Hashem*; he refreshes himself to enhance his ability to learn properly. In essence, his sleep is *avodas Hashem*.

"But if you sleep for just two hours, that is not enough for your body, and it hardly helps you because you are still not calm and relaxed. So it is just a waste of time. If the sleep didn't do what it was supposed to, then two hours is a lot of squandered time."

A Rosh Yeshivah and a Kindergarten

After immigrating to America, Rav Reuven Grozovsky became rosh yeshivah of Yeshivah Torah Vodaath and Beth Medrash Elyon. He once addressed the founding gathering of a day school in Providence, Rhode Island, with the following words:

"What role does a rosh yeshivah have in the establishment of a kindergarten?" he asked. "Doesn't the have other things on his mind? But that isn't the case," he explained. "There's a long-standing rule in the Torah that saving lives assumes priority over everything else. Without Torah study, the children of this community are being buried alive. Without this kindergarten, they will, of course, go to school and learn about George Washington and Thomas Jefferson, but they will never know about Avraham, Yitzchak, Yaakov, or Moshe Rabbeinu. First and foremost, we must ascertain that these children will live.

"Do you know at what point light radiated from Moshe Rabbeinu's face? Not when Hashem first spoke to him, but when he became the intermediary between Hashem and His people, teaching His Torah to Yidden.

"If, as a result of this event, we manage to teach Torah to but one child, we will be worthy of being blessed with the light of Torah."

Lack of Emunah

A 15-year-old approached the great *Yerushalmi tzaddik* and *mechaber sefarim*, Rav Zundel Kroizer, and told him that he was not able to learn.

Rav Zundel looked at him and said, "It isn't the learning that's your problem. The problem is that you don't have *emunah*."

The *bachur* was horrified. His *emunah*? He was quite a serious boy. As far as he was concerned, his *emunah* was not at all compromised.

Rav Zundel smiled and continued: "Don't we say, '*Tov li Toras picha mei'alfei zahav va'chesef* — The Torah of Your mouth is better for me than thousands of gold and silver coins' (*Tehillim* 119:72)? If you truly believed that every word of Torah was worth a dollar, you would learn all day long."

A powerful, if difficult, lesson.

Yeshivah Policy

Atalmid of Beth Medrash Elyon had set up a demanding personal regimen that did not conform to the yeshivah schedule. When the rosh yeshivah, Rav Reuven Grozovsky, took him to task, the young man offered what he thought was an effective defense.

Rav Reuven replied, "You must understand: First of all, there are two types of yeshivos: *hanhalah un nit-hanhalah*, those run by the administration and those not run by the administration. In this yeshivah, which is run by the administration, it is expected that you conform to the directions of the *hanhalah*.

"Second, everyone needs a rebbi for guidance. Do you realize that long after he was established as a rosh yeshivah, my sainted father-in-law, Rav Baruch Ber Leibowitz, still consulted with both the Chofetz Chaim and Rav Chaim Brisker? And after Rav Chaim's passing, he consulted with his son, Rav Velvel, even though he was my father-in-law's junior in years? I am fulfilling this function for you by advising you to adhere to the yeshivah schedule.

"Third, even if the yeshivah tells you to do something that is not in your best interests, once the yeshivah has taken a stand, your action involves defiance of yeshivah policy, which can only be harmful to you. It is now to your benefit that you listen."

Of Beds and Bachurim

Rabbi Yosef Meir Katzburg, a resident of the Bayit Vegan neighborhood in Yerushalayim, learned at Yeshivas Kol Torah and later served there as a madrich. The job of a madrich was to awaken the bachurim in the morning for davening and to supervise them during bein hasedarim. He related the following story.

"The rule in the yeshivah was that if I saw that a *bachur* hadn't made his bed, I was to call him out of *shiur* to take care of it. There were even times when a *bachur* who was called out of *shiur* to make his bed wasn't allowed to return to the *shiur*. I always did my job dutifully, but I never dared go into the *shiur* of the rosh yeshivah, Rav Shlomo Zalman Auerbach. I did not have the courage to interrupt his *shiur*.

"One day, I was informed that Rav Shlomo Zalman wanted to see me. 'Listen to me,' he said. 'If a boy from my *shiur* hasn't made his bed, you must come get him — even in middle of my *shiur*!' "

Mealtime Nourishment

A *talmid chacham* once approached Rav Akiva Eiger and asked him for the source of a certain story that he had seen quoted in *sefarim* in the name of a Midrash.

Rav Akiva responded that he had a *sefer* where the story is mentioned, but it was at the very top of his bookcase, near the ceiling. He asked the gentleman if he could kindly climb on a small ladder in order to retrieve the volume. Once the man was standing within reach, Rav Akiva directed him toward the volume he had in mind.

The man was surprised when Rav Akiva pointed to none other than the *Tzenah Ur'enah*. First printed in the early 1600's, *Tzenah Ur'enah* is a commentary on the Torah in Yiddish, based on the Midrash, Gemara, and other sources, designed primarily to be studied by women.

The man couldn't contain himself. "Why," he asked Rav Akiva, "would you have learned *Tzenah Ur'enah*?"

Rav Akiva related that he recalled the words of the *Tzenah Ur'enah* from his youth. When he was a child and his mother would feed him, she would read to him from the *Tzenah Ur'enah*. With his innate desire to know and to learn, young Akiva Eiger listened to every word, drinking in the wisdom and messages of Torah imparted by his mother through the *Tzenah Ur'enah*.

With his remarkable memory, he remembered years later what he heard at that juncture.

It is never too early to engage in the spiritual nourishment of one's children. It is an investment whose dividends are eternal.

What to Teach and What Not to Teach

After Rav Reuven Grozovsky would deliver his *shiur* to his *talmidim*, they would crowd around him and question various points. Sometimes, he would concede an area of doubt. A colleague once asked him, "Why do you confuse your *talmidim* by conceding your doubts? A *shiur* should teach absolutes."

Rav Reuven replied, "At times, it is more important to teach that which I do not really know."

Admitting to one's uncertainties can teach as much as deep discourses and brilliant dissertations.

A rosh yeshivah recalled a *shiur* he delivered in Rav Reuven's presence. Rav Reuven asked him, "Why did you quote the *Hagahos Asheri*?"

Hagahos Asheri is the commentary written by Rav Yisrael of Krems, Austria, on the halachic commentary of the Rosh, serving as a source for many otherwise unknown decisions of the Baalei Tosafos.

"I thought it was interesting," the *maggid shiur* said.

"Yes, it was interesting," Rav Reuven said, "but it didn't explain anything. Whatever doesn't add distracts attention from your major thesis and can only spoil your presentation."

Back to the Board

Rav Hirsch Kaplan was a sixth-grade rebbi at Yeshiva Torah Vo-daath in the 1940's. Hailing from the town of Mir, Rav Kaplan communicated with his American students in Yiddish as he taught them Gemara, Chumash with Rashi, and other subjects.

When his students would misbehave, Rav Kaplan would sometimes write their names on the blackboard on a "bad boy" list, as an incentive for them to correct their behavior. When their conduct improved, he would erase their names.

One day, a number of names were written on the board when the principal, Dr. David Stern, walked in unannounced. Immediately, Rav Kaplan pressed his back to the chalkboard in order to hide the names of the boys who had misbehaved. He pressed tightly and moved slowly, left and right, erasing the names with his *kapote*. Dr. Stern spent a few moments with the boys, and as he spoke to them, Rav Kaplan kept his back flush against the blackboard, slowly shifting back and forth, ensuring that all that was left of the names on the board was a big smudge.

Dr. Stern soon left the room escorted by Rav Kaplan. The boys, saw his chalk-white back, and with it they saw how far their rebbi would go to protect their dignity.

— *heard from Rav Nosson Scherman*

Turned Away

Rejection by schools and yeshivos is by no means a new phenomenon. Rav Yerucham Levovitz, the great mashgiach of Mir, pointed to one such rejection as a watershed in his life.

Shortly before the onset of the 20th century, Yerucham, a *bachur* in his 20's, was already known as "the *mechasheif*," the spellbinder, because of his extraordinary ability to influence others. It was at that point that he decided to go to the famous Talmud Torah of Kelm, led by the Alter of Kelm, Rav Simcha Zissel Ziv.

The Alter was very selective about whom he accepted into the yeshivah. He chose carefully and then embarked on molding those *talmidim* into giants of Torah and *mussar*. Most of the applicants to his yeshivah were turned away, and even those who were ultimately accepted were rejected the first time they tried to gain entry. Yerucham was no different.

When he arrived at the Talmud Torah in Elul 1897, he was not even permitted in the door. He stood outside the Talmud Torah crying in bitter disappointment for several hours.

"If there is anything in me," he later told his *talmid*, Rav Dovid Povarsky, "it is because of those hours that I spent crying outside the Talmud Torah in Kelm."

When Yerucham was allowed to enter the yeshivah, he was still not permitted in the *beis midrash* when the Alter delivered his *shmuess*. Finally, after seven months, the Alter gave his official permission and Yerucham was accepted as a regular member of the Talmud Torah.

> *Rav Yerucham taught with his own conduct how to use rejection as an impetus for personal growth and advancement, not allowing obstacles to impede us from reaching our goals.*

Honor for People, Honor for Children

A group of 13-year-olds at Yeshivas Eitz Chaim went to the rosh yeshivah, Rav Isser Zalman Meltzer — with their rebbi — to be tested on what they were learning. Rav Isser Zalman asked them about a certain Tosafos, and one of the students was quick to respond — with the wrong answer. With a smile, Rav Isser Zalman answered, "Wonderful! You surely meant such and such…," and he began to explain the Tosafos properly.

The young boy countered, "No, Rebbi, that's not what I meant…," and he reiterated his incorrect response.

Unruffled, Rav Isser Zalman said, "I understand. Come, let's see…" He then proceeded to explain the Gemara in detail, returning eventually to the question of Tosafos. Afterward, he explained Tosafos's answer in such an erudite fashion that its meaning should have been very clear.

Yet the boy stood his ground. "Why doesn't the rebbi understand? I explained it differently!"

By now the other boys in the class were grinning, and their rebbi was becoming increasingly upset. Still, for the next 10 minutes, Rav Isser Zalman kept trying to explain it to the boy, asking again and again: "You probably meant this, right?"

But the boy would not relent: "No, no…"

Finally, when the situation had gone beyond all reasonable limits, Rav Isser Zalman excused himself and left the room. Curious to see where Rav Isser Zalman had gone, the rebbi opened the door quietly and peeked into the hallway. He saw Rav Isser Zalman pacing the hallway, saying over and over, "When the Torah commanded us to have honor for other people, it was referring to children also."

Shortly thereafter, Rav Isser Zalman reentered the room, returned to his place, and turned to the student with a shining face. Once again, he asked, "Please tell me, how do you explain the words of the Tosafos?"

— *heard from Rabbi Dov Brezak*

Nuggets *of* Wisdom

On Not Giving Up

Rav Yechezkel Abramsky, *dayan* in England and famous author and *talmid chacham*, related how people would often swim across the English Channel, which separated England from France, and then be awarded a prize. One time, just before reaching the French side, one swimmer declared that he absolutely could not swim any farther. The bystanders tried to encourage him and convince him of the folly of giving up his prize after having invested so much time and energy, and just before reaching his goal.

Similarly, said Rav Abramsky, we have suffered so many tragedies during this long exile and we would be foolish to give up now, after all we have invested thus far. All we have to do is keep going just a little bit more, with determination and perseverance.

Because we are almost there.

On True Unity

The Midrash (*Midrash Tannaim, Devarim* 33) tells us that at the time of *Matan Torah*, there was a great noise in the world (*Tehillim* 29:3-9), and the people from the other nations asked Bilaam, the evil prophet, "What is going on? Is another *mabul* coming?" (ibid. v. 10). Bilaam answered that Hashem is giving the Torah to His people, as it says: "*Hashem oz l'amo yitein* — Hashem will give might [a reference to Torah] to His nation." The nations then responded, "*Hashem yevareich es amo va'shalom* — Hashem will bless His nation with peace" (ibid. v. 11).

Rav Meir Shapiro explained that people come together for two reasons. If a tragedy occurs, people often gather to deal with the tragedy. At other times, Torah is what brings people together. But there is a key difference between these gatherings, he said. When people come together in time of danger, then when the danger is over, the people disperse and are no longer united. However, when people come together because of Torah, the Torah causes them to coalesce; they then become a single unit with permanence.

When the nations of the world heard that the Jews were gathered for the purpose of receiving the Torah, they responded by blessing them with *shalom*, peace — the everlasting type of unity, which is forged through Torah.

On Doing for Others

The great Chassidic Rebbe, Rav Moshele of Pshevorsk, once invited a guest into his home. After arranging a full meal for him, he proceeded to prepare a bed for his guest.

The guest was embarrassed and protested, "Please, Rebbe, you do not have to spend your valuable time preparing my bed."

Rav Moshele responded, "I am not preparing your bed. I am preparing my bed."

On Using Time Wisely

The Chofetz Chaim once explained to Rav Elchanan Wasserman how life is like a postcard. At the beginning, you don't conserve space, because you still have a lot of room. But as you start running out of space, you begin to write smaller and smaller to fit in as much as you can.

Similarly, when a person is young, he wastes time, because his whole life is ahead of him. However, as he grows older, he tries to cram in as much Torah and as many mitzvos as he can and regrets all the time he wasted in his youth.

On Currency

Feivel, who was blessed with vast wealth, was getting on in age, so he called his children together in order to impart an important message.

"Dear children," he began, "in the other room, there's a safe containing currency from countries all over the world. Throughout my life, I collected bills and coins from many countries. Soon, I am going to ascend to the Heavenly realm, and I don't know what form of currency is used there. After I die, please open the safe and deposit in my grave all the money I have amassed. This way, I will be able to purchase what I need in the *Olam HaEmes*."

As his children listened carefully, Feivel continued: "In addition to currency, you will also find diamonds wrapped in paper. Please place those into my grave, as well. Who knows? Perhaps none of the money I have collected will be considered legal tender in the next world, and these precious gems will be accepted."

Upon Feivel's death, his children followed his instructions, placing the money and diamonds in his grave. As soon as he arrived in Heaven, Feivel felt thirsty, so he headed to a nearby stand and asked for a drink.

But when it was time to pay, he ran into trouble. The angel in charge would not accept any of his money as payment. Feivel pulled out a variety of bills and coins; he tried a dollar, a *peso*, a *dinar*, and then a *ruble*, but the *malach* shook his head. So he presented a *franc*, a pound, and a *shekel*, but none of them were acceptable either.

All the money he had collected was worthless.

Finally, Feivel reached into his pocket and pulled out a diamond wrapped in paper.

The *malach* smiled. "There you go," he said, as he reached out to accept the payment. "That will work."

To Feivel's surprise, though, it wasn't the diamond that the angel took hold of, but the piece of paper in which it was wrapped.

"This," said the *malach*, waving the paper, "will get you a drink."

Seeing Feivel's bewildered expression, the *malach* explained, "This piece of paper, as you can see, is actually a receipt that you were handed after giving 10 *shekels* to *tzedakah*. This is legal tender here."

This parable, related by the Chofetz Chaim, conveys an important lesson: What we give to others is being deposited into our spiritual bank account for eternity.

Everything else we amass is for naught.

On Taking Responsibility

av Moshe Eliezer Rabinowitz related a question asked by his rebbi, Rav Chaim Shmulevitz. The Gemara in Maseches Rosh Hashanah (17a) tells us that if someone is maavir al middosav — does not insist that things be done according to his wishes — then the Heavenly Tribunal forgives all his sins. We also learn (see Rashi, Bereishis 36:3) that on the day of his chuppah, a chassan is forgiven for all of his aveiros.

We can understand that someone who is maavir al middosav would have his sins forgiven, but why does a chassan deserve this?

Rav Chaim explained that a person who gets married accepts an entirely new level of achrayus. He accepts the physical and emotional responsibility of another person, and that alone is an enormous accomplishment, and enough of a reason to have his sins forgiven.

On Becoming a Leader

journalist once asked Rav Moshe Feinstein why he was regarded as the greatest halachic authority of the generation. Rav Moshe shrugged and said simply, "People come to ask questions, and if they like the answers, then other people come."

No one appoints or elects the gadol hador; Klal Yisrael has an instinct. The nation instinctively and unerringly recognizes its gedolim.

On Giving Advice

When asked why a millionaire would want to consult with him on matters that did not seem to pertain to Torah or halachah, a rav replied with a story:

There was once a king who had a sore throat. His advisers told him to drink oil, but this only made matters worse. Doctors told him to drink vinegar. This made the pain even worse. Then a simple old man suggested that king should just drink water. Of course, this had been the solution all along.

"People create their problems," the rav said. "The rav's job is to explain, with love and compassion, that these problems are only small things, and that the solution has been right in front of them all along."

On Appreciating Our Leaders

When Yaakov Avinu heard that Yosef was still alive in Mitzrayim, he exclaimed, "How great! My son Yosef still lives! I shall go and see him before I die" (*Bereishis* 45:28). Why did Yaakov stress that he must see Yosef before he dies?

When Yaakov Avinu heard that his beloved son Yosef was still alive — spiritually alive and true to the teachings of his home — after all of the *nisyonos* he had undergone, he said, "I must go meet my son Yosef before I die, because by surmounting his *nisyonos*, he has reached such a high level that in the afterlife I may not be able to go near him."

Rav Shmuel Berenbaum, rosh yeshivah of the Mirrer Yeshivah in

Brooklyn, explained that it is well known that Rav Elchanan Wasserman encouraged *talmidim* to visit the Chofetz Chaim, saying, "Go meet the Chofetz Chaim now while he is alive in this world, for in *Olam Haba* he will be in such an exalted place that we won't be able to go near him." The Chofetz Chaim used those exact words when he told his *talmidim* to visit the great *mekubal*, the Baal HaLeshem, Rav Shlomo Elyashiv.

> *In every generation, we are blessed with leaders who have reached lofty levels. We are fortunate to be able to benefit from and be inspired by their wisdom, holiness, and purity. Let us take advantage of the opportunities to be in the presence of these exalted individuals.*

On Garbage Trucks

Writer and speaker David J. Pollay has a popular essay called "The Law of the Garbage Truck." He writes as follows:

> *How often do you let other people's nonsense change your mood? Do you let a bad driver, rude waiter, curt boss, or insensitive employee ruin your day? For an instant, you're probably set back on your heels. However, the mark of a successful person is how quickly he can refocus on what's important. Sixteen years ago I learned this lesson. I learned it in the back of a New York City taxicab. Here's what happened. I hopped in a taxi and we took off for Grand Central Station. We were driving in the right lane when, all of a sudden, a black car jumped out of a parking space right in front of us. My taxi driver slammed on his brakes, skidded, and missed the other car's back end by just inches. The driver of the other car, the guy who almost caused a big accident, whipped his head around and started yelling at us. My taxi driver just smiled and waved at the guy. And I mean, he was friendly. So I said, "Why did you just do that? This guy almost ruined your car and sent us to the hospital!" This is*

when my taxi driver told me about what I now call "The Law of the Garbage Truck."

Many people are like garbage trucks. They run around full of garbage, full of frustration, full of anger, and full of disappointment. As their garbage piles up, they need a place to dump it. And if you let them, they'll dump it on you. When someone wants to dump on you, don't take it personally. Just smile, wave, wish him well, and move on. You'll be happy you did. So this was it: "The Law of the Garbage Truck."

I started thinking: How often do I let garbage trucks run right over me? And how often do I take their garbage and spread it to other people: at work, at home, on the streets? It was on that day that I said, "I'm not going to do that anymore." …Successful people do not let garbage trucks take over their day. What about you? What would happen in your life, starting today, if you let more garbage trucks pass you by?

Here's my bet. You'll be happier. In fact, I guarantee it.

On Strength in Numbers

Rav Yaakov Kamenetsky notes that the plural form of the Hebrew word for man, איש, should be אישים. Yet throughout *Tanach*, the plural is אנשים, a word that seems to highlight the creation of an altogether new entity. This is because people joining together don't create a union of many different members — איש to אישים — but rather a new *metzius*, a new entity, labeled by a brand new word: אנשים.

In contrast to a single individual, the koach of a tzibbur, a group of people, is not merely in the sum of its varied parts, but an altogether new koach, one that equals far more than the quantitative outcome of the strengths and aptitudes of its members.

On Swimming Against the Tide

The Mishnah in *Maseches Kiddushin* (29a) lists the obligations that a father has to his son. At the end, the Mishnah states that a father is obligated to teach his son how to swim. Why is that listed with all the other vital obligations?

Rav Yosef Shalom Elyashiv explained that any piece of wood can float. That is not called "swimming." The art of swimming is the ability to propel oneself against the tide.

> *It is the obligation of a father to give his children the ability to swim against the tide.*

On Admonishing Others

"*Vayikra Yitzchak el Yaakov va'yevareich oso va'yetzaveihu va'yomer lo, lo sikach ishah mi'bnos Canaan — And Yitzchak called to Yaakov and blessed him and commanded him saying, 'You shall not take a wife from the daughters of Canaan' *" (Bereishis 28:1).

The Chofetz Chaim explained that we can learn from Yitzchak the most effective way of admonishing others. Before Yitzchak warned Yaakov what not to do, he blessed him.

> *If you first show a person that you truly care about his welfare, he will be much more receptive to your recommendation or reproach.*

On Persistence

International business strategist Dan Waldschmidt, author of "Edgy Conversations: How Ordinary People Achieve Outrageous Success," points out that great people throughout history have *often failed, quite miserably, before finally reaching their goals. Some examples:*

Vincent Willem van Gogh, the Dutch Post-Impressionist painter, sold only one painting during his lifetime.

Winston Churchill lost every public election until becoming British prime minister at age 62.

Henry Ford, founder of the Ford Motor Company, went bankrupt five times.

Physicist Albert Einstein, who developed the theory of relativity, was a very poor student and was expelled from school.

Ideas, brilliance, and genius, says Waldschmidt, all mean nothing without the guts, passion, and tenacity necessary to make one's dream a reality.

One of the foremost teaching principles is to encourage others not to fall back on excuses and give up, but to be persistent in trying to reach one's goals.

On Knowing Your Own Greatness

Margaret Thatcher, the prime minister of England, once attended a state dinner in Buckingham Palace. As soon as the prime minister entered the banquet hall, the 2,000 guests in attendance suddenly fell silent. Mrs. Thatcher soon realized why: She was wearing the same dress as Her Royal Highness, the queen of England.

After the dinner, Mrs. Thatcher sent a letter to the queen apologizing for her faux pas, assuring her majesty that in the future she will coordinate her wardrobe with the queen's office.

Mrs. Thatcher received the following reply from the queen's secretary: "Her Royal Highness, the queen, does not notice what commoners are wearing."

In a similar manner, our youth must be taught, and we ourselves must internalize, that we are royalty and the actions of those of the outside world have no bearing on us.

On Influencing Others

"And Yaakov settled in the land of his father's sojournings" (*Bereishis* 37:1).

Chazal (*Bereishis Rabbah* 84:4) derive from this *pasuk* —which employs the term *megurei* — that Yitzchak Avinu had been responsible for producing converts (*geirim*, which has the same root as the word *megurei*). We know that Avraham, who epitomized the trait of *chesed*, brought many people closer to Hashem, but our image of Yitzchak is that of a holy, self-contained individual, so how are we to understand this statement of Chazal?

Rav Moshe Shternbuch quoted Rav Moshe Yehudah Schneider, who noted that there are two types of righteous individuals. Some, like Avraham, actively engage in various public activities to disseminate *Yiddishkeit*, whereas others, like Yitzchak, have an influence by virtue of their personal *avodah*, which is performed with dedication and self-sacrifice. Unlike his father, Yitzchak did not travel from place to place and actively spread the word of Hashem, but he still managed to create converts, because his very *avodah* exuded holiness and truth and had an immense influence on those who witnessed it.

On Toiling in Torah

Some people erroneously assume that *ameilus* in Torah is reserved for the *shevet* of Levi. After all, how can all of Klal Yisrael engage in *limud haTorah*? Who will fill the roles of the professionals needed to service us? Who will be the tailors, grocers, doctors, and shoemakers?

Rav Yehoshua Leib Diskin utilized a *pasuk* in the *parashah* of *Kabbalas HaTorah* to explain why the very premise of this question is based on error. The *pasuk* (*Shemos* 19:5) says, *"Vi'h'yisem li segulah mi'kol ha'amim ki li kol haaretz* —You shall be to Me the most beloved treasure of all peoples, for Mine is the entire world." What is the connection between the first part of the *pasuk* and the second?

Rav Yehoshua Leib explained that the Ribono Shel Olam is telling us, *"Vi'h'yisem li segulah*, all of you are to be a nation devoted and involved in Torah. And should you worry about who will service you and fill the jobs needed to address your needs, know that *'ki li kol haaretz,'* I have all the 70 nations of the world available to engage in the work and labors needed so you can live your lives engaged in Torah."

Not just a few. But all of us.

On Showing Gratitude

A person must be so careful about the things he says, especially when it relates to the blessings Hashem bestows upon us. This is evidenced by the feelings of Rav Shlomo Zalman Auerbach regarding an oft-used phrase at the end of the year: *"Tichleh shanah v'killeloseha —* May this year, and its curses, end." Rav Shlomo Zalman felt that saying this makes a person appear to be a *kafuy tov*, one who is ungrateful and unappreciative. Rav Shlomo Zalman frowned upon the custom of printing these words at the end of yearly calendars, especially since the calendars are printed before the year has even begun.

One who does express this sentiment of "tichleh shanah v'killeloseha," said Rav Shlomo Zalman, should at the very same time express his thanks to the Ribono Shel Olam for the many gifts and wonderful experiences of the past year, asking Hashem to continue showering those berachos during the coming year, as well.

A Taste of Shabbos

The Shabbos Desecrator

*R*av Mordechai Yoffe, one of the first talmidim of Rav Aharon Kotler in White Plains, New York, and later in Lakewood, New Jersey, opened a yeshivah in Kansas City, Missouri. Rav Mordechai's son, Rav Baruch Ber Yoffe, recalled a poignant exchange that took place between his mother and the great Lakewood rosh yeshivah, who was the one who encouraged the Yoffes to move to Kansas City.

"My mother told Rav Aharon that she's concerned about the chinuch of her children in Kansas City," related Rav Baruch Ber. "Rav Aharon listened to her concern and told her, 'For the sake of Klal Yisrael, you have to demonstrate mesirus nefesh regarding your children, too. But if your actions are l'sheim Shamayim, your children will turn out fine and they will bring you much nachas.'"

With those words of encouragement, the Yoffes made the move to Missouri. The burden of covering the budget of the new yeshivah in Kansas City fell squarely on the shoulders of Rav Mordechai, who would travel to towns across the country raising funds.

Rav Nechemya Kaplan related the following story.

During a visit to a certain town, Rav Mordechai was advised that the community wasn't particularly religious, but there was one Jew who was scrupulous in kashrus and mitzvah observance, and Rav Mordechai would be able to stay at that man's home. Rav Mordechai made his way to the fellow's house and, looking through the window, saw a pious-looking Jew with a long white beard, hunched over a Gemara. Rav Mordechai knocked on the door and explained that he was in town for Shabbos and had been directed to this address.

"I was told that you are an *ehrliche Yid*, who is careful with kashrus, and that you get kosher meat from New York," said Rav Mordechai.

"Me?" asked the man innocently. "An *ehrliche Yid*? Why, I am a *mechallel Shabbos*! How can you stay at my home?"

Rav Mordechai was puzzled. He looked the man up and down — yarmulke, white beard, and all — and politely asked what he meant. "You don't look like a *mechallel Shabbos*," said Rav Mordechai plainly. "And how can one who is so scrupulous regarding kashrus be a Shabbos violator?"

"Come inside," said the man, "and I'll explain."

Once Rav Mordechai was settled, the man proceeded to tell his tale.

When I came to the United States from Russia as a young boy of 10, my American uncle helped me settle down and got me a job. I very quickly learned that in America, if one doesn't work on Shabbos, he will have to find a new job every week. Every Friday, when I informed my boss that I would not be coming to work the next day, I was told not to bother coming on Monday either; if I did not work on Shabbos, I would be unemployed. This is the way it went, week after week.

After a few weeks, my uncle rebuked me and said that this could not continue: "You have to work on Shabbos if you are going to survive. You will starve otherwise." He then added, "And soon, getting a new job each week will become harder and harder. As employers find out that you don't work on Shabbos, they won't want to hire you in the first place."

Realizing that I was running out of options, I headed out and got a new job in a factory. That Friday, when I left work, I didn't say anything to my boss. I planned on returning the next day. I felt that I had no alternative; I couldn't starve.

The next morning, I woke up early and, after davening, head-

ed for the trolley, which would take me from the Lower East Side, where I lived, to upper Manhattan where I worked. When I got to the trolley, I said to myself, "I have to go to work so that I don't starve, but why must I desecrate Shabbos by riding the trolley?" I decided instead to walk to my place of employment.

When I got to the multistory building that housed the factory, I was about to enter the elevator that would take me to the right floor. But I stopped. I said to myself, "I have to go to work so that I don't starve, but why must I desecrate Shabbos by riding the elevator?" So I walked the many stairs until I reached the floor of the factory.

I slowly opened the door of the factory and was greeted by the sight of dozens of frum Yidden working at their machines — on Shabbos Kodesh — and I froze.

I could not bear to look. I immediately slammed the door, turned around, and ran. I ran and I ran and I ran until I reached a park, where I collapsed on a bench, exhausted and shaken. I kept muttering to myself, "I won't work on Shabbos. I won't work on Shabbos." I could not believe that I had even contemplated working on Shabbos.

A short while later, a man sitting on an adjacent bench spotted me, a young boy, forlorn and downcast. He asked me who I was and what I was doing there.

I told him my whole story. I described the poverty I was experiencing and the challenge of maintaining a job while keeping Shabbos.

The man explained that he owns a factory and that he would be happy to employ me. "This will be the end of your problems. You can work for me and you won't have to work on Shabbos."

After the man concluded his story, Rav Yoffe thought for a moment before turning back to his host. "I am confused," he said. "Where was the *chillul Shabbos*? Why did you say that you are a *mechallel Shabbos*?"

"Don't you understand?" said the man. "True, perhaps I wasn't actively *mechallel Shabbos*, but the entire Friday night, I slept with the knowledge that the next morning I would awaken and head out to work — on Shabbos. Shabbos morning, as I was walking to the factory, I did so with the mindset that I was going to work on Shabbos. As I headed up the steps of the factory building, I did so with the plan of working on Shabbos. I entered the factory intending to work on Shabbos. At the last moment, the Ribono Shel Olam saved me and prevented me from working. But a *mechallel Shabbos* I am! How can you trust me and eat in my home?" the man asked with utter sincerity and purity.

This, concluded Rav Kaplan, is the beauty of a Yid, who holds himself to such exacting standards, and who wishes to fulfill the will of his Creator, come what may.

The Shabbos Cigarette

After her marriage, Chana moved to the Meah Shearim neighborhood of Yerushalayim, where she became a beloved friend to many. An especially close relationship was formed with Bracha, who was 10 years her senior. Bracha was not a native Israeli, having relocated from the United States over a decade earlier. Neither she nor her husband had any relatives in the country, but thanks to their upright characters, they had a wide circle of friends and acquaintances. Bracha's many fine characteristics endeared her to Chana. In addition, her children were exemplary; their modesty and humility stood out, and they were all exceptional students at well-known institutions of learning.

Chana would visit Bracha's home often, whether it was to borrow an ingredient for a recipe or to ask her friend's advice. During one of their conversations, Bracha revealed a fact that startled Chana.

"I've never told you this," said Bracha, "but I am a *giyores*, a convert."

Chana was stunned. She wanted to shout, "It cannot be!" but she remained silent.

Upon returning home, she couldn't contain herself. "You will be surprised to learn," she told her husband, "that our neighbor Bracha is a convert! I knew she was not born here, but I was sure that she was born in the United States to a devout Jewish family. Her modesty, humility, wisdom, and kindness are all so remarkable."

Every Shabbos afternoon, Chana would visit Bracha at her home. Bracha always received her warmly and sat with her on her porch, enjoying light-hearted banter while partaking of some refreshments. One Shabbos, Chana was delayed and did not arrive at Bracha's home until about an hour before the conclusion of Shabbos. Accompanied by her 2-year-old daughter, she knocked on Bracha's door. When no one answered, Chana figured that Bracha was preoccupied, so she planned to wait several minutes before trying again. But then, to her chagrin, her young daughter pushed on the door and it opened. Apparently, it hadn't been locked. Chana was embarrassed to have barged into her neighbor's home, but her toddler was happily unaware and marched right in.

Chana entered Bracha's home in order to take hold of her daughter and make a hasty exit, but as she did so, she was shocked by what she saw. There, in an adjacent room, was Bracha, sitting and smoking a cigarette!

Chana could not believe her eyes. She grabbed her daughter and scurried out of Bracha's house, running all the way home. She was out of breath, not to mention frazzled and confused, as she got to her own house.

"What's the matter?" her husband asked as he opened the door for her. "Are you all right? You look like you saw a ghost!"

Chana was panting. She stammered as she tried to speak. "You — you're never going to believe this."

Chana went on to explain that she had seen her righteous neighbor Bracha smoking a cigarette on Shabbos. "How can it be? How can it be?" she kept repeating.

Chana didn't want to believe it, but she knew what she saw.

On Motza'ei Shabbos, there was a knock on Chana's door. It was Bracha, looking pale and faint, her eyes red from crying.

"May I come in?" she asked feebly.

Chana nodded and welcomed Bracha in, offering her a glass of water. Once Bracha was comfortable, she addressed her trusted neighbor.

"There's something I must tell you," she began. "I already told you that I'm a convert, but I did not tell you about the phenomenon you witnessed before the end of Shabbos. I wish I did not have this problem — but I am a compulsive cigarette smoker.

"But don't judge me just yet. As Chazal say, '*Al tadin es chavercha ad she'tagia limkomo* — Do not judge your fellow until you have reached his place' (*Avos* 2:5).

"Let me tell you what I deal with every week," she continued. "Every Shabbos, about an hour before the end of the holy day, I experience a burning urge to smoke a cigarette. I try with all my might to resist, but I cannot. It is inexplicable. I cannot describe to you what the feeling is. It is like I am completely unable to control myself. This occurs every week like clockwork, as if an external power overtakes me and forces me to do what I don't want to do, transgressing the Shabbos in this fashion."

Bracha took a deep breath and continued, "I consulted with psychologists, who gave me all kinds of advice, but none of their suggestions helped. I am trapped in this quagmire and cannot find my way out."

Bracha lowered her head in shame.

Chana put her hand on Bracha's shoulder and tried to offer her some encouragement.

"Perhaps you should consult with some rabbanim or seek out a *berachah* from a *tzaddik* or a *mekubal*," suggested Chana.

"I've done that," said Bracha, "but no one was able to help me."

That night and the next day, Chana was not herself; she was so disturbed by her friend's challenge. It seemed so strange, for she knew Bracha to be as genuine and real as anyone she had ever met. She wanted to help her. She just didn't know how.

Chana began to make inquiries among various people, carefully guarding the identity of the person she was seeking to help. Ultimately, she was advised to contact Reb Dovid, the director of an outreach organization, who dealt with many *baalei teshuvah* and *geirim*. After hearing the details, Reb Dovid advised, "You live not far from Rav Yisrael Yaakov Fisher, of Zichron Moshe. I will take your neighbor to see him, and he will guide her through the prism of Torah. Let's see what he advises."

Bracha went with Reb Dovid to consult with Rav Fisher. But after describing her predicament, both Reb Dovid and Bracha were astonished by Rav Fisher's reply.

"You are not a convert," said Rav Fisher decisively. "You are a non-Jew."

After getting over the initial shock, Reb Dovid finally spoke. "This is a woman who is G-d-fearing and known for her modesty and honesty among all her neighbors," Reb Dovid said. "And according to what I have ascertained, she converted 24 years ago. Ever since that time, she has conducted herself as a bona fide Jew, adhering to the laws of halachah with scrupulousness and precision. How can it be that she is not a Jew?"

Rav Fisher stated again, "She is not a Jew!"

Bracha was devastated. Reb Dovid told her to go home and rest while he pursues the matter further. If the venerated rav said that Bracha was a non-Jew, then he had to find out more. After conducting an intensive investigation, he returned to Rav Fisher's home.

"The rav must have *ruach hakodesh*!" exclaimed Reb Dovid. "I looked into this matter thoroughly and discovered that, unbeknown to Bracha, her conversion was conducted by a member of the Reform community, in a fashion that is not acceptable according to halachah. As the rav indicated, she never underwent a proper *geirus*.

"However," continued Reb Dovid, "I don't understand what her faulty conversion has to do with the issue at hand; namely, her obsessive and neurotic need to smoke on Shabbos in violation of halachah."

Rav Fisher smiled and explained, "As you surely know, Chazal state, '*Nachri she'shavas chayov misah*' (*Sanhedrin* 58b; see Rambam, *Hilchos Melachim* 10:9). A non-Jew who observes Shabbos is deserving of capital punishment by the hand of Heaven. Because this woman is truly virtuous, righteous, and G-d-fearing, Heaven arranged that she would not be able to observe Shabbos fully, so that she would not be subject to the dictate regarding a non-Jew who keeps Shabbos."

Bracha was told to undergo an authentic conversion, and she did. Her impulse to smoke on Shabbos — which she had suffered from for years — suddenly disappeared. She was finally able to enjoy Shabbos as she had wanted to, adhering fully to its laws.

What His Grandmother Taught

Rav Yaakov Feitman, rav of Kehillas Bais Yehudah Tzvi in Cedarhurst, New York, told the following story, which he heard from his rebbi, Rav Yitzchak Hutner, rosh yeshivah of Yeshivas Rabbeinu Chaim Berlin.

A young rabbi in Eretz Yisrael was attempting to institute some liberal innovations into certain aspects of *hilchos Shabbos*. Some of these were designed to ease the Shabbos restrictions on religious soldiers in the Israeli Army.

When he presented some of these leniencies to Rav Yosef Tzvi Dushinsky, *av beis din* of the Eidah HaChareidis, the rav was not impressed. The young scholar persisted in offering proofs to his approach from obscure Talmudic sources.

Finally, somewhat exasperated, the sage banged his cane on the floor and concluded, "Young man, I know only one thing. My bubbe told me that you are not allowed to be *mechallel Shabbos*."

What Money Can't Buy

Though now he lives in Atlanta, Georgia, Kivi Bernhard was born and raised in Johannesburg, South Africa. After relocating to the United States in 1997 with his wife and family, Kivi went on to build a multimillion-dollar international wholesale diamond business.

He is also the author of the internationally acclaimed business book Leopardology: The Hunt for Profit in a Tough Global Economy, a best-seller that received accolades from top CEO's and prominent authors. With the aid of award-winning footage, Kivi uses the hunting habits and techniques of the African leopard, perhaps the most successful feline predator on earth, to draw metaphors for personal and corporate leadership, trust, and success.

As a sought-after speaker, Kivi was once contacted by a speakers' bureau, inviting him to deliver the opening address at an important Microsoft conference. Hundreds of prominent individuals, including Microsoft founder Bill Gates, were going to be there. This was a huge opportunity for Kivi.

But then he noticed that the conference was scheduled for a Saturday. Kivi immediately responded that he is Sabbath observant and wouldn't be able to make it.

Shortly thereafter, Kivi received a phone call from a senior vice president at Microsoft, who offered him an exorbitant amount of money to speak at the conference. "Double? Triple? How much do you need? I'll send you a check and you fill it in!" the Microsoft rep said.

"John," Kivi answered, "it's not about money. It's about Sabbath observance."

The senior vice president slammed down the phone in frustration.

Ultimately, the executives at Microsoft were left with no other option, and they changed the date of the conference to Sunday so that Kivi could deliver his talk.

A few months later, Kivi received another phone call from the senior vice president, who related that he had just been with Bill Gates and some other Microsoft top executives on Mr. Gates's private jet, and they were discussing Kivi and the conference.

"We had this guy, Kivi, who was supposed to be the opening keynote speaker," John told Gates and the others, "and we just couldn't get him to commit to the Saturday platform, all because he's Sabbath observant. We even threw money at him, but he wouldn't budge! He just wouldn't budge off the Sabbath."

John shared with Kivi that when Bill Gates heard this, he responded, "That's what happens when you have something that money can't buy."

The Main Thing

When Dr. James David Weiss and his wife first moved to Monsey, neither of them were Torah observant. After a few years, Mrs. Weiss began attending a local shul, Bais Torah, headed by Rabbi Berel Wein, and soon afterward she began to keep Shabbos.

Dr. Weiss was a diehard secular humanist, who did not believe in anything except every man's right to believe in what he feels is important. So while he remained irreligious, he respected his wife's Shabbos and Yom Tov observance and tried not to contaminate her kitchen.

Slowly, Dr. Weiss was affected by his wife's religiosity. Each Shabbos, when Dr. Weiss got home from golfing, his wife would regale him with words of inspiration and fascinating stories from her rabbi. One week after golfing, he showered, changed his clothes, and went to hear Rabbi Wein deliver his Shabbos HaGadol *derashah*.

Dr. Weiss was inspired. He was enraptured. In short, his journey to Orthodox Judaism was ignited by the speeches of Rabbi Wein, who offered a perspective so compelling and enriching that he could not ignore it.

Yet, Dr. Weiss still held back from committing to halachic Judaism. After about two years of listening to Rabbi Wein on Shabbos and learning a little during the week in his classes, Dr. Weiss had not yet embraced *shemiras hamitzvos*.

That summer, Dr. and Mrs. Weiss traveled to Eretz Yisrael. Part of their itinerary included touring the community of Bnei Brak and visiting Yeshivas Ponovezh. When he was a rabbi in Miami, Rabbi Wein would drive Rav Yosef Shlomo Kahaneman, the Ponovezher Rav, to the homes of wealthy individuals to raise funds for the yeshivah. Dr. Weiss had heard Rabbi Wein tell many stories about the rav. In fact, he heard so many stories that he felt he knew the rav personally; he just did not realize that the rav was no longer alive.

On the eve of his departure, Dr. Weiss called Rabbi Wein and told him that he planned to visit Yeshivas Ponovezh, and if the

Ponovezher Rav was going to be there, he would give him Rabbi Wein's regards. Not wishing to discourage Dr. Weiss from his plans, Rabbi Wein said with an enigmatic smile, "Go ahead."

Dr. and Mrs. Weiss arrived in Bnei Brak at 10 a.m. After walking the streets of Bnei Brak, Dr. Weiss was taken to the *beis midrash* of Yeshivas Ponovezh. Upon his arrival, he was immediately impressed by the 500 *talmidim*, young and old, who filled the *beis midrash* with the sound of Torah.

Dr. Weiss wanted to deliver Rabbi Wein's message to Rav Kahaneman. Knowing a little Yiddish, he kept asking the *talmidim* he encountered, "*Vu iz der Ponovezher Rav*? Where is the Ponovezher Rav?" They looked at him quizzically but eventually waved him to the back of the *beis midrash*.

At first, Dr. Weiss searched in vain. All he saw were white-shirted *talmidim*. Then, drifting near one densely packed cluster, Dr. Weiss thought he had struck gold. There, a bigger than usual group was hunched over an elderly man. Dr. Weiss heard one boy announce that the rav was answering questions. Dr. Weiss approached and had to peel off about six boys to get a glimpse of the central figure. A small, white-bearded, aged man was talking to the boys, who were pressed close to him, hanging onto his every word. Dr. Weiss had no idea that the man was the rosh yeshivah, Rav Elazar Menachem Man Shach, and not Rav Kahaneman.

Dr. Weiss waited for a break in the learning and then said, "*Ich breng a gruss fun America, frun Rav Wein.* I bring regards from Rabbi Wein in America."

"*Ich ken nit Rav Wein.* I don't know Rabbi Wein," said Rav Shach.

Rav Shach was about to turn away when he looked into Dr. Weiss's eyes and asked kindly, "*Uber du — du bist a Yid?* But you — are you Jewish?"

Dr. Weiss assured him that he was. "*Avada. Avada geviss.* Of course. Of course I am." Then he repeated, "*Ich breng a gruss fun Rav Wein in Monsey. Ihr kent em fun Miami.* I bring regards from Rabbi Wein. You know him from Miami."

Rav Shach explained, "*Ich hub dir gezugt ich ken em nit. Du meinst Rav Kahaneman. Ich bin Rav Shach un ich bin keinmol nit geven in Miami.* I told you already that I don't know him. You must mean

Rav Kahaneman. I'm Rav Shach and I have never been to Miami."

Rav Shach broke off the conversation with a soft piece of advice, *"Uber gedenk, der ikker zach mit a Yid iz tzu zein shomer Shabbos. Dos iz der ikker zach.* But remember, the main thing for a Jew is to keep Shabbos. That is the main thing."

Rav Shach smiled and then gave Dr. Weiss a *berachah*: *"Zolst du zein ah gebentchte Yid.* May you be a blessed Jew."

The accuracy with which Rav Shach assessed Dr. Weiss's level of observance left him speechless and stunned. How did he know who Dr. Weiss was and where he was holding?

> *One of the points Rabbi Wein would stress, Dr. Weiss later recounted, is that we may think we're doing something for one reason, but, in truth, Hashem is sending us out to accomplish an entirely different goal. Dr. Weiss thought Rav Shach was the Ponovezher Rav, who had passed away many years before, in 1969. Yet even though he did not know who Rav Shach was, Rav Shach seemed to know all about Dr. Weiss. Although over 90 years old at the time, Rav Shach still had penetrating intelligence and used it to size up the good doctor, fearlessly but gently telling him the truth about himself. Dr. Weiss could not be a Jew without Shabbos. That was the covenantal truth.*
>
> *"So," concluded Dr. Weiss, "there I was, thinking I was bringing greetings to a famous rabbi from a trusted friend. It turned out that neither had ever met the other, but both of them had my number. In the end, I was the one who got the message. I left Bnei Brak that summer an unsettled man, and before the Yamim Tovim that year I decided to become shomer Shabbos."*

Honoring Shabbos

*B*eing a Yid goes beyond the externalities, at times even beyond the Shulchan Aruch. It's about feeling like a Yid.

It was Friday night at the Yerushalayim home of Rav Moshe Twersky, and some of his *talmidim* from Yeshivas Toras Moshe were waiting for him to arrive. That night, contrary to her usual custom,

Rebbetzin Bashi Twersky came out of the kitchen and entered the living/dining room where the *bachurim* were sitting and schmoozing. She told them the following:

> We had some painting done in the house this week, and all the furniture in the living room was pushed to the center of the room and draped. The painters didn't finish yet and are going to be returning this coming week to complete the job. It felt like too much work to uncover and move all the furniture back in place for Shabbos, since we would have to move it back and cover it again right afterward, so we decided to just leave it.
>
> When my husband returned home this afternoon, he asked what was going to be with the furniture for Shabbos. I told him that it was too much work to move all the furniture, so we'll just eat in the kitchen this Shabbos.
>
> He didn't say anything, but as soon as I got back to my Shabbos preparations, I heard some noise and realized that he was uncovering and moving all the furniture back in honor of Shabbos.
>
> As soon as my children and I realized what he was doing, we tried to help him. He categorically refused and insisted on doing it himself, saying, "It's my k'vod Shabbos. Let me do the work."

"This is a lesson," the rebbetzin concluded, "that you won't learn from a rebbi while he is giving a *shiur*, but it is a lesson that one has to learn: what it means to be responsible for a household and the *kedushah* of a home."

Just as she finished speaking, Rav Twersky walked in with his usual enthusiastic *"Gut Shabbos"* greeting. The rebbetzin returned the greeting and nonchalantly went back into the kitchen to finish up with her preparations.

— *heard from Rabbi Yehoshua Berman*

A Taste of Your Love

It's Elul

Rav Nosson Meir Wachtfogel once attended a wedding in Monsey that ended at a very late hour. As soon as the wedding was over, Rav Nosson told his driver that he would like to visit Rav Mordechai Menachem Schwab. The driver was somewhat taken aback, because 1 o' clock in the morning is an unusual time to visit anyone, especially an aging person. He respectfully asked Rav Nosson if he was sure that it was an appropriate time for a visit. Rav Nosson assured him that it was no problem.

As they approached Rav Mordechai's house, it appeared that all the lights were out. The driver pointed out that it looked like everyone in the house was asleep. But Rav Nosson insisted that it was a fine time for a visit. They got out of the car and knocked gently on the door. Soon they heard footsteps, and then Rav Mordechai opened the door for them and invited them in.

After spending some time together, Rav Nosson finally got up to leave. Back in the car, the driver asked Rav Nosson how he was so sure that Rav Mordechai was still awake.

Rav Nosson looked at his driver quizzically. "I don't understand your question. It's Elul; of course he would be up late at night."

Bonus Boost

Zvi Leiberman is a student at Saba University School of Medicine, a medical school located in Saba, a municipality of the Netherlands in the Caribbean.

Zvi is the only religious Jewish student at Saba. Maintaining his religion while simultaneously maintaining good grades is highly challenging. Yet Zvi has managed to accomplish this, and has even done it with a smile, knowing that he is fulfilling his passion to pursue a career in medicine while not compromising his religious principles.

In 2016, the two days of Rosh Hashanah fell on the dates of Zvi's school exams. As Saba doesn't have a shul of its own, Zvi arranged to fly to St. Martin, an island in the northeast Caribbean, for the Yamim Noraim. The conflict was clear: Zvi couldn't be davening in St. Martin and at the same time be taking his exams in Saba.

The school's administration understood Zvi's plight, but the school's policy is to not reschedule exams solely for religious purposes. There wasn't much they could do aside from commiserate with Zvi, as was made clear in the dean's written response to his request for accommodation:

> *Dear Zvi,*
>
> *Since we met, I discussed your request to postpone the exams of October 3 and 4 with my advisory council. When you and I spoke, it seemed a straightforward request, stemming from a deep religious conviction, which I honor and respect. My council, however, warned of a significant precedent were I to grant this. There are many faiths represented in the various classes at our school, and some students are strong adherents to their faith with deep convictions, such as yourself. If we set a precedent with your request, others would justifiably request equal treatment, yet it would be impossible to assess the strength of their convictions. And so, as painful as it is for both you and me, I must deny your request. I am sorry for this, Zvi, because I know how much this means to you.*
>
> *Respectfully,*
> *Dean*
> *Saba University School of Medicine*

Zvi submitted the paperwork for his withdrawal from the fall 2016 semester. While his withdrawal was a step back in the progress of his studies, Zvi felt that it was vital and necessary, and would only make him stronger in his values and faith, helping to mold him into the successful physician he one day hopes to be. Some people learned of Zvi's sacrifice and his email inbox began to fill with kind words from well-wishers and *chizuk* from people he never met, encouraging him to uphold his beliefs no matter what.

Withdrawing from the semester and having to start from scratch was within Zvi's control; the financial loss associated with his decision was not. As per school policy, when one withdraws from a semester, one loses the financial-aid status given for that semester. As Zvi had taken a leave of absence, this rule clearly applied to him. Nevertheless, since Zvi's withdrawal and subsequent financial-aid status were based on his religious convictions and not due to any scholastic issues, he was able to work out a manageable plan regarding his tuition.

His lodging arrangement, though, was a different story entirely. As his apartment was on a multiple-semester contract with a landlord unaffiliated with the school, Zvi was unable to terminate the contract, sublet the apartment, or work out any sort of financial arrangement. While working out his tuition was daunting enough, finding a way to pay the full rent on time for a vacant apartment was just too much.

But then something amazing happened: Zvi merited a smile from Heaven.

One Friday morning, Zvi awoke to an email alert from Chase Bank. He logged into his account to find a direct deposit from HCS, a Jewish organization servicing the special-needs population in Zvi's local community, where he had been employed prior to attending medical school.

Zvi assumed they had made this deposit by accident, so he spent some time inquiring about it and discovered that, for some reason, HCS was distributing bonuses. Since he had been on their payroll at the beginning of that calendar year, Zvi was eligible for the bonus. In the three-plus years that he had worked for HCS, he had never, ever, received any sort of bonus.

Zvi took a look at the total amount of the bonus check he received. It matched, dollar for dollar, the amount of money needed for rent until he would again be eligible for financial aid. Zvi couldn't believe how the numbers fit so perfectly, so he redid the math about a dozen times to confirm.

They matched.

His bonus was $2,224. His total rent balance was $2,214. There was a mere $10 difference — money that he decided to use toward purchasing a new *mezuzah* for his apartment.

Zvi already knew that he had done what was correct. But this nod from Above was a meaningful affirmation for this growing young man.

The Greatest Zechus

The Chasam Sofer once called a *talmid* into his study on Erev Yom Kippur and said, "I want to speak to you about something very important. There is an orphan girl who has reached marriageable age. No one is making any effort to help her, and I want you to marry her."

The *talmid* agreed.

The Chasam Sofer's face lit up with joy and he announced, "With this merit I will enter the Day of Judgment!"

Eating on Yom Kippur

Rav Avraham Tzvi Hirsch Kamai was rosh yeshivah and rav of Mir in Poland. His sister, Rebbetzin Malka, was the wife of Rav Eliezer Yehudah Finkel. One year, as the Yamim Noraim were approaching, the rebbetzin became seriously ill. The doctors told her not to fast on Yom Kippur and warned her that doing so could endanger her life. The rebbetzin was distressed at this and told her brother how she felt.

"I am prepared to make an exchange with you," said Rav Tzvi

Hirsch, as he was known. "I will fast on the holy day and gladly give you the merit of my mitzvah of fasting. But you must give me the merit of your mitzvah of eating on Yom Kippur! Not only that, but I'll also add the merit from other mitzvos of mine."

This offer greatly encouraged the rebbetzin. For the first time since hearing the doctors' instructions, she accepted the fact that she had a mitzvah to eat on Yom Kippur.

The Seat Mate

The first month at Yeshivah Toras Moshe in Yerushalayim did not go very well for Yossi. He was homesick and altogether not very happy.

That Elul, Yossi was the only Kohen in the yeshivah, so for Rosh Hashanah and Yom Kippur, he was assigned a seat near the front, providing him easy access to the area where he would be saying *Bircas Kohanim*. That seat assignment placed him right next to Rav Moshe Twersky, a beloved rebbi at the yeshivah, with whom Yossi was not yet acquainted.

Before *Kol Nidrei* on Yom Kippur eve, Rav Twersky turned to Yossi and asked him a few questions about himself, including his name, where he came from, and how he was faring at the yeshivah. Rav Twersky then explained that it is a commonly accepted practice before one embarks on a long plane ride to get to know the person sitting in the next seat.

"Now," he said to Yossi, his face already glowing with the holiness and awe of the holy day, "we are about to take a plane ride — to *Shamayim*."

Yossi later said that his davening was more special that Yom Kippur than it had been in previous years, and soon after, he began to enjoy being in the yeshivah as well.

Rav Twersky would conclude his annual Motza'ei Yom Kippur shiur with the following message. After describing the korbanos brought by a nazir upon completing his course of nezirus, the pasuk (Bamidbar 6:20) says, "And afterward shall the nazir drink wine." Why does the pasuk still refer to him as a nazir at this stage, if he is now "back to normal"?

The answer, said Rav Twersky, is that a nazir doesn't lose himself and revert to his old self, as if nothing has happened. It's not like being on a diet and then bingeing the next day. Because of his experience of nezirus, the nazir is a changed man, even as he returns to his routine.

"So, too," said Rav Twersky, "as we continue our lives after Yom Kippur, we go back to our food and our lives as different people, not the same ones we were on Erev Yom Kippur."

An Opening Like No Other

It was Yom Kippur 5775. The usual pre-*Kol Nidrei* selling of *aliyos* at Agudath Israel of the Five Towns had proceeded uneventfully, until the bidding began for the final *kibbud, pesichah l'Ne'ilah.* A few men began bidding. One by one, most of them dropped out as the dollar amount began to rise. It soon became clear that two *baalei batim* were vying for this *kibbud* and neither was prepared to back down.

Reuven was relatively new to the *kehillah*, so this was his first real interaction with Shimon. The proceedings continued with mounting drama — even tension — as the bidding became an all-out war, and the numbers climbed to figures the shul had never seen before. It was clear that both men were determined to acquire this *kibbud* and were willing to take this as far as they had to.

Finally, Shimon called out an exceptionally high sum. After a moment, to the shock of the entire shul, Reuven outbid him by $200. Then it was silent. Shimon stopped and the bidding came to an end with the *gabbai*'s announcement of "*Zachah lo!*" Reuven now possessed the *kibbud* of *pesichah l'Ne'ilah.*

On Yom Kippur afternoon, Reuven approached his bidding "opponent," Shimon. "I'm the person who outbid you last night," he said. "Do it together with me."

Then, for the second time in 24 hours, the men began to negotiate. Shimon would only agree to the offer if he could pay half. This time, Shimon won, and the two approached the *gabbai*, who sent them to speak to the rav of the shul, Rav Yitzchok Dovid Frankel, to iron out the details. They asked Rav Frankel if there was any problem with performing the *pesichah* together, and he gave them the green light.

Rav Frankel was overwhelmed as he watched these two men, virtual strangers until that moment, approach the *aron kodesh* together and jointly open it. The selflessness of Reuven, who obviously wanted that *pesichah* so badly and rightfully earned the *kibbud* fair and square, was deeply inspiring.

At the *eis ne'ilas shaar*, the time that the gates of Heaven are closed, as the *kehillah* stood trembling, begging for one last chance for true *kapparah* for themselves, their community, and Klal Yisrael, Rav Frankel was exhilarated by the thought that these two men standing before the *aron kodesh* were, most likely, causing all sorts of commotion in *Shamayim*.

What made this all the more inspiring was Reuven's reaction when the rav spoke to him about it after Maariv. While Rav Frankel found this so stirring, to Reuven it was matter of fact.

> *"We can all learn from this to aspire to think and feel as Reuven does," Rav Frankel later shared. "We all encounter moments when we can apply such a lesson and garner zechuyos. Even if not with an expensive kibbud, surely elsewhere in our daily lives we can do so. A parking space, perhaps? Our place in line to a person who looks rushed or harried?*
>
> *"The sky is the limit, but we must be looking for the opportunities, as they are surely there, waiting for us to grab them."*

Specifically on Yom Kippur

Rav Chaim Walkin, mashgiach of Yeshivas Ateres Yisrael in Yerushalayim, learned at Yeshivas Mir Yerushalayim in his youth. He related that one Yom Kippur, during the short break between Minchah and Ne'ilah, he was making his way out of the *beis midrash* of the yeshivah, when he spotted the rosh yeshivah, Rav Nachum Partzovitz, seated in a nearby room. Rav Nachum was already very ill and weak at the time, and he had been brought to a room near the *beis midrash* so that he could hear the *tefillos*.

Chaim Walkin was uncertain if it was an appropriate time to approach Rav Nachum and wish him a good year. Ultimately, he decided to go in. Rav Nachum greeted him warmly and immediately asked, "How is your mother?" Chaim's father had passed away a short time earlier, leaving his mother a widow.

"I could not believe it," Rav Walkin later related. "I was astonished that this was what was important to him on Yom Kippur."

But the great Rav Nachum demonstrated that it was specifically on Yom Kippur that the subject was on his mind.

Rav Moshe Mordechai Chodosh related that he experienced a similar incident with his own father, Rav Meir Chodosh, one Yom Kippur night. After *Kol Nidrei*, Rav Meir delivered a *shmuess* in the yeshivah.

Rav Moshe Mordechai pointed out: "Every person — hundreds of *bachurim* and alumni of the yeshivah, along with the entire faculty — was certain that my father was going to speak about the greatness of the day, inspiring them with a moving *derashah*. But instead, the *shmuess* focused primarily on the subject of *bein adam la'chaveiro*.

"I later took the opportunity to tell him that everyone was surprised by the subject of his speech, and he said to me, 'Moshe, do you also not understand? What else is there to talk about on Yom Kippur?' "

That Type of Husband

During one of her famous lectures, Rebbetzin Zahava Braunstein, the renowned and beloved *mechaneches*, described an incident that occurred on the first Yom Kippur after her wedding, the first time that she davened in a yeshivah. She was not a good faster and didn't realize how late the davening would be over, and her frustration increased as the davening continued with no end in sight. Finally, when the congregation got to "*L'shanah Haba'ah B'Yerushalayim*," she closed her *machzor* and said to herself, *Let me be in Yerushalayim next year, but not back here again*!

And then she heard a noise from the men's section. Curious, she went over to the *mechitzah* and looked out, observing rebbeim and *talmidim*, hand in hand, dancing and singing with much *leibedikeit* and enthusiasm. And this was after they had been fasting for over 25 hours.

She stared at them, mesmerized. It was like Simchas Torah. She had never seen anything like it before. She even forgot how hungry she was and just stood there transfixed, elevated by the sight.

"And the next Yom Kippur," she told her audience, "I was still not a good faster. But I came back, and I came the next year, too."

After Rebbetzin Braunstein related this story, a secular woman who had attended the lecture was introduced to her. Soon after, the woman became a frequent Shabbos guest at the Braunstein home. Though she kept coming, she would challenge everything she saw and heard: from mitzvos, to *hashkafah*, to philosophy. The conversations and the arguments went back and forth. Finally, she agreed to go and learn in Eretz Yisrael.

She said to the rebbetzin, "Do you know when I made up my mind to be *frum*? Do you remember that story that you shared about when you saw the men dancing on Yom Kippur? Right then and there, I decided that that's the type of husband I want, one who can dance like that after Yom Kippur."

One at a Time

In Warsaw during World War II, obtaining a set of *dalet minim* was no simple task. Rav Berel Soloveitchik, knowing how strongly his father, the Brisker Rav, desired to fulfill the mitzvah, set out to acquire a full set of *dalet minim*. A few days before Succos, he heard of a place near a river where *mehudar aravos* were growing. The act of cutting down the *aravos*, however, was fraught with danger, as the area was teeming with Nazi soldiers, so Rav Berel arranged for a non-Jew to cut them for him. This wasn't carried out until close to Yom Tov, and it was subsequently determined that the non-Jew had actually cut the *aravos* after nightfall of the first night of Yom Tov, rendering them *muktzeh*. Therefore, the rav had to use a set of *aravos* that were kosher but less *mehudar*.

When the Imrei Emes, Rav Avraham Mordechai Alter, heard that the Brisker Rav had a set of kosher *aravos*, he dispatched one of his Chassidim to ask the rav if he could use the *aravos* as a *matanah al m'nas l'hachzir* (a gift given on condition that it is returned), as required by halachah, as his own *aravos* had dried out completely. The rav happily acquiesced and sent Rav Berel with the *aravos* to the Imrei Emes.

Upon arriving at the home of the Imrei Emes, Rav Berel observed that the Rebbe's *minyan* was about to start *Hallel*. The Rebbe began to engage Rav Berel in conversation, when his son, Rav Yisrael, commented that the Brisker Rav was likely waiting for Rav Berel to return home with the *aravos*. The Imrei Emes indicated that his son's point was valid and immediately commented, "The halachah (*Shulchan Aruch, Orach Chaim* 651:12) is that if one takes the *dalet minim* one at a time, he has fulfilled the mitzvah [although this is not the best way to perform the mitzvah]." The Rebbe then shook the *aravos*, even though he was not holding the *lulav, esrog*, and *hadassim*.

When recounting this story, Rav Berel would comment on the sensitivity of the Imrei Emes and how careful he was not to unnecessarily trouble or inconvenience another person, even at the expense of his own optimal mitzvah performance.

The House

In 1958, the Brisker Rav sent a messenger to Morocco to obtain a high-quality, non-grafted *esrog* for Succos. However, when the man returned to Eretz Yisrael with the fruit, it was confiscated by customs officials, due to fear of infestation from produce grown out of the country.

The rav called on Rabbi Shlomo Lorincz, the trusted emissary of many *gedolei Yisrael*, to get involved. Despite his efforts, though, Rabbi Lorincz was unable to make contact with the official who had the authority to release the *esrog* in time for Yom Tov. On Chol HaMoed, the rav again implored Rabbi Lorincz to gain permission to bring the *esrog* into the country; at least the rav would be able to fulfill the mitzvah for the rest of Yom Tov. Rabbi Lorincz's additional efforts bore no fruit — literally and figuratively — and he was ultimately told by the official to speak to the agriculture minister.

The minister was hospitalized at the time, so Rabbi Lorincz went to meet him in the hospital. However, the official didn't have with him the papers needed to issue the release. After a while, though, the proper documents were obtained and the minister signed a release form, allowing the *esrog* into the country. Rabbi Lorincz made his way to the airport to retrieve the precious fruit, but by the time he arrived, the department holding the *esrog* was already closed.

It appeared that, after all, the rav would not be able to fulfill the mitzvah of *dalet minim* with the *mehudar esrog* from Morocco. Rabbi Lorincz was very disappointed and unsure how to break the news to the rav.

When he worked up the courage to tell the rav that all his efforts had come up empty, the rav responded with a smile. Rabbi Lorincz commented that he had expected the rav to be extremely disappointed. Why the cheerful mood?

The rav explained his feelings with a story.

In the city of Shavel, there resided an elderly woman, Rachel, whose children lived in Brisk. After her husband's passing, her children visited on a rotating basis, spending Shabbos with her and tending to her needs while keeping her company. This system initially worked well for all parties. Rachel loved her home and its surroundings, and her devoted children did not mind traveling every few weeks to spend Shabbos with their mother in her hometown.

After some time, however, the arrangement became more challenging. Traveling between Brisk and Shavel — a distance of about 375 miles — was no simple matter. On some weekends, none of the children were able to make the trip and their mother was forced to spend Shabbos alone.

Rachel's children were torn. They wished to spend Shabbos with their mother, but they also had obligations — familial and *parnassah* related — back in Brisk, and traveling was physically taxing and time consuming.

The children discussed the situation and decided that it would be best if their mother relocated to Brisk, where she would be surrounded by her children and grandchildren. They even found a suitable apartment for her in Brisk. Now they just needed her approval.

They were in for a surprise; their mother flatly refused their offer. "I must stay here in Shavel," she averred. "I cannot leave this home."

The children tried to explain the challenges involved in the trip to Shavel from Brisk. They told Rachel that in Brisk, she would be surrounded by family around the clock, and that her new lodging would be more comfortable than her little house in Shavel. But their begging and cajoling accomplished nothing.

With no other choice, the children continued their rotation, except for the Yamim Tovim, when they would pick up Rachel in Shavel and bring her to Brisk to spend the holidays in the company of her entire family, on their turf. After the Yom Tov, she would pack her suitcases and head back home.

One Yom Tov, while Rachel was in Brisk, one of her sons arranged for her to meet the Brisker Rav, who greeted the family matriarch and gave her a heartfelt *berachah* for *gezunt* and *nachas*, praising her children, respected members of the *kehillah*. He then asked Rachel why she doesn't move to Brisk to be close to her family; he said it would be an honor for the community to welcome her.

Though Rachel was flattered by the rav's invitation, she insisted that she must remain in her home in Shavel.

"I see that you have a particular reason to stay where you are," the rav said to her. "What is it? Perhaps we can accommodate you here in Brisk and provide you with whatever is keeping you connected to your hometown."

Rachel responded, "In fact, there is something very special about my humble home. I refrained from sharing it, because I was not sure that others, including my own children, would understand. But maybe the rav will understand."

Then she told her story:

> My grandfather was a talmid chacham and a righteous man, who devoted his days to Torah and avodas Hashem. Though he lived in poverty, he was most satisfied with his spiritual assets; he felt blessed to be living a life of G-dliness. He also appreciated his wonderful children, who never complained about the indigence in the home, as they understood that this world is merely a passageway to the next world.
>
> The mitzvah of dalet minim meant a lot to my grandfather. Despite his strong desire, however, every year he was forced to suffice with the few brief moments that he got to hold the communal esrog in shul. Hence, in order to be able to fulfill the precious mitzvah the way he envisioned, he began to put away money. For years, my grandfather set aside funds, kopek after kopek.
>
> Finally, one year before Succos, when he was already an older man, he went to a dalet-minim seller to purchase an esrog. How dismayed he was to learn that the money he had saved up was not enough to purchase an esrog.

He came home dejected. Seeing her husband's pain, my grand-mother suggested, "We have a large home, but we can surely make do with a smaller house. Let us sell this home, and with the profit we earn, you can purchase the esrog you so desire."

That is what they did. In just a few days they were able to sell their house and move to another, smaller abode. My grandfather took the money they made on the sale and purchased a beautiful esrog. His joy was boundless!

Word spread that my grandfather was in possession of a flaw-less esrog. Neighbors and friends vied for an opportunity to see and touch the beautiful fruit, hoping to hold it on Yom Tov. One day before Yom Tov, a neighbor came by and asked if he could see the special esrog. My grandmother granted his wish, carefully and cautiously handing it to him. He took the esrog and began examining it from all sides. Apparently, he was not accustomed to handling an esrog, and before my grandmother knew it, the precious fruit had slipped from his fingers and landed on the floor.

The esrog was now pasul. It was ruined!

My grandmother stood there in shock, not able to utter a word. She began to cry uncontrollably. What would she tell her husband when he returned home? How would her husband deal with this disappointment after all that they had sacrificed?

My grandmother continued to cry and cry until her husband returned. Seeing her tearstained face, my grandfather under-stood that something awful had happened. When asked what was wrong, my grandmother took him to the closet, opened the door, and revealed his precious esrog — which was no longer usable for the mitzvah. She told him what happened, expecting him to respond with immense frustration, perhaps even anger.

Instead, to her astonishment, my grandfather remained calm, showing no anger whatsoever. With complete equanimity, he said to his wife, "What did we want to accomplish here? What was the purpose of buying the esrog? Did we need a physical fruit? No, all we desired was to please Hashem Yisbarach. We wished to fulfill the mitzvah — faithfully, and with our heart and soul.

"We did our job perfectly. We saved money from our meager earnings, we even sold our house, and we expended great effort to fulfill the mitzvah. From our vantage point, we created great pleasure for Hashem Yisbarach.

"If, for whatever reason, He didn't want us to fulfill the mitzvah with our own esrog this Succos, are we to complain and be plunged into sadness? Absolutely not. If we don't have an esrog, then we are exempt from the mitzvah." And that year, the simchas Yom Tov in my grandparents' home was greater than ever.

The rav of the city, like many others, was most impressed when he heard about my grandfather's composure and tranquility, after such sacrifice and amid seeming disappointment. He went out of his way to visit my grandfather at home, and brought a set of dalet minim for my grandfather to bentch on.

This is what he said to my grandparents, "The nachas that you created for Hashem with your second act, not getting angry or even annoyed by what occurred, was superior even to your first act, sacrificing to purchase the esrog. In the merit of your first act of self-sacrifice, you were zocheh to pass — with flying colors — the second and greater nisayon when the esrog became unfit for the mitzvah. This was a remarkable kiddush Hashem, which surely created great joy in the Heavenly realms."

The rav told my grandparents that their new, smaller home, which had been bought solely to make funds available to purchase the esrog, was now itself a "cheftzah shel mitzvah," an object used for a mitzvah, because it was bought only to facilitate the performance of a mitzvah.

Tears filled Rachel's eyes as she concluded her tale. "I feel that it is a special *zechus* to reside in my grandparents' house, which is considered a *cheftzah shel mitzvah*. The walls, the ceiling, and even the floor are objects of a mitzvah. Every day that I am in the house, I hear the rav's words ringing in my ears, and I feel a special closeness to Hashem. In addition, every time I pass my grandparents' previous home, I am filled with the happiness that my grandparents felt at being granted the ability to sacrifice for the sake of Hashem's mitzvah.

"It is for this reason that I cannot leave my home to relocate to Brisk. My house represents my grandfather's *ahavas Hashem*, his love for Hashem's mitzvos, his willingness to sacrifice for a mitzvah, and, perhaps above all, his ability to maintain his equanimity at a time when most of us would feel justified expressing indignation."

Rachel remained for the rest of her life in that home, a dwelling that represented the greatness that man can achieve.

The Brisker Rav turned to Rabbi Lorincz. "Reb Shlomo, we did all we could to get that *esrog*. But now we see that there's no way for us to obtain it. Like the grandfather in the story, if we've tried our hardest and we don't have an *esrog*, then we are exempt from the mitzvah. And the only thing left for us to do is to be happy!"

Remaining an Am Haaretz

When he was already in his 90's, Rav Michel Yehudah Lefkowitz held his customary *kabbalas kahal* on Chol HaMoed Succos, greeting every person individually. Rav Michel Yehudah's warmth and sensitivity were legendary, and he took the time to wish each person *ah gutten moed* and inquire about his welfare.

Day turned into night. After about four-and-a-half hours of greeting people, Rav Michel Yehudah davened Maariv and then turned to his grandson, Reb Yossi Karlansky, and said that he was very worn out. "But I have not yet learned today," he added. Rav Michel Yehudah had indeed learned earlier, but he was apparently not satisfied with that. "I am going to sleep," he told his grandson. "Please wake me up in an hour so I can learn."

Rav Michel Yehudah went to sleep in the *succah*. An hour passed, but his grandson didn't have the heart to wake him, since he was clearly exhausted. After several hours, Rav Michel Yehudah woke up on his own and realized that he had "overslept." He called his grandson, who explained his stance. "*L'maaseh*," Reb Yossi rationalized, "you were sleeping in the *succah* and were thus being *mekayeim* a mitzvah."

Rav Michel Yehudah wasn't pleased with the answer. "*Mit azeleche mitzvos, vell ich bleiben an am haaretz ah gantze leben*. With mitzvos like these," said the nonagenarian rosh yeshivah, "I'll remain an ignoramus my entire life."

Mazel Tov

*B*ais Medrash Yaakov Moshe, a small shul in Flatbush, lacked material trappings. But its physical deficiencies were more than compensated for in the spiritual arena, under the quiet leadership of Rav Shamshon Brodsky, whose diminutive build seemed to match his modest demeanor.

In this shul, as in many others, each Simchas Torah, the *kehillah* customarily honored the rav with the *kibbud* of *Chassan Torah*. The *mispallelim* would watch their rav slowly make his way to the *bimah* and recite the *berachah* on the Torah, while the children reveled in the joyous atmosphere of the day, taking in the rav's shining countenance at this most festive time.

The *kriah* would end and the rav would recite the *berachah* of *Asher Nassan Lanu*. The *kehillah* would spontaneously erupt in cheerful singing, celebrating the great *simchah* of *Chassan Torah*. But the rav was already on his way across the room.

Where was he headed? He wasn't going toward his seat. What had suddenly captured his interest?

Mispallelim watched as he walked toward the *mechitzah* and the women's section. A moment later, the rav was seen approaching his wife, the rebbetzin of the shul.

"Mazel tov," the rav would say with a big smile on his face, and then he would repeat, "Mazel tov."

Having wished his wife mazel tov on the occasion of her husband receiving the honor of *Chassan Torah*, the rav turned around and headed to his seat.

A small deed.
An act of greatness.
An eternal lesson in mentchlichkeit.

The Ezras Nashim

One year, in Yeshivas Kamenitz in Europe, some of the *bachurim*, in an act of misplaced zealotry, decided that the women's section of the yeshivah should be closed for Simchas Torah; they felt it was not modest for women to come to the yeshivah.

Every year on Simchas Torah night, the *bachurim* would gather at the home of the rosh yeshivah, Rav Baruch Ber Leibowitz, and then they would escort him to the yeshivah for *Hakafos*, singing and dancing all the way to the building.

That year, however, the rosh yeshivah refused to go to the yeshivah. When questioned, Rav Baruch Ber explained that he would not go to the yeshivah, because the *ezras nashim* had been shuttered.

"This is the only time of the year that the glory of Torah can be demonstrated and magnified for the women. It is the one time that they get to see how *bnei Torah* celebrate with the *heilige Torah*.

"In our times," continued Rav Baruch Ber, "the honor accorded to the Torah is so limited. Not every girl comprehends the importance of Torah and those who learn it. Here, once a year, we have a chance to demonstrate how we rejoice over the Torah — and specifically on this day you close the *ezras nashim*?!"

Only once the *bachurim* said that they would open the women's section as usual did Rav Baruch Ber agree to go with them to the yeshivah.

A Pesach Release

Dudi, a G-d-fearing Jew, owned a printing press in Yerushalayim. He would daven each day *k'vasikin* and then learn
Daf Yomi before heading to his printing shop. He earned a modest
living and was beloved by his customers, whom he greeted with
kindness and good cheer. Each evening, after he departed from his
business partner, Yaakov, he would return to the *beis midrash* to
conclude his day by studying the holy words of Torah.

Once a year, Dudi was summoned for reserve duty in the Israel Defense Forces. He was blessed to serve as a watchman, a job
that allowed him to spend his time learning. One year, when he
received his summons for reserve military duty, he realized that the
three-week stint would fall out on Pesach. He was devastated. Who
would lead the Seder for his wife and children? What would Pesach
be like for him without his family? It was a Friday, though, and
there was no time for him to sulk. He had to prepare for Shabbos.

After the Shabbos *seudah*, Dudi ventured out into the Yerushalayim streets for a walk, seeking to clear his mind. His stroll took
him past the storied Zichron Moshe shul, where he would often
hear words of *chizuk* from the *maggid* of Yerushalayim, Rav Shalom
Schwadron. He hesitated, unsure if he should just continue on his
walk or if he should enter Zichron Moshe. Somehow, he felt drawn
to the shul.

He entered the lobby of Zichron Moshe, which opens up to smaller *batei midrash*, as well as the main larger shul. As Dudi walked
along the book-lined wall, he heard the thundering voice of Rav
Schwadron, who was delivering a discourse.

He turned his head to hear Rav Schwadron remark that he had
just thought of a story. "Although this story is not related to the
topic we are discussing," Rav Schwadron was telling his listeners,
"I must share it with you."

Rav Schwadron then related the following:

> When yeshivah bachurim visited the Chofetz Chaim in Radin
> for advice on how to avoid being drafted into the Polish Army,

they would receive varied responses. In some instances, the Chofetz Chaim would place his sefer Machaneh Yisrael — a guide for Jewish army conscripts — in the bachur's hand and wish him well, and the bachur knew that he would be drafted.

In other cases, the Chofetz Chaim would take the young man's hand in his own and tell him the words of Pirkei Avos (3:6), "If someone takes upon himself the yoke of Torah, the yoke of government and the yoke of worldly responsibilities are removed from him." The bachur knew that he must not let up in his Torah learning, having been assured by the Chofetz Chaim that he would not be drafted.

"If someone takes upon himself the yoke of Torah, the yoke of government and the yoke of worldly responsibilities are removed from him!" bellowed Rav Schwadron. "If someone takes upon himself the yoke of Torah — this means in all circumstances!"

Rav Schwadron went on to relate several instances involving *bachurim* who accepted the burden of Torah upon themselves and escaped the draft. After Rav Schwadron concluded the story, he returned to the topic he had been discussing previously.

Dudi stood there, suddenly sweating profusely. He felt that he had just experienced amazing *Hashgachah Pratis*. He sensed that it was not coincidental that at the very moment he arrived at Zichron Moshe, Rav Schwadron had launched into a tale that he himself told his listeners had nothing to do with the matter at hand. In fact, as Dudi listened to the rest of Rav Schwadron's *derashah*, it became clear that the story about the Chofetz Chaim had no connection to his speech.

Dudi felt uplifted by what Rav Schwadron had said; his message spoke to him in a personal way. On the spot, he accepted upon himself to add one hour of Torah learning to his daily schedule. And rather than waiting until the next day to implement his brand-new *kabbalah*, he sat down right there to learn for an hour. Afterward, he headed home, suddenly worry-free, buoyed by the mantra that was now directing his life: "If someone takes upon himself the yoke of Torah, the yoke of government and the yoke of worldly responsibilities are removed from him."

That Sunday, Dudi told his business partner, Yaakov, that he had received a draft summons for the upcoming month of Nissan. He then made a surprising request of Yaakov: "I'd like to close our store an hour early each day so that we can utilize that time for extra Torah learning."

His partner agreed.

Several weeks later, Yaakov arrived at the shop, eager to speak to Dudi. "Dudi, you're never going to believe it. I just received my own draft notice — and it is in the month of Nissan, as well."

Army regulations dictate that business partners do not have to fulfill their draft duties simultaneously. Either Dudi or Yaakov would be exempt. The two partners headed to the draft office, where they explained their predicament. They were assured by the clerk that their summonses would be reexamined. It was about a week later that Dudi received a letter in the mail stating that he would not have to report during the month of Nissan. Yaakov, however, would have to fulfill his draft duties at that time.

Dudi couldn't believe his good fortune. He'd be spending the Yom Tov of Pesach with his family after all. He almost danced his way home, struggling to hide his smile from passersby.

Little did he know that the Providential orchestration of events was only beginning.

The day Yaakov parted from Dudi was bittersweet. Dudi was relieved to be staying home, but his heart went out to Yaakov. The next morning, when Dudi arrived at his shop, he was surprised to find that the door was unlocked. He opened the door gingerly, and there was Yaakov, hard at work.

"Yaakov?! What are you doing here?" he asked. "Weren't you supposed to report to the base? Have you ignored the order?"

Yaakov grinned. "Listen to this! When I arrived at the base yesterday, a supervisor came over and told me that that my draft notice was really for two months from now, and it was sent to me in error. I couldn't believe what I was hearing, but he apologized for making me schlep down to the base and then promptly sent me home!"

Yaakov paused. He was very emotional as he continued.

"Dudi, do you realize what we have witnessed with our own eyes? We can attest to the potency of the words: 'If someone takes upon himself the yoke of Torah, the yoke of government and the yoke of worldly responsibilities are removed from him.' In order for you to have been exempt from your draft duties, I had to get a draft summons erroneously."

Some months later, Dudi and Yaakov were going through the finances of their store. As they reviewed the books, they realized that from the day they began closing their store early to spend an extra hour learning, their profits had increased significantly.

This wasn't a coincidence, they told each other. It was a product of their adherence to the principle that was now their guiding light: "If someone takes upon himself the yoke of Torah, the yoke of government and the yoke of worldly responsibilities are removed from him."

Pride in Our Own

Rav Chaim Soloveitchik of Brisk was once walking with his son, Rav Yitzchak Zev (Velvel), past a shul on the night of the Seder when sounds of *Hallel* were heard. Rav Velvel remarked to his father that he wishes he could say *Hallel* in shul on the Seder night like these Yidden who observe this custom.

Rav Chaim was unhappy with this comment and said to his son, "True, some of our brothers have a beautiful custom to do so, but the Rema is our family's spiritual father and guide. If he told us not to say *Hallel* in davening on the Seder night (*Orach Chaim* 487:4), then that's what is best for us. We should take pride in our own customs and bring passion and enthusiasm to the things we do, not try to find satisfaction and growth in the customs of others."

Purified by Torah

Some years ago, the community of Ramat Elchanan was reeling from tragedy after tragedy, including a number of untimely *petiros*. The rav of the neighborhood, Rav Yitzchak Zilberstein, approached his brother-in-law, Rav Chaim Kanievsky, and asked him to recommend an area in which the local residents could be *mechazeik* themselves, in order to acquire the necessary *zechuyos* to halt the *tzaros*.

Rav Chaim responded by referring to a *Yerushalmi* in *Maseches Rosh Hashanah* (4:8), which states that regarding all *korbanos*, the term *cheit*, sin, is used by the Torah, but not regarding the *korbanos* of the Yom Tov of *Atzeres*, meaning Shavuos, the day of *Kabbalas HaTorah*. Why? The *Yerushalmi* explains that HaKadosh Baruch Hu said, "Since you have accepted upon yourselves the yoke of Torah, I consider it as if you have never sinned in your lives."

> *Rav Chaim explained that when one accepts the yoke of Torah, he is purified. Accepting the primacy of Torah and making it part of our lives has unparalleled power.*

The Merit of Righteous Women

It was Erev Shavuos 5774. Most schools were closed. Playgroups and babysitters were off. This presented a challenge for many kollel fathers, whose wives had a regular work schedule. They were forced to stay home from yeshivah in order to watch their broods.

Is that the best way to prepare for *Kabbalas HaTorah*?

That's a question one Lakewood woman asked, and she responded admirably.

This woman presumably had her own family to care for and her own Yom Tov to prepare. Nevertheless, she hung a sign on the bulletin board of Beth Medrash Govoha, offering babysitting and childcare free of charge to the families of those *yungerleit* whose wives were working but wished to have their regular morning *seder* on Erev Yom Tov.

It was with this zechus that this eishes chayil and her family entered Zman Matan Toraseinu, a beautiful manifestation of the heroism and self-sacrifice of those who, from behind the scenes, enable the learning of Torah each and every day.

No Cake

*T*he greatness of Rav Zundel Kroizer, a man who knew kol haTorah kulah and authored volumes on all of Tanach and Shas, was laced with down-to-earth simplicity and humor. When inscribing a sefer, he would sign his initials in English, "Z. K.," just to elicit a smile from his American visitors.

A *bachur* once asked Rav Zundel: Why don't people stay up the entire night of Pesach, when there is a Biblical mitzvah to engage in *sippur Yetzias Mitzrayim*, while the custom to stay up the entire night of Shavuos is observed almost universally?

Rav Zundel enjoyed the question. Stroking the *bachur*'s face, he said, "Because on Pesach night after eating the *afikoman*, it is forbidden to eat and no one gives out cake!"

Too Precious to Sleep Away

T he following story was related by Rav Shmaryahu Yosef Finkel about his father, Rav Nosson Tzvi Finkel, rosh yeshivah of Yeshivas Mir Yerushalayim.

An *avreich* used to learn with Rav Nosson Tzvi Finkel every evening during night *seder*. The night before Shavuos, Rav Nosson Tzvi asked this *chavrusa* to return the next afternoon to learn.

When the *chavrusa* arrived, he found that Rav Nosson Tzvi had just finished learning first *seder*. The *avreich* was surprised and asked why Rav Nosson Tzvi wasn't resting to conserve his energy for the night of Shavuos.

Rav Nosson Tzvi responded, "How could a person not learn on such an important day?"

And he learned until Yom Tov began.

That night, of course, Rav Nosson Tzvi learned in the yeshivah's *beis midrash* throughout the night, along with everyone else. "How can a person sleep on a night like this?" he asked. He learned hour after hour, with virtually no energy left, until davening in the morning, not stopping even when his family members pleaded with him to rest a bit before Shacharis. When he took his leave of the *avreich* who had learned with him, he asked him to come back immediately after Havdalah, so that they could continue learning from where they had left off. The *avreich* inferred that the rosh yeshivah planned to sleep during the day in order to have the strength to learn after Yom Tov.

Instead, Rav Nosson Tzvi sat down to learn again after davening, and he returned home only in time for the *seudah*. After the *seudah*, he said to everyone, "Who could go to sleep on such an important day?" And he sat down at the table in his living room and learned until Minchah.

After Minchah, he davened Maariv and made Havdalah, and then there was a knock at the door. The *avreich* had come to learn with the rosh yeshivah.

Rebbetzin Finkel could not understand what was happening. Her husband had spent the entire day learning. He had no energy left, after a full 24 hours without sleep, and it was clear that he could not continue. However, when Rav Nosson Tzvi heard that the *avreich* had come, he immediately sat down at the table to learn with him. They learned until the rosh yeshivah collapsed, and then he went to sleep.

> *Such levels of mesirus nefesh are often told about Torah giants of bygone eras. Rav Nosson Tzvi demonstrated that such lofty levels could be attained in today's day and age as well.*

Overcome by Grief

*A*t the time of bentching, there is a minhag to cover the knives *that are on the table (Orach Chaim 180:5). One reason is that once, when a person came to the berachah of Bonei Yerushalayim, he was so overcome by grief over the destruction of the Holy City and the Beis HaMikdash that he stabbed himself.*

A *yungerman* questioned Rav Chaim Kanievsky about this halachah. "We have never heard of anyone, in our times, harming himself upon mentioning the *churban Beis HaMikdash* and the destruction of Yerushalayim," remarked the *yungerman*, indicating that the requirement to cover knives seemed strange.

"This *din* is not strange," replied Rav Chaim. "At one time, every person understood the severity of the *churban Beis HaMikdash*, and he thus lost his composure upon contemplating the depth of our loss. Hence, there was a genuine concern that he may also react in a manner that is life threatening.

"We are the ones who are strange. Not the halachah."

For Just a Year

*R*av Tzvi Hirsch Kamai once entered a bookstore in Poland to buy a *Kinnos* for Tishah B'Av. Rav Tzvi Hirsch noticed that the volume cost 40 *zlotys*. He went over to the storeowner and began to bargain.

"Would you sell me this volume for 20 *zlotys*?" asked the rav.

The storeowner was surprised by the question. The rav had bought many *sefarim* from him before and had always paid the asking price without a problem.

"You've never bargained with me," said the man. "Why now?"

Rav Tzvi Hirsch explained: "Every other *sefer* I bought from you was meant to last an entire lifetime. This volume," Rav Tzvi Hirsch said, raising the *Kinnos*, "will be needed for only one year, because, G-d willing, Mashiach will arrive by next year. Since I am buying it for only one year, can you offer me a lower price?"

Rav Tzvi Hirsch imparted a lesson in truly believing in the imminent arrival of Mashiach.

Glossary

achrayus — responsibility; liability; guarantee.

adam gadol — lit., *a great man*; a prominent personage.

Admor (pl. *Admorim*) — leader of a Chassidic community

afikoman — 1. portion of matzah hidden during the Passover Seder and eaten toward its conclusion. 2. the Pesach offering.

Aggados — homiletical, non-halachic teachings of the Sages.

agunah (pl. *agunot*) — lit., *chained*; a woman who cannot remarry because she has not received a halachic divorce or because her husband is missing.

ah gutten moed — (Yiddish) "have a good Chol HaMoed."

ahavas Hashem — love of Hashem.

ahavas haTorah — love of the Torah.

Aibeshter — (Yiddish) lit., *the One Above*; G-d; Hashem.

Akeidah, Akeidas Yitzchak — the Binding of Yitzchak.

al kiddush Hashem — for the sake of sanctifying Hashem.

aleha hashalom — peace be on her.

aleph-beis — the Hebrew alphabet.

aliyah (pl. *aliyos*) — lit., *going up*. 1. spiritual elevation. 2. act of being called to recite a blessing at the public reading of the Torah. 3. ascent.

aliyah baTorah — success in one's Torah studies.

almanah (pl. *almanos*) — a widow.

alter heim — (Yiddish) lit., *the old home*; pre-war Europe; *shtetl* life.

am ha'aretz — unlearned, illiterate person.

am Hashem — the nation of Hashem; i.e., Israel.

amah (pl. *amos*) — a cubit (approximately two feet); a cubit, unit of measure.

Amora (pl. *Amoraim*) — Sage whose opinion is cited in the Gemara.

amud — 1. lectern or podium. 2. one folio of the Talmud.

anivus — humbleness; humility.

aravah (pl. *aravos*) — willow twig; one of the Four Species taken on Succos.

arichas yamim — lit., *lengthened days*; a long life.

aron — a coffin.

aron kodesh — holy ark in which Torah Scrolls are kept.

Asarah B'Teves — the Tenth of Teves, a public fast day

askan (pl. *askanim*) — a community activist.

atzeres — a gathering.

aufruf — act of a bridegroom being called to recite a blessing at the public reading of the Torah or a boy on his bar mitzvah.

av beis din — the head of a religious court.

aveilim — mourners.

aveirah (pl. *aveiros*) — a sin; a transgression.

avodah — work, effort, service.

avodas hakodesh — holy service.

avodas Hashem — service of Hashem.

Avos — the Patriarchs; Avraham, Yitzchak, and Yaakov.

avreich (pl. *avreichim*) — a young married man.

baal habayis (pl. *baalei batim*) — lit., *householder*; layman; homeowner.

baal kishron — a gifted Torah scholar.

baal kriah — the person who reads the weekly Torah portion aloud on behalf of the congregation.

baal menagen — a gifted singer who is often called upon to lead communal singing.

baal simchah (pl. *baalei simchah*) — celebrant; one who hosts a celebration.

baal teshuvah (pl. *baalei teshuvah*) — one who repents; one who returns to Torah-true Judaism.

baal tzedakah — one who is a generous donor to charity.

baalas chessed — a woman who performs acts of loving-kindness.

bachur (pl. *bachurim*) — young man; an unmarried young man, often used to denote a student in a yeshivah.

bar chiyuva — one who is obligated to perform the mitzvos.

bar mitzvah — 1. a 13-year-old boy. 2. the ceremony marking the coming of age of a Jewish boy.

baruch Hashem — lit., *Blessed is Hashem;* an expression of appreciation of Hashem's goodness.

bas mitzvah — 1. a 12-year-old girl. 2. the ceremony marking the coming of age of a Jewish girl.

Bavli — lit, *Babylonian;* the Babylonian Talmud.

b'chavrusa — with a study partner.

b'derech hateva — in the way of the natural world.

b'ezras Hashem — with Hashem's help.

b'seiver panim yafos — pleasantly; with a pleasant expression.

b'tzibbur — communally; together with the congregation.

bechinah (pl. *bechinos*) — a test.

bechor — firstborn male.

befeirishe din — a clearly stated law.

bein adam la'chaveiro — between man and his fellow.

bein hazmanim — vacation time between semesters in yeshivah; intersession.

beis avel — a house of mourners.

beis din — a Rabbinical court.

Beis Din Shel Maalah — lit., *the court above;* i.e., the court of Heaven.

Beis HaMikdash — the Holy Temple in Yerushalayim (Jerusalem).

beis midrash (pl. *batei midrash*) — a study hall where Torah is learned, often used as a synagogue as well.

ben Torah (pl. *bnei Torah*) — 1. one who studies and observes the teachings of the Torah. 2. a yeshivah student.

bentch — (Yiddish) 1. recite Grace after Meals. 2. to bless someone.

berachah (pl. *berachos*) — a blessing.

bimah — table or platform in the synagogue from which the Torah is read.

Bircas Kohanim — the blessings recited by the *Kohanim* during a prayer service.

bitachon — lit., *trust;* trust in Hashem.

bitul Torah — idle use of time that could be used for Torah study.

bizayon (pl. *bizyonos*) — disgrace; humiliation.

bnos Yisrael — Jewish girls.

bris, bris milah — circumcision of male infants, generally performed on the eighth day after birth.

bubbe — (Yiddish) grandmother.

chaburah — 1. a group (usually a group that studies together). 2. lecture or discourse delivered to a group.

chacham (pl. *chachamim*) — (l.c.) a wise person; wise man. (u.c.) a Sage quoted in the Mishnah or Gemara.

chachmei Yisrael — the Sages of Israel.

chag (pl. *chagim*) — a holiday; a festival.

chakirah (pl. *chakiros*) — an investigation.

chametz — leavened foods prohibited during the Passover festival.

chanukas haMishkan — the inauguration of the Tabernacle.

chareidi — strictly religiously observant.

chas v'chalilah — Heaven forbid.

chas v'shalom — Heaven forbid.

Chashmonaim — the Jewish warriors, led by Yehudah HaMaccabee, who rebelled against the Syrian-Greeks, as noted in the history of Chanukah.

chashuve — important; prominent; renowned.

chassan — a bridegroom.

Chassan Torah — lit., *the bridegroom of the Torah*; the one given the honor of being called to the Torah on Simchas Torah when the last Torah portion is being read.

Chassid (pl. *Chassidim*) — followers of a Chassidic leader (Rebbe); a pious individual; the followers of the Chassidic movement founded by Rabbi Yisrael Baal Shem Tov.

Chassidus — the study of chassidic thought.

chasunah — a wedding.

chavrusa — a study partner.

chavrusashaft — (Yiddish) a study partnership.

Chazal — acronym for *chachameinu zichronam livrachah*, "Our Sages of blessed memory."

cheder — school, usually an elementary school (spec. for Jewish studies).

chesed — acts of kindness; lovingkindness; charitable giving.

chesed shel emes — lit., *true act of kindness*; e.g., attending to the needs of a deceased person, such as arranging a funeral, when there is no ulterior motive but simply a pure act of kindness.

cheshbon — an accounting.

cheshbon hanefesh — spiritual accounting; accounting of one's deeds.

chevrah kaddisha — a burial society.

chiddush (pl. *chiddushim*) —Talmudic or halachic novellae.

chiddushei Torah — novel explanations of Torah subjects.

chillul Hashem — desecration of Hashem's Name.

chillul Shabbos — desecration of the Sabbath.

chinuch — Jewish education; the obligation for a parent to train a child to perform mitzvos.

chinuch habanim — educating children; raising children.

chizuk — encouragement; strengthening; corroboration.

Chol HaMoed — The intermediate days between the first and last days of Pesach and of Succos.

chov (pl. *chovos*) — a debt.

Chumash — one of the Five Books of the Torah; the Five Books collectively.

chuppah — 1. a wedding canopy. 2. the marriage ceremony.

churban — destruction of the Holy Temple.

daas Torah — Torah knowledge; one who assesses situations solely through the perspective of Torah.

daf — lit., *page*; one folio of the Gemara.

dalet minim — the Four Species taken on Succos.

daven — (Yiddish) to pray.

dayan (pl. *dayanim*) — halachic decisor or judge.

derashah (pl. *derashos*) — a Torah lecture; sermon or Torah discourse.

derech — 1. path. 2. method. 3. a way.

derech haTorah — the path of Torah; righteousness.

dikduk — Hebrew grammar.

din — (Jewish) law.

din Torah — 1. case brought to a halachic court. 2. decision rendered by a halachic court.

dirah — an apartment.

dvar mitzvah — 1. an item used to perform a mitzvah. 2. anything which it is a mitzvah to perform.

dvar Torah (pl. *divrei Torah*) — a lesson from the Torah; a Torah thought.

ehrliche — (Yiddish) upright; honest.

eidelkeit — refinement.

einikel — (Yiddish) a grandchild.

eishes chayil — 1. woman of valor; a worthy wife. 2. (u.c.) *Proverbs* 31:10-31, traditionally recited before the Friday-night Shabbos meal.

eitzah (pl. *eitzos*) — advice.

eizer k'negdo — lit., *a helpmeet opposite him*; term used for a wife.

elter zeide — great-grandfather.

emunah — faith; belief in G-d; faithfulness.

emunas chachamim — belief in the advice of Torah scholars.

Eretz Yisrael — Land of Israel.

Erev — the eve of the Sabbath or a holiday.

esrog — a citron, one of the Four Species

taken in hand during the Succos Festival.

ezras nashim — women's section in a synagogue.

farher — (Yiddish) oral test or examination, often required for admission to a yeshivah.

frum — (Yiddish) religious; Torah observant.

frumkeit — (Yiddish) the state of being religious.

gaavad — (acronym) *gaon av beis din*; lit., *the revered scholar, the "father" of the court*; title of the head of a rabbinic court.

gabbai (pl. *gabbaim*) — (Yiddish) synagogue sexton; personal attendant; person responsible for the proper functioning of a synagogue or other communal body.

gadlus — greatness.

gadol (pl. *gedolim*) — 1. an adult according to halachah 2. an outstanding Torah scholar.

gadol baTorah — a great Torah scholar.

gadol hador (pl. *gedolei hador*) — spiritual leader of the generation.

Gan Eden — the Garden of Eden.

gaon (pl. *gaonim*) — revered Torah scholar.

gartel — (Yiddish) belt worn to distinguish between the upper and lower parts of the body.

gedolei Yisrael — outstanding Torah scholars.

Gehinnom — Hell.

geirus — conversion (to Judaism).

Gemara (pl. *Gemaras*)— (u.c.) the Talmud. (l.c.) a volume of the Talmud.

ger (pl. *geirim*) — a convert to Judaism.

geshmak — (Yiddish) (n.) zest. (adj.) appealing.

gezeirah — an edict; a decree.

gezunt — (Yiddish) health.

goral — lottery; throwing of lots.

guf — lit., *the body*; the material side.

gvir — (Yiddish) a rich man.

hachnasas kallah — sponsoring a bride with items or money she needs in order to marry.

hachnasas orchim — hospitality; inviting guests.

hachzakas Torah — strengthening Torah observance.

hadas (pl. *hadassim*)— a myrtle branch; one of the Four Species taken in hand on Succos.

hadlakas neiros — candle-lighting.

hadrachah — guidance; instruction.

hagbahah — the raising of the Torah Scroll for all to see after the public reading; the honor of raising the Torah Scroll after the Torah reading, before it is wound and tied.

HaKadosh Baruch Hu — lit., *The Holy One* (i.e., Hashem), *Blessed Is He.*

Hakafos — the encircling of the *bimah* seven times on the holiday of Simchas Torah, while dancing with the Torah Scrolls.

hakaras hatov — gratitude; expressing gratitude.

halachah — Torah and Rabbinic law.

halachic — pertaining to Jewish law.

Hallel — lit., *praise*; a thanksgiving prayer comprised of selected Psalms, recited on Rosh Chodesh and most festivals.

hanachas tefillin — putting on *tefillin.*

hanhagah (pl. *hanhagos*) — customs; manners of behavior.

hanhagas hachaim — the manner in which one conducts one's own life.

hanhalah — school administration; administration.

Har Sinai — Mount Sinai, the mountain where the Jewish People received the Torah.

harbatzas ha Torah — spreading of Torah.

hasagas gevul — infringing on one's boundaries.

Hashem Yisbarach — Hashem, the blessed One.

Hashgachah — Divine Providence.

Hashgachah Pratis — Divine intervention.

hashkafah (pl. *hashkafos*) — outlook; ideology; worldview; a concept of *emunah;* perspective.

hasmadah — 1. consistency and persistence. 2. diligence in learning.

hataras nedarim — negation of vows.

hatzlachah — success.

Havdalah — lit., *separation*; prayer recited as the Sabbath or Festival comes to an end.

havtachah — a promise.

hazmanah — an invitation.

Heichal HaNeginah — the celestial Chamber of Music.

heilige — (Yiddish) holy.

hesped (pl. *hespeidim*) — a eulogy.

heter — permission; something permitted.

hiddur mitzvah—beautifying a mitzvah; e.g., by buying the most beautiful *esrog* or an expensive *mezuzah*.

hilchos Shabbos — the laws pertaining to Sabbath observance.

hislahavus — enthusiasm; zest.

iluy — a genius.

Imeinu — our mother, usually used in reference to one of the Matriarchs.

K'vod habriyos — respect due to people.

k'vod harav — lit., *his honor, the Rabbi*; a respectful title used when addressing a Rabbi.

k'vod haTorah — the honor and respect due to the Torah.

k'vod Shabbos — the honor of the Sabbath.

k'vod Shamayim — the honor of heaven.

kabbalah — lit., *acceptance*; the act of taking on a specific action to elevate oneself spiritually; an obligation taken upon oneself.

Kabbalas HaTorah — receiving the Torah at Mount Sinai.

kabbalas kahal — set time for an audience with a rabbi.

Kaddish — prayer said in memory of the dead.

Kaddish Yasom — mourner's prayer.

kappitel (pl. *kapitlach*) — a chapter of *Psalms* (*Tehillim*).

kapote — long coat worn by certain chassidic men.

kapparah — atonement.

kasha — a query.

kasher — to make fit for use according to Torah law; purified; purged (a utensil) of absorbed nonkosher taste.

kashrus — relating to Jewish dietary laws.

kavanah — intention, esp. when reciting a prayer or performing a mitzvah.

k'vasikin — at sunrise.

kedoshei — the holy ones of....

kedoshim — lit., *holy ones*; martyrs who perished in the Holocaust.

kedushah — 1. holiness. 2. a prayer recited during the repetition of the *Shemoneh Esrei* (it may be said only in the presence of a *minyan*).

kehillah — a congregation; a community.

kesher — a connection; a bond; ties that bind.

kesubah — a marriage contract.

kever (pl. *kevarim*) — a grave.

kevurah — burial.

kibbitz — tease; joke with.

kibbud (pl. *kibbudim*) – lit., *an honor*; the honor of being called to the *bimah* during the reading of the Torah or to be a participant at a religious ceremony.

kibbutz — a communal farm.

Kiddush — 1. mandatory blessing over wine expressing the sanctity of Shabbos or Festivals. 2. (l.c.) a reception after Sabbath morning prayers at which *Kiddush* is recited and refreshments are served. 3. the blessing over wine recited before the Shabbos and Yom Tov meals.

kiddush Hashem — sanctification of Hashem's holy Name.

kinder (pl. *kinderlach*) — (Yiddish) children.

Kinnos — a book of elegies read on the Ninth of Av.

kiruv — outreach; outreach movement drawing people to Torah observance.

kiruv rechokim – lit., *bringing near those who are far away*; outreach movement drawing people to Torah observance.

kisharon — ability.

klal — the community.

Klal Yisrael — Jewish people in general; the Jewish nation.

koach (pl. *kochos*) — strength; ability; energy.

Kohen (pl. *Kohanim*) — a member of the priestly tribe descended in the male line from Aaron.

kol haTorah kulah — the entire Torah.

Kol Nidrei — opening prayer recited at the onset of Yom Kippur.

kol Torah — the sweet sound of Torah learning.

kol tuv — lit., *everything good*; all [should be] good; often used when saying farewell.

Kol Yachol — the Omnipotent (Hashem).

kollel — academy of higher Jewish learning, whose students are mostly married men.

korban (pl. *korbanos*) — a sacrificial offering.

Kosel — the Western Wall.

kriah — 1. reading. 2. reading the weekly Torah portion during prayer services in a shul.

Krias Shema – 3 paragraphs of the Torah recited twice daily, beginning with the words "*Shema Yisrael,* Hear, O Israel."

kuntz — trick; art.

kvittel (pl. *kvittlach*)— a written petition for help or spiritual guidance.

lashon hara — lit., *evil speech;* derogatory speech; slander; gossip.

l'chaim — 1. party celebrating an engagement 2. toast over a drink of wine or whiskey.

lechem hapanim — the twelve loaves placed on the Table in the Sanctuary of the Beis HaMikdash.

leibedige — (Yiddish) lively; living.

leibedikeit — (Yiddish) liveliness.

lein — (Yiddish) to read the Torah portion in the synagogue.

levayah — a funeral.

limud haTorah — the learning or teaching of the Torah.

l'maaseh — practically speaking; from a practical viewpoint.

lomdei Torah — those who learn Torah.

l'sheim Shamayim — lit., *for the sake of Heaven;* a selfless action done solely for the sake of Heaven.

lulav — palm branch, one of the Four Species taken in hand on Succos.

maamarei Chazal — Torah discourses of the Sages.

Maariv — the evening prayer service.

machlokes — an argument; a dispute; discord.

maggid — speaker or lecturer who uses stories to teach moral lessons.

maggid shiur — a lecturer.

makolet — a small grocery store.

malach (pl. *malachim*) — a heavenly angel.

malach Elokim — an angel of Hashem.

Malach HaMavess — the Angel of Death.

mamme — (Yiddish) mamma; mother.

manhig — a leader.

marbitz Torah (pl. *marbitzei Torah*) — one who disseminates Torah.

mareh makom (pl. *mareh mekomos*) — source.

masechta (pl. *masechtos*) — tractate of Talmud.

mashal — a parable; an example.

mashgiach — 1. (cap.) dean of students in a yeshivah who oversees students' spiritual and ethical development. 2. kashrus supervisor.

Mashiach — Messiah, the awaited redeemer of Israel, who will usher in an era of universal recognition of the Kingship of Hashem.

mashpia — (n.) one who has a positive influence on others. (v.) to affect and influence.

masmid (pl. *masmidim*) – 1. an exceptionally dedicated Torah scholar who spends much time immersed in Torah study. 2. exceptionally diligent student.

maspid (pl. *maspidim*) — (n.) one who delivers a eulogy. (v.) to deliver a eulogy.

Matan Torah — the Giving of the Torah at Sinai.

matanah — a gift.

matir neder — annulment of a vow.

matzah — unleavened bread.

matzliach — successful.

mazel tov — congratulations.

mechaber sefarim — one who authors books, esp. books on Torah topics.

mechallel Shabbos — one who desecrates the Sabbath; the desecration of the Sabbath.

mechanech (pl. *mechanchim*) — an educator.

mechaneches (pl. *mechanchos*) — a female educator.

mechazeik — to strengthen, often spiritually.

mechilah — forgiveness.

mechitzah — a partition separating men and women during prayer; a partition.

mechutan (pl. *mechutanim*) — parent of one's in-law children; one's relative through marriage.

mehudar — beautiful, of higher halachic quality.

mekach ta'us — an error in halachah or interpretation.

mekadesh Sheim Shamayim — to sanctify Hashem's Name.

mekayeim — to fulfill.

mekomos hakedoshim — holy places.

mekomos haTorah — places where Torah is studied.

mekubal — a Kabbalist.

melaveh malkah — meal eaten on Saturday night in honor of the departure of the Sabbath Queen.

menachem avel — to comfort a mourner; to pay a condolence call.

menahel — a school principal; a supervisor.

menorah — candelabrum used to hold the Chanukah lights.

mentchlichkeit — the quality of exemplifying integrity, respect toward others, and decency.

menuchas hanefesh — peace of mind; spiritual calm.

mesader kiddushin — the one who officiates at the marriage ceremony.

mesamei'ach — to make happy; to gladden.

mesirus nefesh — self-sacrifice; total and unlimited devotion.

mesivta (pl. *mesivtas*)— yeshivah high school.

mesorah — Jewish heritage; the received tradition.

mevater— to nullify.

middah (pl. *middos*) — character trait; attribute.

middos tovos — positive character traits or attributes.

Midrash — homiletical teachings of the Sages.

mikveh — ritual bath.

Minchah — the afternoon prayer service

Minchah Gedolah — an early time in the afternoon for davening Minchah.

minhag (pl. *minhagim*) — custom.

Mishnah — (u.c.) teachings of the Tannaim that form the basis of the Talmud, the Oral Torah; a segment of *Pirkei Avos*; writings of the early Talmudic sages (circa 200 B.C.E – 00 C.E.). (l.c.) (pl. mishnayos) the germinal statements of law elucidated by the Gemara, together with which they constitute the Talmud; any paragraph from this body of law.

mishpachah — a family.

mishtateif — to take part in.

mispallel (pl. *mispallelim*) — 1. to pray. 2. one who prays.

mitzvah min haTorah — a mitzvah specifically commanded in the Torah.

mizrach — east.

mochel — to forgive.

morah — a woman teacher.

moreh hora'ah — a Rabbinic decisor.

mosdos haTorah — Torah institutions.

Motza'ei — nightfall following ....

muktzeh — an object that may not be handled on Shabbos or Yom Tov.

Mussaf — additional prayer service recited after Shacharis on Shabbos, Rosh Chodesh, and Festivals.

mussar — ethical teachings geared toward self-refinement; reproof.

mutar lach — "it is permitted to you."

muvhak — primary.

nachas — pleasure, joy, usually from one's children; spiritual or emotional pleasure.

nachas ruach — spiritual satisfaction.

navi (pl. *nevi'im*) — a prophet. (u.c.) one of the Books of the Prophets.

nazir — a Nazarite; one who has vowed, for a defined period, to refrain from cutting his hair and to abstain from (a) grapes and grape products and (b) contact with a grave or corpse.

nechamah — comfort; consolation.

Ne'ilah — concluding prayer service of Yom Kippur.

neis — a miracle.

ner tamid — a candle or light that is kept burning permanently, especially in a shul.

neshamah (pl. *neshamos*) — soul.

nezirus — the state of being a *nazir* (see above).

nichum aveilim — lit., *comforting mourners*; making a consolatory visit to a mourner.

niftar — (n) a person who passes away. (v.) passing away.

niggun — tune; Jewish tunes or melodies, often sung during special occasions.

nimshal — the moral of a parable.

nisayon (pl. *nisyonos*) — a test, esp. a spiritual test.

nogei'a b'davar — involved in the matter;

having a personal stake in the outcome.

nu — (interjection) well?

Nusach Sefard — style of prayer service used by Jews of Eastern European descent.

off the derech — straying from the path of Torah-true *Yiddishkeit*.

Olam Haba — the World to Come.

Olam HaEmes — the World of Truth; *Olam Haba*.

olam HaTorah — the Torah world.

onein — one whose close relative has died but the funeral has not yet taken place, in which case the person is not obligated to perform the positive mitzvos.

oveid Hashem — a servant of G-d.

oy vey — (Yiddish) (interjection) what a pity!

parashah (pl. *parashiyos*) — the weekly Torah portion.

parashas hashavua — the Torah portion read during a particular week.

pasken — to answer practical questions in halachah; to render a halachic ruling.

pasuk (pl. *pesukim*) — verse in the *Tanach* or liturgy.

perek (pl. *perakim*) — a chapter.

Pesach — Passover.

pesichah — opening the holy ark where the Torah Scrolls are kept.

Pesukei DeZimrah — lit., *Verses of Praise*; a section of the morning prayer service.

petirah (pl. *petiros*)— lit., *departure*; death; the moment of death.

pidyon shevuyim — the mitzvah to redeem prisoners.

pikuach nefesh — a matter of life and death; a life-and-death situation.

pintele Yid — (Yiddish) the flickering remnant of Jewishness inherent in a Jewish person.

poel — a worker.

poritz — landowner; nobleman.

posek (pl. *poskim*) — halachic authority. authoritative Rabbinic decisor.

potch — (Yiddish) slap.

psak — a halachic ruling.

pshat — basic explanation.

pushka — (Yiddish) a charity collection box.

rabbanit — *Rebbetzin; wife of the Rabbi.*

Rabbeinu — our Teacher.

rabbosai, rabbotai — lit., *gentlemen*, a polite term of address.

rachmanus — pity; mercy.

rav (pl. *rabbanim*) — a rabbi; a spiritual leader.

Rebbe — a rav; a rabbi or teacher.

rebbetzin — (Yiddish) rabbi's wife; also used to refer to a respected Jewish woman.

rebbi (pl. *rebbeim*) — a male Torah teacher.

refuah — cure; recovery.

rekidah — a dance.

Ribono Shel Olam — lit., *Master of the World*; i.e., Hashem.

Rosh Chodesh — the first day of a new month.

Rosh Hashanah — the Jewish New Year.

rosh kollel — the dean of a kollel.

rosh yeshivah — the dean of a yeshivah; senior lecturer in a yeshivah.

ruach hakodesh — Divine inspiration.

ruchniyus, ruchniyusdike — spirituality; spiritual growth.

s'chach — the roof of a *succah*, generally made from leaves, branches, or bamboo.

s'gan nasi — deputy leader.

sakanah — danger.

sandak — person who holds the baby while the *bris* is performed.

schep — lit., *draw* (as water); to derive (satisfaction) from.

seder (pl. *sedarim*) — 1. study period. 2. study session. 3. (u.c.) Pesach-night ritual during which the Haggadah is recited. 4. set time, usually for learning. 5. any of the six Orders of the Mishnah.

sefer (pl. *sefarim*) — a book, specifically a book on holy subjects or a learned topic.

sefer Torah (pl. *sifrei Torah*) — a Torah Scroll, written on parchment.

seichel — insight; intelligence; common sense; rationality; one's rational side.

Selichos — prayers said during the Ten Days of Repentance.

semichah — Rabbinical ordination.

seudah (pl. *seudos*) – a meal; esp. a meal served on Shabbos or Yom Tov.

seudah shelishis — the third Shabbos meal, which is eaten on Shabbos afternoon.

sevarah (pl. *sevaros*) — logical reasoning.

shaatnez — 1. the prohibition against wearing garments containing both wool and linen. 2. a fabric made of the prohibited mixture of wool and linen.

Shabbos HaGadol — the Great Shabbos, which precedes Pesach.

Shabbos Kodesh — the holy Sabbath.

Shabbos Shuvah — lit., *the Sabbath of the return*; the Sabbath before Yom Kippur.

Shacharis — the morning prayer service.

shadchan — a matchmaker.

shailah (pl. *shailos*) — question asked of a rabbinical authority regarding a halachic issue

shalom — peace; often said on meeting or leave-taking.

shalom aleichem — lit., *peace be on you*; traditional greeting; (u.c.) Friday-evening song of welcome to the ministering angels.

shalom bayis — peace and harmony in the home; marital harmony.

Shamayim — Heaven.

Shas — the Talmud as a whole.

Shas Yid (pl. *Shas Yidden*) — someone who has learned through the entire Talmud.

shechitah — the ritual manner in which an animal is slaughtered.

Sheim Hashem — Hashem's holy Name.

Sheimos — the Names of Hashem.

shekiah — sunset.

shemiras hamitzvos — observance of the mitzvos (commandments).

shemiras Shabbos — Sabbath observance.

Shemittah — the Sabbatical year, occurring every seventh year, during which the land is not worked. This law pertains only to the Land of Israel.

Shemoneh Esrei — lit., *18*; the prayer, originally eighteen blessings but now nineteen, that forms the central core of each weekday prayer service

shidduch (pl. *shidduchim*) — 1. match, esp. a marriage match. 2. proposed marriage match. 3. one's betrothed.

shiur (pl. *shiurim*) — (a) a Torah lecture. (b) the required amount (e.g., of eating forbidden food to be considered a punishable act).(c) halachic amount.

shivah — lit., *7*; the seven-day mourning period immediately following the death of a close relative.

shliach mitzvah — someone on his way to perform a mitzvah.

shmeck taback — a pinch of snuff.

shmuess (pl. *shmuessen*) — (Yiddish) lecture on Torah topics; Torah discourse.

shoin — (Yiddish) now; already.

shomer Shabbos — one who observes the laws of Shabbos.

shomrei Torah u'mitzvos — those who observe the Torah commandments.

shteig — (Yiddish) to advance in learning.

shteller — (Yiddish) a position, especially a rabbinical post.

shtender — (Yiddish) a lectern.

shtetl — a small European village

shtickel Torah — (Yiddish) a "piece" of Torah; a Torah thought.

shtriemel — the fur hat worn by certain Chassidic Jewish men.

shul — (Yiddish) synagogue.

Shulchan — the Golden Table in the Mishkan (Tabernacle) and *Beis HaMikdash*.

Shulchan Aruch — *Code of Jewish Law*, compiled by R' Yosef Karo (16th century).

shver — (Yiddish) 1. a father-in-law. 2. difficult.

siddur kiddushin — officiating at a wedding, which is considered the most prominent honor.

simchah (pl. *simchos*) — 1. happiness, joy; a joyous occasion. 2. a happy occasion; a celebration, esp. a celebration of a family milestone such as a wedding, bar mitzvah, or a birth.

Simchas Beis HaSho'eivah — gathering held on the intermediary days of the Succos holiday, which includes music, dance, and refreshments, commemorating the Water Libation Ceremony performed in the Holy Temple in Jerusalem.

simchas haTorah — the joy inherent in learning Torah.

sippur yetzias Mitzrayim — retelling the

events of the Exodus from Egypt.

siyata d'Shmaya — Divine assistance.

sofer — a religious scribe; scribe who writes religious materials such as a Torah Scroll, a *mezuzah*, *tefillin*, etc.

stam — (Yiddish) simply.

succah — booth in which Jews are commanded to dwell during Succos.

Succos — Festival of Tabernacles; the festival during which one dwells in a *succah;* Tabernacles; the festival during which one dwells in a *succah* and takes the Four Species.

sugya (pl. *sugyos*), *sugyos haShas*— (Aramaic) topic; conceptual unit in Talmud study; topic in Talmud.

taanis (pl. *taaniyos*) — a fast day.

taanis dibbur — lit., *a "fast" of speech;* resolving not to speak for a certain period.

taharas hamishpachah — the laws of family purity.

tallis — a prayer shawl.

tallis zekel — (Yiddish) a bag to hold one's *tallis.*

talmid (pl. *talmidim*) — a disciple; a student.

talmid chacham (pl. *talmidei chachamim*) — lit., *the student of a wise person;* a person learned in Torah and Talmud; a Torah scholar.

talmidah (pl. *talmidos*) — a female student.

talmud Torah — learning Torah.

Tanach — acronym for *Torah, Neviim, Kesuvim;* the written Torah, including the Five Books of Moses, the eight books of Prophets, and eleven books of Writings.

Tanna (pl. *Tannaim*) — one of the various authorities quoted in the Mishnah.

tefillah (pl. *tefillos*) — Jewish prayer.

Tefillas HaDerech — the wayfarer's prayer.

tefillin — phylacteries, leather boxes containing select Torah verses, worn by men on the arm and on the head.

tehorah — one who is ritually pure.

tekias shofar — the sounding of the shofar.

temimusdik — (Yiddish) having integrity.

terutz — (Yiddish) an answer.

teshuvah (pl. *teshuvos*) — 1. answer. 2. repentance. 3. rediscovery of Torah Judaism. 4. a response to a halachic query.

tinokos shel beis rabban — young children learning in a *cheder.*

tisch — (Yiddish) lit., *table;* a Chassidic gathering around a Chassidic Rebbe.

Tishah B'Av — [the fast of] the Ninth of Av; day of mourning for the destruction of the Holy Temples.

Toras chaim— a Torah of life; Living Torah.

Tosafos — 1. critical and explanatory notes on the Talmud by French and German scholars of the 12th–14th centuries. 2. the authors of those notes, collectively.

treif, treife—colloquial term for nonkosher.

tzaar — pain; suffering.

tzaddeikes — a righteous woman.

tzaddik (pl. *tzaddikim)* — a righteous person.

tzarah (pl. *tzaros*) — problems; difficult, painful situations.

tzedakah — compassion; charity.

tzetel — (Yiddish) a note; a piece of paper.

tzibbur – congregation; the community as a whole; the public.

tzidkus — righteousness.

tzitzis — fringes required by the Torah to be placed on a four-cornered garment.

tznius — standard of modesty with regard to speech, behavior, and dress.

upsheren — (Yiddish) lit., *shearing;* the first haircut given to a boy at the age of 3.

Viduy — confession recited on Yom Kippur and before death.

vort — lit., *word;* a Torah thought.

yahrtzeit — (Yiddish) the anniversary of a person's passing.

Yamim Noraim — lit., *Days of Awe;* Rosh Hashanah and Yom Kippur.

yasom (pl. *yesomim*) — orphan.

yegiah — effort; work.

yemos haMashiach — the era of Mashiach.

yerei Shamayim — one who fears Heaven.

yerushah — an inheritance.

Yerushalmi — 1. Jerusalemite. 2. The Jerusalem Talmud.

yeshivah — a school of Jewish studies; a Torah academy.

yeshivah ketanah — an elementary school.

yeshuah (pl. *yeshuos*) — salvation; rescue;

remedy.

yesod (pl. *yesodos*) — a basic principle; a foundation.

Y'hi Ratzon — May it be His [Hashem's] will.

yichus — lineage.

Yid (pl. *Yidden*) — a Jew.

Yiddishe – (Yiddish) Jewish.

Yiddishe kind — (Yiddish) a Jewish child.

Yiddishkeit — (Yiddish) Judaism; the Jewish way of life.

yirah — fear; awe of Hashem.

yishuv — a settlement.

Yom Kippur — the Day of Atonement.

Yom Tov (pl. *Yamim Tovim*) — a Jewish holiday; a Festival

yungerman (pl. *yungerleit*) — (Yiddish) young married man, usually referring to one studying in a yeshivah or kollel.

zachah lo — he merits it.

zechus (pl. *zechuyos*) — merit; privilege.

zeide — (Yiddish) grandfather.

zemiros — songs, esp. those sung at Shabbos and festive meals.

Zichronos — part of the Mussaf prayer on Rosh Hashanah.

zman (pl. *zmanim*) — lit., *time*; 1. the time the Sabbath or a holiday begins. 2. a school semester.

Zman Matan Toraseinu — the time of the Giving of the Torah; i.e., Shavuos.

zocheh — to merit.

This volume is part of
THE ARTSCROLL® SERIES
an ongoing project of
translations, commentaries and expositions on
Scripture, Mishnah, Talmud, Midrash, Halachah,
liturgy, history, the classic Rabbinic writings,
biographies and thought.

For a brochure of current publications
visit your local Hebrew bookseller
or contact the publisher:

Mesorah Publications, ltd.

4401 Second Avenue
Brooklyn, New York 11232
(718) 921-9000
www.artscroll.com